Community,
Violence, and Peace

Community, Violence, and Peace

*Aldo Leopold,
Mohandas K. Gandhi,
Martin Luther King Jr.,
and Gautama the Buddha
in the Twenty-First Century*

A. L. Herman

State University of New York Press

Published by
State University of New York Press, Albany

For information, address State University of New York
Press, State University Plaza, Albany, N.Y., 12246

Production by E. Moore
Marketing by Anne Valentine

Library of Congress Cataloging-in-Publication Data

Herman, A. L.
    Community, violence, and peace : Aldo Leopold, Mohandas K. Gandhi,
Martin Luther King Jr., and Gautama the Budha in the twenty-first
century / A. L. Herman.
        p.   cm.
    Includes bibliographical references (p.   ) and index.
    ISBN 0-7914-3983-6. — ISBN 0-7914-3984-4 (pbk.)
    1. Social history. 2. Community. 3. Violence—History.
4. Violence—Philosophy. 5. Violence—Forecasting. 6. Nonviolence.
I. Title.
HN18.H395 1998
306'.09—dc21   97-47500
                                                                    CIP

10 9 8 7 6 5 4 3 2

*This book is for
Carolee Cote*

Contents

Preface   ix

Introduction   1

1. Something about Community   5

2. Aldo Leopold and the Biotic Community   47

3. Mohandas Karamchand Gandhi and the
   Ashramic Community   76

4. Martin Luther King Jr. and the Beloved Community   116

5. Gautama the Buddha and the Karmic Community   149

6. Conclusion: Community and the Twenty-First Century   181

Notes   217

Some Suggestions for Further Reading   233

Index   239

Preface

This book is an investigation into the relation between community and the problems of violence (of which there is too much) and peace (of which there is too little). It begins in the first chapter with a preliminary inquiry into what a community is and it turns to Plato of Athens and Aldous Huxley, two utopian community builders in the West, for their answers. With Plato and Huxley we raise and attempt to answer three central questions: What is a community? How does one become a member of a community? And can the problems of violence and peace in the twenty-first century be solved through the way of community? Following the identification of several problems and questions regarding these two *fictional* communities, the next four chapters take these central questions to four *historical* communities, the biotic community of Aldo Leopold, the American naturalist and ecomystic, the ashramic community of Mohandas K. Gandhi, the Hindu statesman and prophet of nonviolence, the beloved community of Martin Luther King Jr., the Christian social activist and civil rights leader, and, finally, the karmic community of Gautama the Buddha, the religious reformer and founder of Buddhism. Our three questions are pursued by a naturalist, a Hindu, a Christian, and a Buddhist, and we find that they all seem to share several common characteristics and several problems: chief among the common characteristics is a philosophy of ethical altruism, a belief that community will work and solve the problems of violence and peace but only if the members of the community are willing to engage in activities that put the interests of the community, others, before their own, a position we shall call "communal altruism"; chief among the common problems that they share is the problem of communal altruism, the discovery that communal altruism, as well as the ethical altruism from which it is derived, is logically opaque and empirically and practically incoherent. The book concludes this investigation into community by arguing that since communal altruism can't work, it is vain to try to make it work. Our conclusion is that only the position called "communal egoism" can solve the problems of violence and peace in the twenty-first century, and that all six of our community builders, the fictional as well as the historical, are quite capable of agreeing to and accepting this new and defensible moral position.

Along the way to this conclusion and its defense, the book offers several additional points of interest: an examination of self-transformation, which is the key to the practical workings of both communal altruism and communal egoism; arguments to support the contention that Aldo Leopold, naturalist *par excellence*, can be viewed as an "ecomystic," a position more common among many ecologists than was previously thought; new and unpublished conversations with Mohandas Gandhi that reveal the inner workings of the Wardha ashram in 1933 and that offer new insights into how impossibly difficult people can learn to get along; the source of Martin Luther King Jr.'s extraordinary faith and vitality in solving the problems of communal injustice following a self-transforming experience; finally, the Buddha's remarkable insight into community that enabled him to dramatically recast the law of karma from its two Hindu interpretations called "karmic individualism" ("If you do the crime, then *you* do the time") and "karmic Saviorism" ("If you do the crime then the *Savior* does, or has done, the time") to his own interpretation in Mahāyāna Buddhism called "karmic communalism" ("If you do the crime, then the *community* does the time").

A number of very delightful people have given most freely of their time, talents, and energy to the creation of this work: Carolee Cote, as usual, patiently typed, word-processed, and photocopied her way through multiple versions and reversions of the manuscript; Russell T. Blackwood read the manuscript in its entirety and made extremely valuable comments to almost every page; Barbara Herman, as usual, read and reread various versions of the various stages in the development of the work, all the while offering her impeccably sound advice throughout; Harold Coward of the University of Victoria read the manuscript in its early stages and gave grand suggestions toward its improvement; Frank J. Hoffman of West Chester University chaired a conference on Gandhi and King at which he and Margaret Chatterjee helped me to see valuable things about my approach to community that I had never considered; David J. Kalupahana of the University of Hawaii (Manoa) whose summer and winter seminars on Buddhism and peace provided the impetus and inspiration for this book; my perceptive and eloquent colleagues at the University of Wisconsin, Stevens Point, including Donald Fadner, Michael P. Nelson, Thomas W. Overholt, and John Vollrath, read chapters and versions of the work and gave many valuable comments toward its betterment; in addition, I want to thank Jan Jopling and Arthur Herman for support and encouragement in the early and final stages of the writing, Dôna Warren for outright sound advice on several of its philosophical issues, and Elizabeth Moore for always being there.

The errors that this book contains are entirely my own. Whatever merit the work possesses, and I really mean this, is due entirely to the collective kindness, wit, and attention of all of the above extremely generous persons.

Introduction

This book is about community and it's about the problems of violence and peace in the context of community in the twenty-first century. This investigation of community, violence, and peace will be conducted using four ways or views of community from four remarkable human beings, two from the East, Gautama the Buddha and Mohandas Karamchand Gandhi, and two from the West, Aldo Leopold and Martin Luther King Jr. Each of these men faced similar problems of violence and peace and each proposed singularly different, but at the same time fundamentally similar, solutions to those problems; for while their solutions were uniquely developed within each man's individual view of community, at the same time each presupposed that a selfless and altruistic ethic of service must lie at the foundation of any true community.

These four ways of community, with their putative solutions to the problems of violence and peace, bring both theoretical and practical problems of their own that make understanding, acceptance, and implementation of community difficult. For while each of these four ways of community is an attempt both to solve the problems of violence and peace and to solve the problems that the other competing views of community failed to solve, something seems oddly lacking, finally, that makes difficult, if not impossible, the understanding, acceptance and implementation of community as an altruistic and selfless problem-solving enterprise. That is to say, there may be something radically wrong with any concept of community that rests upon the presupposition that any way of community must have a selfless and altruistic ethic of service at its foundation.

We begin with three central questions: First, What is a community? Or, more accurately, since community depends on something being shared, what is it that is *shared* that makes a community a community? Second, how does one become a member of a community? And third, our predominant question, can the problems of violence and peace in the twenty-first century be solved through the way of community?

In order to answer these central questions, chapter 1 begins by analyzing the concept of community and the *sine qua non* of community, sharing. It does this by examining two classic cases of utopian communities: the first is ancient, the spiritual community envisioned in Plato of Athens's philosophic classic, the *Republic*; the second is modern, the materialistic community created in Aldous Huxley's social satire, *Brave New World*. Both utopian communities pursue our other two central questions, setting the stage for the discussion and exploration of all three questions in the four historical communities that follow.

Chapters 2 through 5 examine four representative historical communities: the "biotic community" of Aldo Leopold; the "beloved community" of Martin Luther King Jr.; the "ashramic community" of Mohandas K. Gandhi; and the "karmic community" of Gautama the Buddha. Following the examination of each of these communities, we raise several questions and problems to which each of them would seem to lead. Each of these communities is also at some pains to define for itself what a community is, to state how one secures membership in it, and to suggest, however indirectly, that it is able to solve the problems of violence and peace in the twenty-first century.

Chapter 6 concludes this book by returning to the several puzzles that have arisen from trying to argue that the problems of violence and peace can be solved through the way of community. In particular, we shall be critically examining the nature, the origin, and the defense of the view called "communal altruism." The *altruism* in communal altruism assumes an ethical altruism, that only through selfless service to others will community be possible. The *community* in communal altruism assumes a communal holism, that the community is in some sense metaphysically and axiologically greater than the sum of the members that compose it. An analysis of both of these assumptions reveals that communal altruism is both conceptually opaque and normatively impractical. Consequently, we turn away from communal altruism, the view that the good of the individual is contained in the good of the community, to a critical examination of a more defensible and practicable view that we shall call "communal egoism," the view that the good of the community is contained in the good of the individual. We conclude the chapter and this book by arguing that the problems of violence and peace in the twenty-first century can probably best be solved through communal egoism.

Chapter 1

❧◇❧

Something about Community

Insanity and Community

It is perhaps a tired truism to say that we live in a time of urgent crisis. I don't know of any age, any historical period, about which that assertion could not be made;[1] but our age differs from all others in that at no previous time, not even after the introduction of the battle chariot, the long bow, the musket, or the machine gun, has life seemed so precariously balanced between existence and nonexistence, as it is in the twenty-first century: if nuclear violence doesn't obliterate our community, then environmental violence surely will.

Insanity

What Erich Fromm, the twentieth-century psychoanalyst and critic of Western community, wrote nearly fifty years ago about community is even more poignantly true today. Our society, the whole of Western society, Fromm claimed, was sick, and that sickness was displayed in the intolerably high incidence of psychological depression, alcoholism, drug addiction, homicides, overpopulation, poverty, pollution, and war generated by and within our community. Taking war as an example, Fromm observed:

> Let us, in good psychiatric fashion, look at the facts. In the last one hundred years we, in the Western world, have created a

5

greater material wealth than any other society in the history of the human race. Yet we have managed to kill off millions of our population in an arrangement which we call "war." Aside from smaller wars, we had larger ones in 1870, 1914 and 1939. During these wars, every participant firmly believed that he was fighting in his self-defense, for his honor, or that he was backed up by God.[2]

Fromm continued his 1955 work, which he titled *The Sane Society*, observing:

Happiness becomes identical with consumption of newer and better commodities, the drinking in of music, screen plays, fun, sex, liquor and cigarettes. Not having a sense of self except the one which conformity with the majority can give, he is insecure, anxious, depending on approval.[3]

The kind of person that we have managed to produce and that we take as the norm, as the best that we can produce, is a person "alienated from himself":

He is incapable to love and to use his reason, to make decisions, in fact incapable to appreciate life and thus ready and even willing to destroy everything. The world is again fragmentalized, has lost its unity; he is again worshipping diversified things, with the only exception that now they are man-made, rather than part of nature.[4]

Fromm concluded with the only possible diagnosis: Our society is insane:

This alienation and automatization leads to an ever-increasing insanity. Life has no meaning, there is no joy, no faith, no reality. Everybody is "happy"—except that he does not feel, does not reason, does not love.[5]

Several additional signs of insanity have recently emerged to capture the attention of those concerned about communal madness. These other forms of lamentable and preventable insanity are easily identified on six community levels: on the individual level, where insanity appears as "neuroses and suicide"; on the family level, as "domestic abuse and unemployment"; on the city level, as "urban blight and indifference or neglect"; on the national level, as "disease and injustice"; on the international level, as "terrorism and war"; and, finally, on the ecological level, as "ecospheric degradation and environmental pollution." Each of these communities from the self to the ecosphere shares its madness with levels above and below itself and each represents an area where our communal problems of violence and peace have their origin. The insanity that begins at the individual level grows and spreads to ever wider populations until, for us, in the twenty-first century, it has threatened to devour every living thing on this planet together with the very planet itself.

If something is to be done then that something must begin at the level of community, that is, with the six communities just mentioned. Four philosophers who have had much to say about insanity and community, violence and peace, were Aldo Leopold, Mohandas Karamchand Gandhi, Martin Luther King Jr., and Gautama the Buddha. Each gave us a vision of community and each provided a solution to the problems of violence and peace within community. Each speaks to our communal condition today. But before we turn to their views about violence and peace, it might be well to look very briefly at just what community is.

Community

If all communities[6] share certain properties, properties that make them communities, then what applies necessarily to one community ought to apply to other communities. So we might well ask, first, What is a community?, second, How does one become a member of a community?, and, third, Can the problems of violence and peace in the twenty-first century be solved through the way of community? As to the first, let's assume at the outset, and very roughly and incompletely, that a community (from the Latin *communis*, "common") is a group, set or collection of two or more members who share something-or-other and that it's that sharing that defines them as a community. And let's also assume that the more obvious things that community members share, whether consciously or unconsciously, and in varying degrees or quantities, are a history of, and a loyalty to, their community, together with common properties, languages, feelings, expectations, purposes, respect, stability, integrity, love, or destiny. Thus not only would individuals, families, villages, cities, nations, and the ecosystem be candidates for community status, but so also might lynch mobs, orchestras, the human body, autos, and cuckoo clocks. The key to what our concept of community is must lie in the nature of what is shared together with the sharing itself.

Second, one becomes a member of a community by participating in the sharing or in what is shared: one shares, voluntarily or involuntarily, consciously or unconsciously, in the community's purposes, goals and ends, that is, in its "happiness," and in virtue of that sharing one is said to be a member of that community. In the fourth century B.C.E. the Greek philosopher Aristotle began his *Politics* with these memorable lines, "Every community is established with a view to some good . . . every political community aims at good . . . at the highest good."[7] That "highest good," for Aristotle, was "happiness." In our investigation we shall be employing Aristotle's notion of community and assume that the kind of community that we are seeking is one that is capable of generating the highest human good through some manner of sharing. This allows us to leave out of consideration as candidates for community mobs, autos, and clocks, as well as nefarious human economic, political, and social groups that are themselves obviously insane or inherently self-destructive (*pace* Erich Fromm).

A third question now looms: Can Leopold or Gandhi or King or the Buddha bring about happiness for our communities? That is, can the problems of violence and peace in the twenty-first century be solved through their ways of community? It is this third question, a question about happiness in communities, that will constitute the dominant question to be put throughout this study. This question can be answered by turning to a variant of a Socratic argument first used by Plato in the fourth century B.C.E. That Socratic argument, in turn, is best seen against the background of a community, Athens, caught up in over a century of external violence, its hard-won peace now threatened by internal violence from one of its own members.

Socrates and Community

Socrates of Athens (469–399 B.C.E.) finds himself in the last year of his life brought up on charges by the city of Athens that could end that life. He is charged with endangering the peace, order and traditions of the community: "Socrates is guilty of corrupting the minds of the young and of believing in deities of his own invention instead of the gods of the community."[8]

Traitors and their associates. The three charges reflect the fears and suspicions of the Athenians of the time towards Socrates largely because of his close friendship with two of the community's most notorious traitors. The first, Alcibiades, had been responsible, it was believed, for two anticommunal acts in 415 B.C.E. at the height of Athens's war against Sparta, the Peloponnesian War (431–404 B.C.E.). These acts involved the profanation of the mysteries, a conspiracy to mock the gods of the community, and with it the mutilation of the hermes, the numerous votive statues dedicated to the god Hermes. But this impious attack on the religious foundation of the city was nothing compared to Alcibiades' other acts of treachery. He had been responsible for urging the Athenians to dispatch a large fleet and army against Syracuse, a Spartan ally in far-away Sicily. The venture was a disaster. The expedition was defeated in 413 B.C.E. and thousands of young Athenians were drowned or killed. Syracuse and Sparta triumphed and, back in Athens, everyone blamed Alcibiades. He fled Athens, sought refuge with the Spartans, and proceeded to advise them about their military tactics. Subsequently, he committed yet another treasonous act by joining with Athens's traditional and ancient enemy, the Persians: here was triple treason most foul. Alcibiades was closely identified in every Athenian's mind, once the war was lost, with his infamous mentor, teacher, and friend, Socrates.

The second traitor, Critias, had an even more nefarious anti-community reputation. Following the defeat of Athens by Sparta in 404 B.C.E. an oligarchical party of thirty pro-Spartans took over the rule of Athens and quickly instituted a reign of terror. The first order of oppression was to round up the more popular supporters of the defeated democracy and execute them. The ruthless rule of the Thirty Oligarchs led to the massacre of thousands of Athenians. And Critias, the pupil, friend, and associate of Socrates, was identified as the most bloodthirsty of all of the tyrants.

With the restoration of the democracy in 403 B.C.E., and despite a general amnesty, Athenians were in no mood to forgive those who had destroyed their community. Here was a chance to even the score with the equally notorious associate of Alcibiades and Critias, a man who, like them, had undermined the morality and religion, the peace, order and traditions, of the community.

Socrates was also identified with, and seemed to support and defend, another anticommunal tendency known to the Athenians, the cult of individualism. As seen by Plato, Socrates had discovered the *psychē*, the soul, that eternal, immortal, spiritual part of humans that stood, in a sense, separated and above the community. The soul defined a person more distinctively than the community:

one's soul pulled one away from the group, the community pulled one into it. It was, after all, Socrates, alone, who heard the voice of God, his *daimōn*, and, he, alone, who had a sacred mission from God to teach the citizens to discover and care for their individual *psychēs*. The unexamined life, as he tells the Athenian jury at his trial for blasphemy in 399 B.C.E, is not worth living and the examination of that life is directed, above all else, at one's own *psychē*:

> Men of Athens, I honor and love you; but I shall obey God rather than you, and while I have life and strength I shall never cease from the practice and teaching of philosophy, exhorting any one whom I met and saying to him after my manner: You, my friend,—a citizen of the great and mighty and wise community of Athens,—are you not ashamed of heaping up the greatest amount of money, and honor and reputation and caring so little about wisdom and truth and the greatest improvement of the *psychē* which you never regard or heed at all.

Following this opening, Socrates then moves into his defense against the charge that chiefly concerns us here, the charge that he has corrupted the youth of the community. At the same time he reveals himself as God's messenger sent by Apollo himself on a sacred mission:

> For I do nothing but go about persuading you all, old and young alike, not to take thought for your persons or your properties [concerns which, incidentally, hold the community together and which are now sorely threatened] but first and chiefly to care about the greatest improvement of the *psychē*. I tell you that goodness is not given by money, but that from goodness comes money and every other good of man, communal as well as individual. That is my teaching, and if this is the doctrine which corrupts the youth, I am a mischievous person.[9]

In the eyes of the jury that teaching did, indeed, corrupt the youth as well as the community at large. After all, recall what the teaching of individualism and the care of the *psychē* had done to Alcibiades and Critias. Now it threatened the community once again: individualism had led to blasphemy, treason, defeat, and chaos, and Socrates was responsible. Therefore, Socrates deserved death.

Plato has raised a problem that will be with us throughout this book, "the dilemma of the individual and the community": If the individual is too strong, if private rights and personal interest supersede community benefits, then we have anarchy and chaos; if, on the other hand, the community is too strong, if community welfare and the common good supersede private rights, then we have totalitarianism and chaos. It might be argued that Plato's dialogues, from first to last, are all about community. The *Apology*, probably his first written work, is a defense of those private rights as Socrates, the defender of *psychē* and individualism, dies a martyr to that defense. Plato's last written work, the *Laws*, on the other hand, is an attempt to lay down the draconian rules by which what we would regard as a totalitarian society is meant to live and survive. The *Laws*, one of the few Platonic works in which Socrates appears not at all, leaves no doubt that in Plato's mind should any new Socrates arise, any new apologist of individualism, he would be tried for *asebeia*, blasphemy, all over again, and the result, death, would be the same, all over again.[10] Between these two works on community, the *Apology*, a work of Plato's youth, and the *Laws*, a work of his old age, lies the *Republic*, Plato's and the Western world's greatest philosophic work. In the *Republic* Plato attempts to meet the dilemma of the individual and the community and to make the care and the examination of the individual *psychē* possible for all citizens within a community setting.

Some community arguments. A glimpse of Plato's way out of that dilemma is offered in the *Apology* as Socrates turns to an argument to prove that he's not guilty of corrupting the youth of Athens. This "Socratic argument" will lead us into a parallel argument, "the community argument," that attempts to bring the individual and the community together in such a way that the dilemma is solved and the third question that we raised, above, will be answered, Can the problems of violence and peace in the twenty-first century be solved through the ways of community of Leopold or Gandhi or King or the Buddha?

Socrates begins by getting one of his accusers, Miletus, to admit to the jury of 501 citizens that no one wants to be harmed or injured. Next, he gets Miletus to agree that wicked people have a bad effect on those with whom they associate, that is, bad people harm those with whom they are in contact. But, then, Socrates concludes his argument, claiming that he's innocent of spiritually molesting the youth of the city of Athens because no one would intentionally harm those who could then, in turn, harm oneself; this gets Socrates to the conclusion that he never *intentionally* corrupted the youth of the community, so he's not guilty of knowingly harming the young. This *Socratic argument* looks like this:

1. No one would intentionally harm oneself.
2. If one harms others then they will harm oneself.
3. Therefore, no one would intentionally harm others.[11]

The second premise makes sense, it seems to me, only if we accept that those others are in some manner in close association with, in community with, oneself. If I harm you then, if you are going to harm me, I must be in proximity to you, and available for you, to harm me. The argument, in other words, assumes a community of persons capable of doing wicked acts and of being retaliated against as a consequence. This *Socratic community argument* would look like this:

1. No one would intentionally harm oneself.
2. Oneself is those others, one's community (those corrupted youth of Athens, their relatives and friends, the entire angry city, for example, who could harm oneself).
3. Therefore, no one would intentionally harm those others, one's community (those who make up the community).

The nature and force of the "is" in the second premise of the Socratic community argument and in the second premises of the two community arguments that come next, need explanation. It will be our contention that the four major communities to be discussed in this book use the *is* of identity in explaining the relation between community and its members. In other words, for Leopold, Gandhi, King, and the Buddha, the relation between the community and its members is one wherein the community is the same as each member and each member is the same as the community. This organic and holistic interpretation of community together with an analysis of the *is* of identity that accompanies it will be taken up in some detail in chapter 6, below.

Which brings us to the main reason for approaching our discussion of community, violence, and peace from the point of view of Socrates and community. The Socratic community argument about those "others" and community leads to a third argument that we shall call the "community violence argument." This community violence argument will be with us in the chapters that follow. It is an argument upon which Leopold, Gandhi, King, and the Buddha will base their solutions to the problems of violence and peace:

1. No one would intentionally do violence to oneself.
2. Oneself is one's community.
3. Therefore, no one would intentionally do violence to one's community.

While the community violence argument is meant to solve the problem of violence, another argument is necessary to solve the problem of peace. That is to say, the argument just presented shows what is necessary to reduce or eliminate violence. But what about peace, which is not merely the absence of violence? So, a corollary argument is necessary to stand beside the community violence argument. Call this second demonstration "the community peace argument":

1. Everyone would intentionally do peace to oneself.
2. Oneself is one's community.
3. Therefore, everyone would intentionally do peace to one's community.

The justification of these premises parallels the justification of the premises in the community violence argument. The language is a bit clumsy but the idea should be clear. It is not enough just to reduce violence in the twenty-first century. One would hope that making peace, that is, doing acts of love, generosity, and benefit, would also occur. And when they do, the agent believes that he or she is really doing good to himself or herself. Finally, if the cause of both problems is, indeed, unintentional, that is, done out of ignorance, then, as Socrates knew, the solution to both is going to involve attacking that ignorance through education—through enlightenment, self-transformation, or conversion. Education was, after all, what Socrates' sacred mission was about. We shall return to the community violence argument and the community peace argument throughout this book.

If our two community arguments are sound, and Leopold, Gandhi, King, and the Buddha accept the truth of the two premises, then it is imperative, if our third question is to be answered, that we inquire into just what a community is for these four men and just how one goes about defending the view that one's community is oneself—that we are the community.

Community as a Prescription for Liberation from Suffering

If communities are established, as Aristotle suggested, for the sake of some good, then communities are also established to escape some evil. And if we now confine our investigation to purposeful communities, then we ought to be able to name both the good at which they aim as well as the evil that they seek to avoid.

A useful heuristic for dealing with such problems, causes, solutions, and ways has been nicely established in one of the world's ancient religions and we shall make use of that formula here; it is the so-called "Four Noble Truths" of Buddhism. Following his nirvana or enlightenment in 528 B.C.E., Gautama the Buddha journeyed to the city of Varanasi to preach his first sermon. In that sermon he laid out the simple formula that has defined Buddhism and guided Buddhists into the twenty-first century. The four truths to which he drew attention were the following:

1. The *problem* is that all existence is dominated by suffering.
2. The *cause* of the problem is grasping or desire.
3. The *solution* of the problem is nirvana or liberation from suffering.
4. The *way* to the solution that gets at the cause of the problem is the noble eightfold path; eight things that the follower of the Buddha can do right now to bring about that solution, ranging from the right kind of occupation, to the right intentions in action, to displaying the right kind of attention to the world, to the right kind of meditation within oneself.

It is the form of the Four Noble Truths and not their content that will serve us here. That four-stage formula can be used not only to help to define any religion, such as Buddhism, but it can outline any organized, purposeful activity set upon solving problems. And we can employ that outline on our ways of community by simply asking four questions of each: What *problem* does it attempt to solve? What is the *cause* of the problem? What is the *solution* it seeks? And what is the *way* it uses to solve the problem?[12]

In this book we apply this four-stage prescription, or *Rx* (i.e., "recipe") to communities as Prescriptions for Community. But before we push out our critical necks too far, suppose that we test the application of our Rx for Community on two well-known communities and see if our four-stage formula is, indeed, a true and useful heuristic. That is to say, before turning to the four communities of Leopold, Gandhi, King, and the Buddha with which this book is principally concerned, let's have a run at two more familiar, though fictional, communities that have had an impact, political in the first case and literary and social in the second, on the twenty-first century.

Two Communities: Plato's Republic and Aldous Huxley's World State

Aristotle had stated two necessary conditions for community and those conditions, together with our view that communities entail some kind of commonality or sharing aimed at problem-solving, should give us a ground from which to go community-hunting with our four-stage Rx for Community. First, Aristotle assumed, communities are intentionally established, that is, they don't just grow spontaneously or haphazardly, and, second, they are established in order to solve a problem by creating the highest good, namely, happiness or *eudaimonia*. "Happiness" is a grandly ambiguous word and the kind of community one establishes to generate happiness (and Aristotle himself attempted in his *Politics* to describe one such happiness-generating society) varies and depends on what one views happiness to be.

In what follows, we briefly explore two such communities established with two entirely different notions of happiness in mind, self-realization in the first and pure pleasure in the second. But while different, each community believed that it could bring about the greatest good for all of its citizens and thereby solve the problems of violence and peace. Following this exploration we will conclude by presenting a comparison of our two utopias together with an analysis of several problems and puzzles that would appear to arise concerning them. The first community is that of Plato of Athens (427–347 B.C.E.) and the second that of Aldous Huxley (1894–1963).

Plato of Athens: The Community of Republic

Plato set standards in the search for both the meaning of life and the philosophy of community that later generations of philosophers in the West have attempted to follow. In a very real sense Plato invented both "philosophy" and "community" and he took his inventions very seriously, indeed. He says in his greatest work, the *Republic*, "For no light matter is at stake; the question concerns the very manner in which human life is to be lived."[13] Plato anticipated thereby the sentiment of his own pupil, Aristotle, who asked the two practical questions that philosophers have been pursuing ever since: What is the best and most worthwhile *life* that a human being can live? and What is the best and most worthwhile *community* that will make that life possible?

Plato's Life

Plato was born in Athens in 427 B.C.E. His real name was "Aristocles" but a nickname, "Platon," which in Greek means "wide" or "broad," was given to him perhaps because of his thickset, stocky body, which helped to make him a champion wrestler. Plato's family was from the aristocratic ranks, but it strongly supported the administration of a free and democratic Athens. Plato counted among his father's ancestors one of the last kings of Athens and among his mother's ancestors was Solon, the great lawgiver. Plato grew up during the devastating Peloponnesian War and was only twenty-three when it finally ended with totalitarian Sparta triumphant over democratic Athens. As a young man he had fought in three battles of that war and had won a medal for bravery. He excelled in his studies in music, mathematics, rhetoric, and poetry. He wrestled at the Isthmian games and wrote love poetry, tragic verse, and epigrams. Plato, though acquainted with Socrates all of his life, may have been only twenty when he first heard Socrates speak in public. One source says that the experience so moved him that he went home, burned a tragedy that he had just written, and renounced poetry, wrestling, and women in order to follow this odd but compelling personality.

Plato had cherished the hope for a political career, as he tells us in one of his many surviving letters, but gave up politics when he saw what horrors the rule of the notorious Thirty Oligarchs brought to defeated Athens when the pro-Spartans seized power in 404 B.C.E. He was especially horrified when he saw later how the anti-Spartan democracy dealt with his beloved Socrates three years after they recovered power. Athenian politics was no place for a political moderate, a well-educated and promisingly brilliant philosopher. Following the tragic execution of his friend and teacher in 399 B.C.E., Plato fled Athens and spent twelve years traveling the violence-ravaged Mediterranean world.

The Academy: *An Educational Community*

Plato, on his return to Athens in 387, proceeded to establish a school, the Academy, one mile outside the walls of Athens in a place consecrated to a mythological hero, Academus. The place consisted of a grove of trees, gardens, a gymnasium, and several other buildings. It was here in this sacred plot that Plato gathered about him the young men who were to form a religious community, the nucleus of one of the first universities of its kind in the ancient world. The scholars ate their meals in common, and the meals were occasions for long drinking, reading, and talking sessions, "symposia,"[14] as they were called.

Outsiders were welcome to the public lectures and people from all over the civilized world came in large numbers, especially for lectures with catchy titles such as "On the Good," "On the Soul," "On the Best Life," and so on. Having come, they expected, we are told, to hear some wonderful sort of prescription for human happiness and the best life; but, as often as not, they went away disappointed when the master's lectures were all about mathematics and astronomy, Plato's adamantine prerequisites to virtue and happiness. Over the portals of the Academy, carved in the face of the rock, was the motto by which this community, established on hallowed ground and dedicated to the divine Muses of learning, was guided: *Let No One Ignorant of Geometry Enter Here*, a reference to the order and harmony and reality of the numbers and ideal figures that Plato, like his Pythagorean predecessors, revered.

Besides lectures on the good, mathematics, and astronomy, he also taught political theory. The principal aim of the education at the Academy, the sole reason for its existence, was to produce those men and women who would become philosophers, statesmen, counselors, rulers, and even kings, in the communities of the world outside the school's sacred confines. The pupils of Plato, we are told by Plutarch and others, traveled far and wide as political troubleshooters, helping colonies, cities, and towns revise their constitutions, in order to better govern their subjects, citizens, and colonies by adopting milder forms of government with more agreeable and enforceable laws. It is this interest in, concern for, and expertise about community that makes Plato more than capable to speak to the questions we have set for him below. The Academy became a school of political science and diplomacy for the entire Mediterranean world for several hundred years and remained an educational force in the West until its abrupt closing by the Christian emperor of Rome, Justinian, in 529 C.E. The memory of Plato's Academy stands, even today, as a model of educational inspiration and reform, a bright intellectual light that the passage of the years has neither extinguished nor dimmed.[15]

Plato died in 347 B.C.E. and, following a funeral procession at the Academy, was buried within its sacred grounds. The entire city mourned the death of the greatest philosopher and Athenian since Socrates.

The Republic: *A Spiritual Community*

The *Republic* consists of an opening chapter in the style of a Socratic dialogue and nine remaining chapters in the style of Plato's middle period. The subject throughout the *Republic* is *dikē* (pronounced "dee-kay"), "justice," which refers to the best and most worthwhile life that a human being, or a community, can live.[16]

What is justice? The *Republic* is undoubtedly Plato's finest and, except for the *Laws*, his longest work. In it Plato, through his hero Socrates, undertakes to describe the ideal community in which every human being can be happy. It is the first and in many ways the most finely described Western utopia that we have, setting a model that later utopia builders, from Aristotle to St. Aurelius Augustine, to François Rabelais, Jonathan Swift, Karl Marx, Edward Bellamy, and Aldous Huxley, will try to match and surpass.

The *Republic* is a dramatic dialogue set sometime around the year 421 B.C.E. The action takes place at the house of Polemarchus in the Piraeus, the port of Athens and six miles from the city. In addition to Socrates, Plato's two brothers are present along with a company of young, and several older, men. The subject of discussion quickly turns to *dikē*, justice, that is, the best life. The question quickly becomes, What is the best life, happiness, for the soul, *psychē*? and, What is the best life, happiness, for the community? The first book of the *Republic* is a dialogue in the grand old Socratic tradition of Plato's early works, hunting for the meanings of concepts through the analysis of suggested definitions. Before the first book concludes, some seven definitions of *dikē* have been offered and rejected. But what is needed, Socrates has discovered, is a lengthier and larger examination of justice in the context of a community before it can be determined what justice in the soul is all about.

Justice in the large: Utopia as community. So Socrates suggests that in order to see what justice in the small, or in the individual soul, is like, it might be better, first, to see justice magnified. And therefore he recommends looking at justice in the large in the only external place where it can exist, that is, in a community. Now begins Plato's construction of an ideal community, a community which is happy, where all may seek the best and most worthwhile life possible. Here is Plato's *utopia*, a best place (*eu-topos*) that is no place (*ou-topos*).

Plato starts by focusing on the three classes of citizens who will compose the community: (1) the philosopher-kings or rulers, (2) the warriors or defenders, and (3) the craftsmen, farmers, or producers. The warriors are the guardians of the community, and, like the rulers, they possess no private property, wealth, or goods, lest they become corrupted by bribery and greed; they eat in a common mess, share and share alike, live together like campaigning soldiers, and handle no gold or silver. These guardians are the helpers of the rulers and, like the rulers, they are chosen for their vocation according to their inborn, or hereditary, natures. Plato's community is based on the particular natural talents, abilities, and capacities inborn in every person.

Censorship and eugenics. To begin with, everyone over the age of ten must be excluded from the community. Education must start with children only, for adults are already corrupted and uneducable and cannot be trained for utopia. The children of the community will develop and be educated under the watchful eyes of Plato's philosopher-statesmen. Strict censorship exists and even Homer is prohibited lest his immoral tales of the gods corrupt the young. Plato would have been shocked by our sentimental and nostalgic movies about religion, such as *The Ten Commandments*, *The Robe*, *The Silver Chalice*, and *David and Bathsheba*, as well as by the mawkish Saturday and Sunday school stories of biblical heroes. Music is censored and only patriotic military anthems are allowed, not sentimental and romantic melodies; Plato would have been repelled were he living now upon hearing our modern maudlin love songs, as well as by our country-western, rock jazz, and acid rock. John Philip Sousa would probably have pleased him, however. Plato's entire community is to be rigidly controlled in its intellectual, emotional, and religious life in the uncontrovertible belief that what you are exposed to today will help to determine the kind of person that you will become tomorrow. Everything that is done is done to ensure that the young and growing citizens will be surrounded only by the best, at least "the best" as determined by the wisest minds available, at least "the wisest minds" as determined by Plato. The society is a totalitarian community from rulers to farmers, with the sole aim of making all of the citizens happy by producing the best and most worthwhile life for all.

The citizens are trained to accept the class that their inherited soul natures determine they belong in. Through an elaborate "golden lie," the citizens are induced to believe that it is God's will that they remain in the class that they are naturally suited for, but are not necessarily born into, and that that class is the best.[17] Socrates, Plato's voice in the *Republic*, states: "It seems likely that our rulers will have to make considerable use of falsehood and deception for the benefit of their subjects."[18] But the lies are *golden* lies because they are harmless and ultimately for the best, just as our lies to our children are profitable and for the best regarding Santa Claus, the Easter Bunny, the Tooth Fairy, and so on. Community security and social stability are always the ultimate aim.

Eugenics is practiced among the rulers and the guardians since the best will mate only with the best "like race horses," Plato states. Abnormal infants are allowed to die by the chief method of birth control known throughout the ancient world, exposure. But women are treated on an equal level with men, sharing the direction and defense of the community wherever their natural vocations lead them. While men's and women's natures differ, Plato says, it is not the kind of difference that need make a difference to this community.

The organic theory of the community. The utopia that Plato envisions is an organic community in which the citizens are like the cells in a body with the three classes forming the body's major parts.[19] The ruling class is the head, the defenders are the arms, and the farmers-workers-artisans are the loins, stomach, and legs. All the parts are necessary to the happy functioning of the whole. No one part is more important than another, and all are equally important.

Cicero, the Stoic Roman statesman of the first century B.C.E., tells a story that best illustrates this organic theory of the community. It seems that a violent dispute broke out in the body between the head and the arms as to who was the most important. The head maintained that without it, the body would never find food and would wither and die. The arms maintained that the head was wrong for without arms the food would never be gathered and the body would surely perish. And on they shouted and raged at one another until all their wrangling woke up the stomach who sleepily asked what all the racket was about. On being told, the stomach then lazily stated that as far as truth was concerned, it, the stomach, was the most important member of the body. Whereupon the arms and head laughed at the impertinence of this lazy, good-for-nothing interloper in their fight. So the stomach promptly stopped accepting the food that the head found and the arms gathered. The body, after several weeks, began to wither and was only saved from death when the head and arms together acknowledged the equal importance of the stomach to the total health of the body.

That is the very point that Plato is making in his description of his community: all the parts are important to the total well-being of the whole; if each part is happy and doing its assigned task, then the whole community will be happy. Thus the need for strict central control of the classes by censorship and the golden lies: justice (well-being) in the parts yields justice in the whole. That is to say, there will be justice in the community when the ruler is ruling, the defender is defending, and the farmer-artisan-businessman is doing what the state needs, that is, producing and exchanging goods.

But how does one know to which class one belongs? And what does it mean to be happy in following one's vocation, one's calling? And who calls one to one's task or vocation, anyway? The answers to these questions, as we shall see, are, first, that through education one discovers one's appropriate class; to be happy means to have the three parts of one's own soul working in harmony and balance just as happiness in the community means that the three classes of the community are working in harmony and balance; and, finally, each person calls himself or herself to the class and the vocation that one enjoys in the community, that is, your soul calls you and tells you who you are. These questions and answers will be explored as we turn finally to Plato's philosophy of soul-realization in his *Republic*.

Justice in the small: Self-realization. There are four assumptions that underlie Plato's description of his ideal community that, if accepted, would probably make that community work, that is, produce the best and most worthwhile life for all of its citizens.

Taken together, these assumptions constitute Plato's description of justice in the small and his theory of self-realization as the way to that best and most worthwhile life of the soul:

1. Each person has one of three distinct soul natures.

Plato assumed that every human being has a soul, that it has three parts, and that these parts determine the kind of person one will be. The theory of the tripartite soul is essential to both justice in the community, "justice in the large," and justice in the soul, "justice in the small," that Plato is advancing in the *Republic*. The three parts of the soul are: (1) the rational or reasoning part, which predominates in the naturally contemplative and deliberative person; (2) the spirited or active part, which predominates in the naturally pugnacious or aggressive person; and finally (3) the emotional or acquisitive part of the soul, which predominates in the naturally wealth-directed, material-object-loving person. The kind of person that you are essentially, whether a thinking, willing, or feeling person, depends on which of the three parts of your soul is dominant.

2. A person can live the best and most worthwhile life, that is, be happiest, when he or she is living according to his or her own soul nature.

Plato assumed that the soul nature that one had was the key to happiness. There are vocations, in other words, to match soul natures. Part of the task of Plato's educational system, as we shall see, is to match souls to jobs. Plato joins three specific vocations to the three predominant soul natures in the following manner: Corresponding to the soul that is predominantly rational and contemplative is the vocational class of the philosopher-kings whose task it is, like the head of the human body, to lead and direct the community. Corresponding to the soul that is predominantly aggressive and assertive is the vocational class of the guardians and warriors whose task it is, like the arms of the body, to protect and defend the community. Corresponding to the soul that is predominantly appetitive and acquisitive is the vocational class of the artisans, merchants, and farmers, whose task it is, like the stomach and intestines, to nourish the community.

Socrates points out to Glaucon, Plato's brother, that justice in the community and harmony and happiness in the soul depend, in the end, on the same thing, namely, each person, and thereby each class doing what they are best fitted by their own nature to do: The community is the soul writ large:

SOCRATES: Through these waters, then, said I, we have with difficulty made our way and we are fairly agreed that the same kinds equal in number are to be found in the community and in the soul of each one of us.

GLAUCON: That is so.

SOCRATES: Then does not the necessity of our former postulate immediately follow, that as and whereby the community was wise, so and thereby is the individual wise?

GLAUCON: Surely.

And in the same way as the community and the individual are wise, so also will it be with respect to bravery and self-control in the community for the two remaining classes and in the individual for the two remaining parts of the soul. Further, the community will be just in exactly the same way as the individual is just: "that the community was just by reason of each of the three classes found in it fulfilling its own function."[20] From the parallel with the community, then, the soul will be just and happy when all of its parts are performing their proper functions and working in harmony with one another.

3. A person's soul nature can be empirically discovered.

Plato claimed that education in the community could be employed to determine which citizens were by nature best suited to handle the three main tasks of the society: governing it, defending it, and nourishing it. There is to be every opportunity for the demotion of the unworthy and the promotion of the worthy. The educational plan that he developed in the *Republic* and later in his *Laws* worked somewhat as follows:

Ages   Educational Activity

1–5   The children of the workers are kept at home and the children of the rulers and soldiers are raised together in the state nurseries.

5–15   Reading, writing, music, the arts and gymnastics are taught with the teachers keeping a watchful eye in order to see what natures or abilities predominate in their charges. *The working class, the common people, begin to graduate.*

15–17   Mathematics is taught and examinations, verbal, written and physical, are given as future *farmers, craftsmen, and merchants continue to graduate.*

18–20 Military and physical training is taught and more tests are given as future *warriors graduate.*

20–30 Higher mathematics instruction and tests are given as the *lower ranks of philosopher-kings graduate.*

30–35 Pure reasoning is taught and higher training in moral reasoning is given.

35–50 More advanced practical instruction in running the state is given and the *higher ranks of philosopher-kings emerge.*

Socrates describes Plato's aristocratic (literally, "the rule of the best") vision of a community directed by men and women with the highest practical expertise backed by the purest theoretical knowledge:

> Unless, said I, either philosophers become kings in our communities or those whom we now call kings and rulers take to the pursuit of philosophy seriously and adequately, and there is a conjunction of these two things, political power and philosophical intelligence, while the motley horde of the natures who at present pursue either apart from the other are compulsorily excluded, there can be no cessation of troubles, dear Glaucon, for our communities, nor, I fancy, for the human race either.[21]

In his famous allegory of the cave, Plato offers one of the most memorable similes of the ultimate spiritual nature of his educational process. Our souls, he says, are like chained miserable prisoners in a gloomy and enshadowed cave. Unable to move about or to see beyond the shadows directly in front of us, we live in ignorance of our soul's real nature and of our true surroundings. But then one of the souls is relieved of his shackles and forced to stand up, he turns about and sees the causes of the shadows and his bondage. Now begins the soul's ascent to knowledge and enlightenment as it is dragged (by the teacher) up the steep and darkened incline to the brightened mouth of the cave. There the soul suddenly beholds a world of reality and beauty lighted by the most dazzling and resplendent Being of all symbolized by the sun. Gradually raising his eyes, the prisoner beholds the truth, beauty, and goodness of this new world and he is transformed by the experience. If the prisoner, now filled with the vision of his soul's ascent to Reality, which is actually a descent into itself, should return to the unhappy community within the cave and tell his wretched companions what he has seen, what would their reaction be? Socrates answers the question for the world's reformers, mystics, and idealists:

> Would he not provoke laughter, and would it not be said of him that he had returned from his journey aloft with his eyes ruined and that it was not worth while even to attempt the ascent. And if it were possible to lay hands on and to kill the man who tried to release them and lead them up, would they not kill him?[22]

This is the martyr of Athens speaking, of course, and Plato was all too conscious of the irony that Socrates' words must have produced.

Violent communities are caused by violent people, people ignorant of who and what they are, people doing what they are not fitted by their soul natures to do. Ignorant people in the wrong jobs makes them violent, "unjust" in Plato's words, and they cause nothing but trouble for everyone else in the community.

4. *Therefore, in order to find the best and most worthwhile life that a human being can live, that is, in order to be happy, a person must discover his or her soul nature and then live according to that nature.*

Plato assumed that justice in the soul paralleled justice in the community such that to be happy, to live well, one must let reason rule the soul just as the philosopher-king rules the community. All persons can be happy—the key lies, as it did for Socrates, in soul-realization, the examined life.

Plato's Prescription for Community: The Republic

As a way of summarizing our description of Plato's way of community, we turn to our handy four-stage Prescription for Community presented earlier.

The problem. The central problem for Plato is really twofold— a personal problem involving the soul and an inseparable political problem involving the community. There are evils aplenty waiting to seize either the soul or the community and suffering abounds at both levels. Given the history of Plato's times, the Republic, as a community, free of disease and sickness (only the lazy and the leisured get sick), empty of vermin and pests, bereft of dissension and licentiousness, and unafraid of enemies and the future, must have spoken directly for, and to, the war generation of those times. Athens had suffered unspeakably the tragedies of the Persian War (490–479 B.C.E.), the First Peloponnesian War (461–446 B.C.E.), the Great Peloponnesian War (431–404 B.C.E.), and the Corinthian War (395–386 B.C.E.). In addition there were the plagues, the famines, and the dozens of smaller battles and skirmishes that the great empire of Athens endured in the periods during and between these wars. In a sense, Plato was a spokesman for this Peloponnesian lost generation, a generation of despair, fear, and apathy, a generation dominated by a failure of nerve that sought places to hide; and the Hellenistic world that followed produced just such places including Cynicism, Stoicism, Epicurean Hedonism, Skepticism, and, of course, even Platonism. The *Republic* was a response to that first lost generation of hopeless, betrayed and bewildered young men and women, as the Athenian community came crashing down, the product of an insane, violent, and unjust world.

The causes. Injustice, *adikē* (pronounced "ah-dee-kay"), is the concept that Plato uses to describe the imbalance that causes the suffering spoken of previously. Injustice is the imbalance and disharmony within soul or community that leads to the vices of ignorance, dishonor, and intemperance in the former and to the excesses of military oligarchy, tyranny, timocracy, and democracy in the latter. The cause, in turn, of this injustice is primarily ignorance and in particular ignorance of one's own nature through lack of proper education. If the citizens knew who they were, what their soul nature or natural abilities were, then presumably they would follow the vocation for which they were naturally fitted. As a result, the community would be harmoniously balanced as those fitted by nature to rule, to defend, and to produce became rulers, defenders, and producers, respectively. And in following that vocation, they, in turn, would be just and happy, and the community would, in turn, be peaceful, just, and happy.

The solution. The solution to the problem of suffering lay, as it did for Socrates previously, in stopping the ignorance, establishing justice in both the soul and the community, and thereby producing happiness for everyone. The solution is happiness at both levels.

The ways. The ways to happiness in the soul and happiness in the community lay through education and, ultimately, soul-realization, that is, through establishing justice through erasing ignorance, finding one's soul-nature, and working at that vocation that one is suited by one's nature to follow.

Aldous Huxley:
The Community of the World State

Aldous Huxley in his early years was fundamentally a sceptic, that is, he was naturally suspicious of anyone who claimed "I've got it!"—where the "it" was some perfect truth, a complete knowledge, a superior salvation. Huxley, while open to being persuaded by his own experience, that being the test of all such claims, was deeply antagonistic to all absolute declarations, but especially to those that led to fear and extravagance. This naturally sceptical nature was coupled with a bias toward the intellectual life that compelled him to rebel against the grosser emotions and vulgar behavior and to satirize them wherever possible. This nature, combined with an exceptional literary talent, led Huxley to produce some of the finest philosophic novels of the twentieth century. There is, I would suggest, one compellingly central question that drove Huxley through the some five phases of his literary life, a life that spanned the earliest cynical despairing years (1919–30), the utopian years (1931–39), the pacifist years (1937–48), the Vedanta years (1939–45), to the final psychedelic years (1955–63). That question also dominated the lives of Socrates and Plato, and it was simply: What is the best and most worthwhile *life* that a human being can live? Coupled with this dominant question is our familiar second question that all three pursued with equal concern: What is the best and most worthwhile *community* that will make that life possible?

Aldous Huxley's Life

Aldous Huxley was born in England in 1894. He was the biological product of two great English families, each of which contributed something genetically distinctive to his philosophic and imaginative genius. His grandfather on his father's side was the essayist, biologist, evolutionist, and defender of Charles Darwin, Sir Thomas Henry Huxley; his great-grandfather on his mother's side was the educator, Dr. Thomas Arnold of Rugby, father of the poet Matthew Arnold. With such forebears it is small wonder that great things were expected of Aldous, things that were subsequently fulfilled beyond all expectation. Over fifty major works of poetry, essays, plays, short stories, and over a dozen distinguished novels, flowed from his pen beginning with a book of poetry, *The Burning Wheel*, in 1916, and ending with his last novel, *Island*, in 1962 and a final collection of essays, *Literature and Science*, in 1963.

In September of 1908 Aldous entered Eton College, where he planned to begin the pursuit of biology, a pursuit in which his older brother, Julian, was soon to earn honors and international recognition. But then two events in the young Aldous's life conspired to affect him profoundly and unalterably, events that turned him from science into entirely different paths.

In November of 1908 his mother, the educator, Julia Huxley, died quite unexpectedly. Aldous, then fourteen, had been utterly devoted to her and her death brought about a bewildering upheaval in his life. This was followed by another, and in many ways, heavier blow when in 1910 an attack of keratitis punctata left him nearly blind, necessitating his withdrawal from Eton. Huxley was to remain legally blind for the remainder of his life, though the handicap did not prevent him from using his good eye and, like the mythical Theban seer, Teresias, seeing more in one lifetime than most of us could see in several.

Following the tragic suicide of his brother Trev Huxley in 1914, Aldous continued his education at Oxford in English and French literature, his poor eyesight now improved by surgery and strong lenses. He quickly formed friendships with many of the young men who would shortly be slaughtered in the Great War of 1914–18. Aldous was to stand by angrily and helplessly as the cream of Oxford and British intellectual life marched off to battle and to obliteration. He graduated from Oxford in 1916, the year of the first battle of the Somme. In a sense, this battle was the turning point of the war and the end of a way of life in Britain and in the world that would never return. About that single battle of July 1, 1916, A. J. P. Taylor was later to write:

> The Somme had no longer any purpose as a field of battle. No strategical prize would be gained even if there were a great advance. . . . The British infantry had enthusiasm and not much else. These were the men who had answered Kitchener's call; hardly any were conscripts. They had received hasty and rudimentary training. . . . They had been instructed

to rely mainly on the bayonet. When it came to real war, the British infantry on the Somme never saw those whom they were fighting; and the bayonet was used only to kill men who had already surrendered. The junior officers [the young university volunteers Huxley knew] were also recruits recently trained. They, too, had enthusiasm and little else. They had been taught to expose themselves recklessly—hence officer casualties were often six times greater than those of other ranks. They had also been taught to obey unquestioningly and never to show initiative.

And what was the result of the first massive British attack against the German Somme entrenchments?

On 1 July 1916 the British sustained 60,000 casualties, 20,000 of them killed—the heaviest loss ever suffered in a single day by a British army or by any army in the First World War.

Taylor concludes his account:

Strategically, the battle of the Somme was an unredeemed defeat. . . . Idealism perished on the Somme. The enthusiastic volunteers were enthusiastic no longer. They had lost faith in their cause, in their leaders, in everything except loyalty to their fighting comrades. The war ceased to have a purpose. . . . The Somme set the picture by which future generations saw the First World War: brave helpless soldiers; blundering obstinate generals; nothing achieved.[23]

Just as Plato was a spokesman for the Peloponnesian generation, Aldous Huxley was to become the spokesman for the Somme generation, those descendents of despair, cynicism and amorality. And the foundation was laid for a similar commitment to subsequent lost generations of hopeless, betrayed, and bewildered young men and women, the products of insane and unjust communities.

About one of his early and very successful novels, *Antic Hay* (1923), in which he attempted to speak for and to the Somme generation, Huxley was to write:

[*Antic Hay*] is a book written by a member of what I may call the war-generation for others of his kind; and . . . it is intended to reflect—fantastically, of course, but none the less faithfully—the life and opinions of an age which has seen the violent disruption of almost all the standards, conventions, and values current in the previous epoch.[24]

Huxley's early novels, as mentioned above, are loquacious, intellectual, sophisticated, and cynical, with a strong current of hedonism flowing insistently through them. He offers his ideas and the ideas of his generation against a background plot that is oftentimes barely able to sustain the flow of humor, irony, and pessimism. The hero of *Antic Hay*, Theodore Gumbril, for example, has just invented trousers with "a pneumatic seat, inflatable by means of a tube fitted with a valve." One of the recurring themes of the novel is that "tomorrow will be as awful as today." Huxley, in this early phase of his life, was following in the honored tradition of the philosophic novel and treading in the footsteps of other similar cerebral masters such as Herman Melville, Emile Zola, Fyodor Dostoievsky, and Leo Tolstoy, all of whom saw their novel's characters as media for ideas and intellectual controversy.

But it is the commitment of Huxley's fictional heroes to pleasure that makes him and his characters different from the foregoing. Huxley holds the literary mirror up for all of us to peer into and what we see is the hedonism that lives in our own age as a reality as well as an ideal to be pursued. If the hedonist seeks to create a life empty of suffering as well as one full of pleasure, then the former has already been realized in our time: for, despite Huxley's early doubts about any permanent success in escaping from pain into the arms of pleasure, it is becoming nonetheless increasingly possible for us all to go from womb to tomb and never experience one moment of suffering, one moment of anxiety. In the portentous words of the mathematician, musicologist, historian of science, and close friend of Aldous Huxley, J. W. N. Sullivan, writing in 1927:

> To the modern mind suffering is essentially remediable. Suffering is primarily due to physical and moral maladjustment, and with the spread of science and correct social theories we shall be able to abolish it. For an increasing number of people suffering is already practically abolished. They may go through life without meeting one problem they cannot evade until they reach their death bed.[25]

For the hedonist, what Sullivan has predicted constitutes half the struggle, that is, a life without pain. What remains next is to fill that painless void with as much pleasure as possible.

Throughout many of his early and still popular novels, *Crome Yellow* (1921), *Antic Hay* (1923), *Those Barren Leaves* (1925), *Point Counter Point* (1928) and *Brief Candles* (1930), Huxley presents a picture of the pursuit of pleasure by the effete upper middle classes of England and the Continent. While always urbane, witty, and intellectually challenging, these early novels, with their brilliant descriptions of a society devoted to nothing but the seeking of pleasure, all pale beside his memorable utopian satire, *Brave New World*, written from May to August in 1931. It is to this classic work of fiction with Huxley's own prophetic pronouncements about Western communal insanity and injustice that we now turn.[26]

Brave New World: *A Hedonistic Community*

Brave New World dominates the second decade of Huxley's literary life. A splendid hedonism, of course, is the philosophic theme throughout the work, as it depicts an attempt by human beings to prolong life and to make that prolonging as pleasant as possible. The novel remains Huxley's most popular and most controversial book, having the dubious honor of being for many years the second most widely banned novel in high school libraries across the United States (J. D. Salinger's *Catcher in the Rye* wins!).

The setting of *Brave New World* is London some 600 years in the future. The reader is gradually introduced to World State, the new name of the community that dominates the entire globe except for a few isolated primitive reservations and island outposts. The government of World State is a benevolent totalitarian dictatorship run by a carefully bred bureaucracy of its most intrusively caring citizens: Plato's philosopher kings, with a hedonistic twist, may have finally triumphed.

The reader is presented to this ideal state, where "everyone is happy now," through the eyes of a stranger, John, a "savage" from an Indian reservation in Arizona. Brought back to London from a primitive twentieth-century environment, John is slowly indoctrinated into the sights, sounds, principles, and pleasures of this modern hedonistic community where it is forbidden to be unhappy and so simple to be happy. John, from his primitive reservation where the past stood still, brings with him the beliefs and philosophies of the now long-extinct twentieth century. And it is that century with its horrors and sufferings, but with its ancient values and ideals, that has led decades later to the establishment of the World State with its solution to, and dissolution of, the horrors and the atrocities of that century.

One of the dedicated citizens of World State explains to John the rationale behind the New Order with its wonderful consequences for all. For example, there are no literary or dramatic tragedies now, he says, and no books, persons, events, and experiences causing or depicting tragedies and suffering; all of these are banned—pain and Shakespeare are out because sex and soma are in:

> Because our world is not the same as Othello's world. And you can't make tragedies without social instability. The world's stable now. People are happy; they get what they want, and they never want what they can't get. They're well off; they're safe; they're never ill; they're not afraid of death; they're blissfully ignorant of passion and old age; they're plagued with no mothers or fathers; they're got no wives or children or lovers to feel strongly about; they're so conditioned that they practically can't help behaving as they ought to behave. And if anything should go wrong, there's *soma*.[27]

Soma is the pleasure-enhancing, anxiety-reducing super-Prozac that takes away the blues, the pain, the dwindles, the boredom, and the anything-else that sorrowful flesh is heir to. The inhabitants of World State have found the perfect euphoric drug.

The Controller, Mustapha Mond, a sort of twenty-first-century philosopher-king, later explains to John the history of this tightly managed state as John begins to object to the lack of freedom for its inhabitants. John mourns the loss of the nobler virtues drowned by the outrageous sexual license that devours the lives of the citizens in his new-found home:

> "My dear young friend," said Mustapha Mond, "civilization has absolutely no need of nobility or heroism. These things are symptoms of political inefficiency. In a properly organized society like ours, nobody has any opportunities for being noble or heroic. Conditions have got to be thoroughly unstable before the occasion can arise. Where there are wars, where there are divided allegiances, where there are temptations to be resisted, objects of love to be fought for or defended—there obviously, nobility and heroism have some sense. But there aren't any wars nowadays."

And what is the reason for such changes?

> The greatest care is taken to prevent you from loving anyone too much. There's no such thing as a divided allegiance; you're so conditioned that you can't help doing what you ought to do. And what you ought to do is on the whole so pleasant, so many of the natural impulses are allowed free play, that there aren't really any temptations to resist.[28]

In this impulse-driven but rigidly regulated community, total control is maintained over five castes of insanely happy, absurdly contented inhabitants. Their behavior has been fatefully determined by both genetic engineering, everyone is "bottle-born," and psychological conditioning, Pavlovian training abounds, wherein "free will" is simply defined as "liking what you have to do."

The five social castes are patterned somewhat after Plato's three classes of citizens. The *Alphas* are at the intellectual top; they manage and direct the community, and are the least bound by the rules that enclasp the other four castes. The *Betas* constitute the bureaucracy of the community and take their orders from the Alphas above and see to the operations of the other castes below. If the Alphas are the pseudo-philosopher-kings of the World State, then the Betas are the leisured middle class that consumes what the lower Gammas, Deltas, and Epsilons produce and maintain. As the five castes descend in order, so does their literacy, their intelligence, their height, and their individual distinctness and difference, until the lowest Epsilons emerge as physically indistinguishable semi-morons useful for carrying out the monotonous, dirty and onerous work in the community, work that they do with joyous abandon. There is no need for a warrior caste in this warfree community, though there are police. The literary parallel comes closest to Aristotle's utopia in his *Politics*, where Huxley's Deltas and Epsilons emerge as Aristotle's nonrational slaves. In Huxley's World State both of Plato's and Aristotle's utopian political goals have been achieved: everyone is happy now, and everyone is "free" now, because everyone loves what they have to do; and what genetics and conditioning have joined, nature is powerless to put asunder.

But John the Savage is an old-fashioned romantic, a nostalgic conservative, a psychopathic religious and moral fanatic, who clings to the long-dead old-fashioned virtues. John emphatically refuses to trade his painful freedom for the World State's security. In a blistering exchange with the Controller near the close of *Brave New World* they confront each other for the last time. The Savage begins: "Isn't there something in living dangerously?" And the Controller agrees but indicates that there is a compulsory therapy that makes living dangerously not only outdated but impossible. But, he advises John, there is now a drug that makes dangerous living *experiences* possible, personal experiences that harm and injure no one at all:

> "Violent Passion Surrogate. Regularly once a month we flood the whole system with adrenin. It's the complete physiological equivalent of fear and rage. All the tonic effects of murdering Desdemona and being murdered by Othello, without any of the inconveniences."
>
> "But I like inconveniences." [the Savage responds]
>
> "We don't," said the Controller. "We prefer to do things comfortably."
>
> "But I don't want comfort. I want God, I want poetry, I want real danger, I want freedom, I want goodness. I want sin."
>
> "In fact," said Mustapha Mond, "you're claiming the right to be unhappy. . . . Not to mention the right to grow old and ugly and impotent; the right to have syphilis and cancer; the right to have too little to eat; the right to be lousy [to have lice]; the right to live in constant apprehension of what may happen to-morrow; the right to catch typhoid; the right to be tortured by unspeakable pains of every kind."
>
> There was a long silence.
>
> "I claim them all," said the Savage at last.

And the Controller concludes the dialogue with the only possible World State response:

> Mustapha Mond shrugged his shoulders. "You're welcome," he said.[29]

The novel ends, some would say, optimistically. Unlike the hero of George Orwell's *1984*, who is trapped forever in his terrifying and cloying totalitarian state, Huxley's hero has a way out. Unable to withstand the pleasures and the surfeiting security of the World State together with the shame and guilt that its sexual license has awakened in him, John the Savage takes the only way out left to him: He hangs himself.

In 1958 Huxley wrote an afterword to his famous work in which he said, "The prophecies made in 1931 are coming true much sooner than I thought they would."[30] Where *Brave New World*, unlike Orwell's *1984*, had made no mention of nuclear energy and nuclear war and atomic contamination, the possibility of a nuclear holocaust had added a new dimension of horror to be dealt with in assessing our troubled community. Huxley's prophetic satire of a world gone mad with bureaucracy, technology, and pleasure is frightening enough. But even more terrifying, perhaps, is his view of a community that seems even now, to the post-Hiroshima generation of the twenty-first century that has replaced the Somme generation, strangely and compellingly appealing.

Before offering a comparison of our two communities, the Republic and the World State, and the several problems and puzzles to which they lead, let's very briefly summarize our investigation thus far of Huxley's hedonistic community using our four stage Prescription for Community.

Aldous Huxley's Prescription for Community: *The World State*

The problem. The central problem for the World State was, as with Plato, twofold: securing personal happiness for all of its citizens, and political stability within the community. That is to say, the problem before the World State came into existence was human misery on the one hand and community anarchy on the other, conditions that produced the Somme generation with its own despair, fear, and apathy.

The causes. The causes of the suffering are very varied but all involve some form of instability. The instability, in turn, Huxley relates to various physical causes, such as war, famine, old age, disease, the rising new technology, industrialization, and overpopulation together with various psychological causes such as hatred, attachments, lust, anger, solitude, boredom, anxiety, and the fear of change, that is, the unanswered challenge of the new and the different to the old and the habitual.

The solution. The solution to all of these causes of suffering is, of course, happiness, and happiness for everyone, from Alphas to Epsilons. And by "happiness," of course, Huxley means pleasure. The promise and anticipation of future pleasures, sensual pleasures, of course, produce the conformity and the absolute control that bring about the stability, personal and communal, that make the World State work.

The ways. The ways to happiness, personal and communal, lay, on the whole, in the consumption of soma, the attendance at the Feelies, those erotic electrically stimulating and sense-prodding movies beloved by so many, the exciting electronic games, sexual activity, and the public religious worship of Our Ford, the newly adored and technologically inspiring industrial Savior-God. Ford is identified historically with the uniform mass producing and dehumanizing assembly line of the industrial age that has made possible all of the delicious and delirious pleasures in the World State. Each of the castes has, of course, its own particular way of generating pleasure, ways directly related to the intelligence of the caste and to the awareness of the role that each caste plays in the community. But the essence of all of these ways is pleasure. The World State is a totalitarian technocracy, a hedonistically driven, psychologically and politically conditioned, community.

We turn finally to a comparison of our two communities of the Republic and the World State and to the three central questions first broached above regarding communities. Two of those questions were, What is a community? And how does one become a member of a community? For Plato and Huxley, we are really asking, What is it that is shared that makes both the Republic and the World State into communities? And what must one share in order to become a citizen of such a community? Finally, there is our third question that we will also pursue: Can the problems of violence and peace in the twenty-first century be solved through Plato's or Huxley's way of community? The pattern of exploration, investigation, and analysis of community in this first chapter will, as mentioned previously, shape the pattern of presentation for our four remaining communities in the succeeding chapters of this book.

The Communities of Republic and World State: A Comparison

In what follows we'll concentrate on comparing the two Prescriptions for Liberation from Suffering for the Republic and the World State and keep in mind our three previous questions in that comparing.

The Problem

Plato's problem is essentially what we have called "spiritual" since the self-realization that he has in mind as a solution to the problem involves the knowledge of the *psychē* or soul, which is the true Self for Plato. This Self is ultimately Real, it is eternal, unchanging, and independent, Godlike and divine. The way to the knowledge of this Real being is a spiritual undertaking for Plato as it was for Socrates. Hence, if any happiness is to be found it must come from this internal spiritual search within a community of like-minded searchers. It is that shared search for spiritual *well-being* (literally, "*eudaimonia*") that binds the community together and makes the Republic a community. Without that self-knowledge, there must be suffering at the individual level and, with that, suffering at the community level.

Huxley's problem is essentially what we might call a "materialistic" problem. It is solved at the bodily-neurological-psychological level, for that is where pleasure lies. Hence, if any happiness is to be found it must come following the proper *genetic* and *conditioning* technologies applied within the community. Mistakes in either area, and *Brave New World* catalogs a few such errors, can lead to questioning the entire community, with subsequent misery for those recalcitrant citizens not able to conform and fit in. The human automata, for that is what they appear to be, that inhabit the World State are without a doubt happy; being a member of the community really means that one is committed to being happy. And it is that shared pleasure that is the key to individual and, with that, collective happiness; it is that which binds the community together and makes the World State a community.

The Causes

Plato's causes are first, injustice, the imbalance that produces individual soul-suffering as well as public community-suffering; and second, ignorance of who one is, what one's soul, or Self, nature is, and what one's appropriate vocational place is to be in the community; together these produce the anxiety and malaise that makes injustice, eccentricity, that is, suffering, possible.

Huxley's cause is not ignorance of the Self but rather it is a form of *adikē*, instability, a kind of imbalance, once again. But since the problem for Huxley has already been solved through biological and psychological technology, there is no need for each citizen of the World State to fight the battle of Who am I? all over again. The community has already fought the battle of self-identity. If one really wants to know who one is, then one can do it rather painlessly and effortlessly: just look at the color of the clothes that one wears, gray for Alphas, mulberry for Betas, green for Gammas, khaki for Deltas, and black for Epsilons.

For both Plato and Huxley, it is the outsider who suffers and it is ignorance that essentially defines the outsider in both utopias. For Plato, the outsider is the person who is unaware of the laws and the operating mechanism of the new community, who refuses to abide by the rules of the new order, and who is ignorant of the fact that those rules are designed to make him or her happy. John the Savage is ignorant of the fact that the soma will relieve his suffering, he's ignorant of the fact that everyone is happy now, and, finally, he's stupid enough to believe, some readers must feel, that suffering is good, ennobling, and honorable. For John it is the refusal to accept membership in this hedonic club, the citizenship of conformity in this community, that leads to his final desperate escape.

The Solution

Plato's solution is a spiritual solution, Huxley's is a material solution. Each community enforces its solution to the problem of suffering in quite different ways. Plato's commitment to free will suggests, I believe, a strong belief in the power of reason to solve human problems. Plato may distrust the masses, as Huxley certainly does, and both men are, indeed, political conservatives, but Plato feels that each person in the community, if only he or she can be taught what is best for them, will adhere to that best, or can be brought or be led to that best of all possible happy lives. Plato trusts reason and reasonableness, though he remains suspicious of its broad presence in all human souls (it is, after all, weak in both the defenders and the producers in his caste system). Plato, like Huxley, optimistically believes that it is possible for all human beings to be happy. And for Plato, knowing who you are, adopting the vocation that fits your soul nature, and letting reason be your control and guide in the soul, just as the philosopher-kings are the controls and guides in the state, is the surest way of securing that happiness.

Huxley (that is, *Brave New World*), on the other hand, is deeply suspicious of reason. It is, after all, gened-out in the lower classes and highly controlled in the upper. Human beings can all be made happy but they must be driven not led, manufactured and not grown, to that happiness. Only by tinkering with the genes and by conditioning with the whip and the soma can we guarantee that everyone will end up doing what they have to do. Huxley leaves nothing to chance, for it was chance, absence of control, after all, that led to the Somme generation that necessitated the World State. Huxley, in *Brave New World*, is the real archconservative here, and the World State, with its deep distrust of human nature, is the real totalitarian society. By comparison, Plato is the archliberal, arguing that all humans are basically good—they all possess an immortal and real *psyche*, after all. But oddly enough, it's Plato who has been damned over the decades as the originator of communism, fascism, and Nazism, having gotten a bad public rap from his more liberal detractors over the centuries.

The Way

Plato places his faith in both reason, after all he was Socrates' best defender, and education as the keys to the selection process for determining who belongs where in the community's adamantine vocational structure. Each person decides for himself or *herself* who they are and what they thereby owe the community. Plato's commitment to transmigration of the soul lays further stress on the spiritual foundation of his community and places his optimistic belief in a rational free will at the center of his communal *apologia*. Where vocational choices are to be made, choices that will determine one's future place in both present and future communities all set within what is obviously a just universe, the role of education and reason will be of the greatest importance.

Huxley was no Athenian and the alternatives that he presents to the reader as ways of solving the problems of human suffering are *prima facie* unreliable, indefensible, and perhaps unacceptable. No Athenian, no Socrates or Plato, would have embraced the conform-or-kill-yourself options of the World State that face John the Savage no matter how optimistically one interprets his final act. Plato begins his utopia by asking all adults to leave. Huxley does provide reservations of a sort for malcontents, and there is always the hard duty in places like Iceland, even for rebelling and discontented Alphas. So perhaps conform-or-die is not to be taken too seriously as the only choice for those Alphas who had mistakenly had too much alcohol put into their blood surrogate at conception.

John the Savage, however, is the Platonist in the World State.

He is committed to reason, choice, suffering, change, challenge, growth, and salvation. In a community where stagnation and staticity are the norm there will be a premium put upon those ways that entail habit, permanence, repetition, sameness, predictability, and routine. There are no surprises in the World State. There is no place for John the Savage. The World State is a communal hive that just happens to contain human beings.

Problems with the Republic and the World State Communities

There are two problems that stand out and must be solved by anyone considering paying the price for membership in either the Republic or the World State.

The Problem of Lost Virtues

First, John the Savage raises questions for the concerned reader that should have allayed the fears of all those parents of all those high school students forbidden to read *Brave New World*. John asks, quite rightly, what will happen to the other goods of civilization, if pleasure is taken to be the only good as the hedonists have claimed? So what happens to love (women are treated as slabs of meat), knowledge, beauty (the World State is boringly plain and hideously ugly and even Plato's drab Republic seems aesthetically exciting by comparison), accomplishments in overcoming hardships, satisfaction at finishing challenging tasks, rites of passage that induce pride, the sense of honor, and so on? This first problem, which we might call "the problem of lost virtues," spills over into a second problem as we consider the holder of those now abandoned virtues.

The Problem of Communo-fascism

Second, therefore, is the question of what happens to the solitary subject, the individual, faced with the overwhelming power of the collective community? Are the rights of individual persons to be submerged into the will of the collective itself? We might call this second puzzle "the problem of communo-fascism." Huxley, himself, is concerned about the problem of lost virtues and the problem of communo-fascism; and he's troubled by what the collective state mind has done both to the "old-fashioned virtues" and to the individual holder of those virtues. Here, in 1956, he points to the introduction of a new and insidious euphemistic vocabulary designed to make our secure and collective times more palatable:

> A new Social Ethic is replacing our traditional ethical system—the system in which the individual is primary. The key words in this Social Ethic are "adjustment," "adaptation," "socially orientated behavior," "belongingness," "acquisition of social skills," "team work," "group living," "group loyalty," "group dynamics," "group thinking," "group creativity."

And he concludes:

> Its basic assumption is that the social whole has greater worth and significance than its individual parts, that inborn biological differences should be sacrificed to cultural uniformity, that the rights of the collectivity take precedence over what the eighteenth century called the Rights of Man.[31]

The problem of communo-fascism has been recognized by another social critic of our times. Sir Karl Popper identifies the origin of the modern totalitarian state with the philosophy of Plato and, in particular, with Plato's utopian vision contained in the *Republic*:

> Plato was right when he saw in this doctrine [of individualism] the enemy of his caste state; and he hated it more than any other of the "subversive" doctrines of his time.

Popper then comments on two passages from Plato's last work, the *Laws*, which make reference to the *Republic*, first to its community of women and children and, second, to the rule of military leadership in the state:

> Plato describes here the constitution of the *Republic* as "the highest form of the state." In this highest state, he tells us, "there is common property of wives, of children, and of all chattels. And everything possible has been done to eradicate from our life everywhere and in every way all that is private and individual. So far as it can be done, even those things which nature herself has made private and individual have

somehow become the common property of all. Our very eyes and ears and hands seem to see, to hear, and to act, as if they belonged not to individuals but to the community."[32]

From this we can probably conclude that for Plato the individual *is* the community.

On a second, even more outspoken attack by Plato on individualism, Popper points to a passage in the *Laws* on leadership that bears on the *Republic* and its discipline:

"The greatest principle of all," Plato writes, "is that nobody, whether male or female, should ever be without a leader. Nor should the mind of anybody be habituated to letting him do anything at all on his own initiative. But in war and in the midst of peace—to his leader he shall direct his eye, and follow him faithfully. And even in the smallest matters he should stand under leadership. . . . In a word, he should teach his soul, by long habit, never to dream of acting independently, and to become utterly incapable of it. In this way the life of all will be spent in total community."[33]

Popper concludes, "In the field of politics, the individual is to Plato the Evil One himself."[34]

If Popper and Huxley are correct, then the problem of communo-fascism as well as the problem of lost virtues that probably accompanies it, have both an ancient origin and modern instantiations. These problems will be with us as we examine four other attempts to establish utopian, that is, conceptually perfect, communities as ways of solving human social problems.

Having said all of this regarding the problems with the Republic and the World State, where do we stand now with respect to the three central questions posed earlier? We conclude this chapter with a brief response to those questions.

Conclusion: Three Central Questions

What is it that is shared that makes both the Republic and the World State into communities? The Republic is bound together by the common and rational search for happiness. The World State is bound together by the happiness already found. Where everyone in Plato's utopia shares in the search for who they are (barring slaves, if they were, indeed, part of the state), not everyone shares in such a search in the World State: one doesn't have to search for what's already been provided for you. But with Huxley's admission that genetic and conditioning errors are possible, and at least two examples are given, and with the possibility that dissidents and reformers may even now be awaiting birth from one of the state's genetic laboratories, a new dimension, a fear and suspicion of reason and revolt, is added to Huxley's seemingly monotonous, routinized, soma-saturated society: There may be more savage Johns waiting out there, less timid, more insistent. But with those optimistic possibilities aside, what is shared in Huxley's state is a commitment, free or compelled, to a life of pleasure, distraction, and conformity.

How does one become a member of such communities? The Republic, like the World State, gives the impression that merely by being born into or "decanted in," as with the latter, such a totally enveloping community immediately endows one with membership. But I think that there are subtle differences between the two communities. In the Republic, there may be stages of citizenship, given what we know of Plato's educational system. Recall that one progresses through that system to the various levels where the discoveries are made that one is of the *working class*, the *warrior class*, or *philosopher-king class*; whereupon one drops out at each stage in order to drop into one's vocation. It might be argued that those droppings-out *cum* droppings-in constitute rites of passage. As such, they constitute those points at which one secures full membership in the community, for it is at these levels that one begins to actively support the community by full participation in the working tasks, as dictated by one's nature, that will most benefit the community.

The World State operates on a similar principle of vocational training, indoctrination, and conditioning; but the community, in a sense, already owns one, because the state has produced or manufactured one without benefit of nurturing parents or sexual activity between parents, and one now must help to manufacture others just like oneself. There are no choices not to belong, and if there were such anomalies, they would be swiftly dealt with by further conditioning or by exile. So, in answer to this second question, one doesn't do much of anything in order to belong to the World State since it is all done *for* one. In the Republic there are things that one does in finding oneself, in knowing who one is, and in knowing what one's spiritual soul nature is, such that, in order to belong to the Republic, it must all be done *by* oneself. But in the end what one comes to see is that there is an identity between oneself and the community. The community doesn't own one, as in the World State, but one sees the community writ large in oneself and oneself writ small in the community. In both the World State and the Republic the individual has been devoured by the community as one's needs, choices, and desires become directed, controlled, and identified with those of the community.

Third, and finally, we might ask now, Can the problems of violence and peace in the twenty-first century be solved through either of these two ways of community? The answer is, Yes, probably!—though the price may be high. This qualified affirmative answer to our third question can be justified by answering this next question: Why would anyone want to belong to either community? One obvious answer is, of course, that citizens of both the Republic and the World State have been promised pleasure, happiness, well-being, and contentment, a very attractive set of properties, especially for members of the Peloponnesian and the Somme generations.

Both the Republic and the World State hold out another promise that must also prove attractive for all citizens of both communities, and that is *security*, security from suffering in all of its forms. Here, the World State speaks more directly to twenty-first-century anxieties than Plato given his lack of abiding concern for issues that bother us today, for example, rebellion, terrorism, disease, the environment, old age, death, anxiety, famine, and so on. The guaranteed security from the fears and realities of all of these terrors comes at a price, of course. The familiar inverse relation between freedom and security applies to all totalitarian societies such that as security increases, freedom decreases, and vice versa.

So what would one be willing to pay or give up in order to get rid of crime, hatred, war and disease, and violence, once and for all? This is not just a question for college sophomores in these days of big government, big military, and big business. World State uniformity, "Everyone belongs to everyone else," and Republic conformity, "Everyone belongs to the state," are all around us, one might feel; and uniformity and conformity are small, and maybe even acceptable and embraceable, costs for security and peace: freedom-to is a small price to pay for freedom-from.

Both the Republic and the World State promise to reduce violence and to raise peace, and do it through a citizen's identification with the community. Consider our two forms of the community argument, above. First, the community violence argument:

1. No one would intentionally do violence to oneself.

This premise is certainly acceptable to our utopian citizens.

2. Oneself is the Republic/World State community.

Our properly educated utopian citizens would probably accept this premise. Both Plato and Huxley lay a foundation, it seems to me, for accepting this premise. The citizens of the Republic are under an obligation to recognize one more golden lie and to see the community as themselves and to encourage others, through the educational system, to do likewise. Similarly, the citizens of the World State embrace Lenina Crowne's adolescent cry that everyone now belongs to everyone else, which nicely expresses the belief that they are the community and that they also have a duty to instill this recognition in others. Lenina even proselytizes the good news by attempting to seduce John the Savage to this point of view.

But while both communities are committed to a political organicism and to a community dominance over its members, curiously enough both utopias seem grounded in an egoism, a spiritual or hedonic egoism. Each citizen is seeking *my* happiness, *my* self-realization, *my* pleasure, and *my* satisfaction. Consequently, there is no room, given such psychological egoism, for the communal altruism that would seem to generally follow from the members' identification with community. The utopian citizens recognize, it would seem, that in order to secure their own personal ends, an identification with community is necessary, and that's all. What we have then is not a communal altruism so much as a communal egoism. Our two utopias will differ, in this regard, from the four historical and altruistic communities that follow in the next four chapters. There we shall find that each accepts the second premise above, and each embraces the ethical altruism that would seem to follow from the identification of members of a community with their community.[35] We will return to a discussion of the relation between altruism as communal altruism, and egoism as communal egoism, and the claim that oneself is the community when we get to the last chapter of this book.

Our utopian citizens would accept the conclusion:

3. Therefore, no one would intentionally do violence to the Republic/World State community.

For similar reasons, the community peace argument would be quite acceptable to these properly educated citizens, as well:

1. Everyone would intentionally do peace to oneself.
2. Oneself is the Republic/World State community.
3. Therefore, everyone would intentionally do peace to the Republic/World State community.

The language is, again, admittedly clumsy but attention is focused in both community arguments on the role that education or awareness must play in removing the unintentional ignorance and coming to know who one is, and how to get what is best for oneself.

Again, quite apart now from the community peace argument, our utopian citizens are as hereditarily chosen, trained, and conditioned to seek peace as they are to eradicate violence. But here our two utopias would probably diverge in the manner of the peace that they produce and in securing what is best for each citizen. Plato's citizens, after all, produce virtues appropriate to their soul natures, wisdom, courage, self-control and, for all, ultimately, justice. Huxley's citizens have no such virtues, nor do they have the desire to pursue them. The World State produces uniformity, staticity, an absence of violence, but where's the peace? where's the beauty, excellence, integrity, goodness, and admirability of its citizens? John Savage was right, it seems: the price for happiness is too high; one does need the right to be unhappy.

We turn next to four other communities that also aimed at reducing violence and producing peace. These communities will accept the second premise of the community argument, that oneself is one's community, but at the same time avoid some of the difficulties of our two utopian communities in answering the question, Can the problems of violence and peace in the twenty-first century be solved through the way of community?

Chapter 2

⊂◈⊃

Aldo Leopold and the
Biotic Community

The time in which we live has been aptly called the "Age of Ecology." The well-known representatives of this age, Joseph Wood Krutch, Rachel Carson, René Dubos, Ralph Nader, Paul Ehrlich, Allen Ginsberg, and even Al Gore have given powerful voice to the view that the study of the relationships between the organisms of our natural world and their environment is vital to our survival. The ecologists who study such relationships have enjoyed the fame of popular media entertainers, writing best-selling books, starring in movies, singing on radios, determining federal and state conservation policies, and influencing the social, political, and moral lives of millions.

Two major views about the community of nature have influenced these outspoken defenders of "ecology" since that name was invented in 1866. The first describes the whole of nature as a living organism, a holistic entity whose parts are shaped and directed by the entire living environment, a being possessing inherent anthropomorphic properties not unlike reason and feeling. This community of environmental holism was made popular in the early part of the twentieth century by Frederic Clements and S. A. Forbes, who argued that the earth is alive and ensouled, a superperson, that it is indivisible—a community in which each member is necessary to the whole such that if any member is lost the whole suffers irreparably. To this model of eco-*holism* or organicism is juxtaposed a second model that describes the whole of nature as an eco-*system* composed of physical, isolatable, mechanical parts, all reducible to talk about atoms, energy, and economics expressed as quantifiable and measurable units. This community of the ecosystem was made popular in the 1920s and 1930s by Charles Elton and A. G. Tansley, who argued that the ecosystem is like a machine whose parts could be isolated for measuring and study without disturbing the whole since there is no "community" here that is more than the sum of its parts. If the ecoholistic model was dominated by biology, the ecosystem model was influenced by physics. It will be our task to describe the relation of both of these ecological models to the development of Aldo Leopold's life and his concept of the biotic community.[36]

Aldo Leopold's Life

Aldo Leopold (1887–1948), the American educator, ecologist, and nature mystic, who started his career as an ecosystemist and ended as a ecoholist, has left an intriguing and provocative description of community in his posthumously published, and now famous, essay, "The Land Ethic":

> All ethics so far evolved rest upon a single premise: that the individual is a member of a community of interdependent parts. His instincts prompt him to compete for his place in the community, but his ethics prompt him also to cooperate (perhaps in order that there may be a place to compete for).[37]

This phrase, "community of interdependent parts," is what has come to dominate, under very varied synonyms, American environmentalism in our century. Hence, we begin our discussion of Aldo Leopold's concept of community by placing him in the context of that environmentalism and in particular by relating him to one of the first celebrated ecologists of the twentieth century, Rachel Carson. Though she succeeded Leopold in time, she stood within the same holistic tradition, seeing nature as a community of interdependent parts; it is her message and her fame that are largely responsible for people listening to Leopold and his message today.

Rachel Carson: The Web of Life-or-Death as Community

If we were going to pick a date and text and claim for them, "This is where the world's concern about the natural environment began," we couldn't do better than choose 1962 as the date and Rachel

Carson's best-selling, read and reread, quoted and requoted, *Silent Spring* as the text. The book frightened people around the globe; it woke the sleeping and alarmed the awake; it altered the direction of environmental history and wrought revolutionary changes in both United States federal law and then American and worldwide public policy toward our natural surroundings; and it launched the movement that was to make "ecology" a household word.

Silent Spring was written by a trained professional marine biologist who also happened to be a talented technical writer with the United States Fish and Wildlife Service. Rachel Carson (1907–63) possessed both the scientific knowledge and the literary skill to arouse a slothful and indifferent public with an alarming call to environmental arms: We are poisoning and killing our ecosystem with chemicals and ignorance, she declared, we are degrading ourselves and our planet by threatening not only the quality of life of the present generation upon the planet but the very existence of future life itself. The book was an indictment of modern agriculture, the chemical industry, applied entomology, and all the sciences that had made the chemical control of nature a priority:

> The "control of nature" is a phrase conceived in arrogance, born of the Neanderthal age of biology and philosophy, when it was supposed that nature exists for the convenience of man. . . . It is our alarming misfortune that so primitive a science has armed itself with the most modern and terrible weapons, and that in turning them against the insects it has also turned them against the earth.[38]

Carson went on to demonstrate that something could be done about the problem, that the approaching, and seemingly inevitable, ecological holocaust could be averted but only by a wholesale, immediate, and monumental human effort.

Through Rachel Carson and naturalists like her, Americans and then Europeans, began to see ecology as a science of relationships, as another way of talking about "community." The consequences of such a concept, wherein what one does to one minute part of the whole can have horrendous reverberations throughout the whole, were overwhelming:[39]

> For each of us, as for the robins in Michigan [their numbers decimated by spraying for Dutch elm disease and their reproductive lives ended by DDT] or the salmon in the Miramichi

[destroyed by DDT spraying of the spruce budworm aimed at saving evergreen forests in Canada], this is a problem of ecology, of interrelationships, of interdependence. We poison the caddis flies in a stream and the salmon runs dwindle and die. We poison the gnats in a lake and the poison travels from link to link of the food chain and soon the birds of the lake margins become its victims. We spray our elms and the following springs are silent of robin song, not because we sprayed the robins directly but because the poison traveled, step by step, through the now familiar elm leaf–earthworm–robin cycle.

Carson concluded using a phrase that has become the hallmark of those committed to an ethics for the environment and to protecting the biotic ecoholistic community:

These are matters of record, observable, part of the visible world around us. They reflect the web of life—or death—that scientists know as ecology.[40]

Rachel Carson compelled governments and citizens to think about that delicate web of life; and this led many to the enlightening realization that we are all a rather small part of a complex whole that just happens to include humans. It is this rather sobering discovery of human dispensability that has brought the ecological movement into sharp conflict with both the moral and the religious traditions of Western culture. Those traditions initially rejected the idea that the biotic community as a whole may have rights and duties superior to any single member-species within it. This was an especially bitter conflict when it was seen that the moral and religious values of that Western culture were oftentimes the chief and initial cause of the despoiling of the environment. For consider, the holistic web-of-life ecologist is asking the utilitarian, ecosystem naturalist to accept the view that the rightness of an action need not depend on what brings the greatest amount of happiness or pleasure or profit right now to the greatest number of sentient and voting members of the community; in other words, the majority who can count and who bother to be counted could be ethically and morally wrong in determining community policy. The same ecologist is also asking the religious supernaturalist to accept the view that other members of the community, for example those robins and salmon, those gnats and lakes, may have rights equal to, and even superior to, those beings created by God in His own image; metaphysical naturalism of the web-of-lifers and its apparent atheism or agnosticism proved to be insurmountably unacceptable to the ordinary religious person; Carson and others, it seemed to them, were asking for a humility that most Westerners found impossible to accept. "We still haven't become mature enough," Carson said in 1963, "to think of ourselves as only a tiny part of a vast and incredible universe."[41]

Ian McHarg, a professor of landscape architecture and sagacious critic of Western civilization, has argued that the major cause of the world's moral, as well as its environmental, dislocation is to be found in the values espoused by that civilization. McHarg feels, rightly or wrongly, that if practices and actions are a measure of, and have their origins in, a civilization's beliefs and values then one way to discover the causes of wrong practices and bad actions, is to look to their sources in that civilization's beliefs and values. In the West that source lies in our philosophies and religions, especially those religions in the dominant Abrahamic tradition:

> The great western religions born of monotheism have been the major source of our moral attitudes. It is from them that we have developed the preoccupation with the uniqueness of man, with justice and compassion. On the subject of man-nature, however, the Biblical creation story of the first chapter of Genesis, the source of the most generally accepted description of man's role and powers, not only fails to correspond to reality as we observe it, but in its insistence upon dominion and subjugation of nature, encourages the most exploitative and destructive instincts in man rather than those that are deferential and creative.

McHarg concludes, speaking about the dominion-over-all view, a kind of religious anthropocentrism, that has all-too-often sanctioned the attitudes and actions that have proved so environmentally destructive in our time:

> The creation story in Judaism was absorbed unchanged into Christianity. It emphasized the exclusive divinity of man, his God-given dominion over all things and licensed him to subdue the earth.[42]

The web-of-life view, on the other hand, points to an environmental community, an "ecology" in Carson's words. McHarg reminds us that in such a community there is no ranked hierarchy, no dominant and subjugating aristocracy. Forgetting this, we make a community impossible and without community our environmental problems emerge as disastrous repercussions throughout the web.

These repercussions are either immediate or mediate. The former are the easiest to detect, they're with us now; and, unfortunately, they may even be seen as both good and acceptable—no more mosquitoes, no more budworms, no more caddis flies. But the latter, the long range repercussions, constitute the price we pay for the former—polluted waters and soils, unsafe or lethal drinking water and food, reproductive problems in humans, animals, and plants, universal biotic sickness and death, all may come in time because they are all part of the seamless web of life that stretches over the entire planet. It's the nature of an ecology, of webs and nets, of ecocommunities, that nothing is hierarchical, nothing is privileged, separate, unique, or individual.

Rachel Carson was neither the first, nor will she be the last, ecologist to remind us that as members of a community we must all hang together now or we shall surely all hang separately tomorrow. But she was the first to arouse the entire community and to be heard regarding the deadly dangers, both immediate and mediate, confronting it.

Before Carson one other ecologist attempted to arouse a disinterested community to the environmental dangers that it faced. This ecologist was not heard and only lately has the power of his voice and the environmental ethic that he was propounding been listened to, thanks largely to famous and even notorious whistle-blowers and alarm-sounders such as Rachel Carson. Aldo Leopold has become in the last few decades one of the most influential of the environmental ethicists of the twentieth century. It is Leopold's version of the web of life, namely, the biotic community, to which we now turn.

The Life of an Ecomystic

Aldo Leopold was born in Burlington, Iowa, in 1887 and spent most of his life in the Midwest. He was graduated from Yale University in 1909 with a masters degree in forestry and in that same year joined the newly created United States Forest Service. By 1912 he had become supervisor of the one-million-acre Carson Forest in New Mexico. A founder of the Wilderness Society, he initiated the first Forest Wilderness Area in the United States in 1924, an area which eventually became the Gila National Forest. He subsequently moved to Madison, Wisconsin, as associate director of the Forest Products Laboratory. In Madison he founded the profession of game management, authoring the first significant book on the subject in the United States, and in 1933 the chair of Game Management was created for him at the University of Wisconsin. He died of a heart attack in 1948 while fighting a grass fire on a neighbor's farm.

There are two incidents in Aldo Leopold's professional life that have an important bearing on the development of his concept of the biotic community and that transformed him from an ecosystemist to an ecoholist. The first probably dates from 1909 and involves wolves; its significance was not immediately understood nor was it even recorded by Leopold until 1944. The second incident is related directly to the first and involves deer. It falls within the same 1944 time period.

Wolves and Community:
The Only Good Wolf Is a Dead Wolf

In July of 1909 Leopold began work as a forest assistant with the U.S. Forest Service (established in 1905). There the "naturalist and hunter" who just happened to become a forester took up his duties, mostly on horseback, surveying and patrolling portions and beyond of the year-old Apache National Forest in southeastern Arizona Territory. It was probably during September of 1909 that the following incident occurred. Leopold relates it thus as he and several companions see at a distance a playful tangle of writhing, tumbling, half-grown wolf cubs welcoming back to their company what appeared to be their mother:

> In those days we had never heard of passing up a chance to kill a wolf. In a second we were pumping lead into the pack but with more excitement than accuracy: how to aim a steep downhill shot is always confusing. When our rifles were empty, the old wolf was down, and a pup was dragging a leg into impassable slide-rocks.

Leopold closed with the recounting of the experience that was eventually to change his life:

> We reached the old wolf in time to watch a fierce green fire in her eyes. I realized then, and have known ever since, that there was something new to me in those eyes—something

known only to her and to the mountain. I was young then, and full of trigger-itch; I thought that because fewer wolves meant more deer, that no wolves would mean hunter's paradise. But after seeing the green fire die, I sensed that neither the wolf nor the mountain agreed with such a view.[43]

In those days, and for decades beyond, Leopold had been an enthusiastic supporter of the movement initiated by sportsmen and ranchers nationally to exterminate the large carnivores from the ranges of Arizona and New Mexico. Here is what he told delegates to the National Game Conference in New York City in 1920:

It is going to take patience and money to catch the last wolf and lion in New Mexico. But the last one must be caught before the job can be called successful.[44]

The significance of the green fire that he had experienced in Apache Forest in 1909 would have to wait for over thirty years for its true meaning to surface. And what he had seen was to have an impact on Leopold's concept of the biotic community, a web of mutually dependent living and nonliving things, including those large carnivores, existing in a holistic and harmonious balance with nature and nature's way. Which brings us to the second major ecological incident in Leopold's life.

Deer and Community: Bambi *and the Doe Season*

In the winters of 1940–41 and 1941–42 it was discovered that deer populations in Wisconsin had been escalating at an alarming rate. It was also discovered that vegetation and forest damage, starvation among deer together with a significant fawn mortality, were at unacceptably high levels. Nothing was immediately done to deal with the catastrophe, since the disturbing discovery took time to filter up through the natural resources bureaucracy, but finally two committees were organized to confront the disaster. In September of 1942 the Citizen's Deer Committee was formed and in November a second committee was organized, the Committee on Natural Resources for the Wisconsin Academy of Sciences, Arts and Letters. Aldo Leopold was appointed chairman of both organizations. Following his own extensive field investigation and research, Leopold recommended to his committees, to the government, and the public one far-reaching and controversial proposal. Curt Meine has put the matter quite succinctly:

He was teaching a lesson from his own experience of over-populated deer ranges. He was selling the idea that if Wisconsin were to [solve its problem] a substantial reduction in the deer herd was necessary. This inevitably meant a doe season— the first in recent memory, and a move not likely to sit well with any segment of the public. Even hunters, accustomed to the traditional buck seasons, were bound to protest. It did not help, either, that Walt Disney's *Bambi* had just been released.[45]

And then the winter of 1942–43 was an especially hard one. Deer, adults and fawns, again starved and died in record numbers. An insignificantly few of the carcasses were preyed upon. But the public at large would have nothing to do with a doe season, that is, an antlerless deer season, for the approaching autumn. Leopold's real difficulties, as he was to discover, lay with the citizens and voters of the state and not with protecting the natural predators of the deer: "The real problem is one of human management. Wildlife management is comparatively easy; human management difficult."[46] In the end a split season for November 1943 was approved; a four-day forked-buck hunt to be followed by one for antlerless deer. The stage was set for an autumn hunt that would please no one. In some counties herds were reduced by 90 percent when 50 percent would have been sufficient. Reports of illegal kills, bad sportsmanship, black-marketing in venison, and license abuses were all adding to the confusion stemming from killing does. Further, something no one now recalls, meat was then rationed and the fighting in World War II was at a critical stage. The entire hunting fiasco would be branded "the crime of '43." It was a community in chaos. And Leopold would never hunt deer again.

Leopold's state of mind during this first period of his ecologic pilgrimage is best captured in his book, *Game Management* (1933). He was teaching in the Department of Agricultural Economics, whose name alone probably indicates more than anything else the ecosystemist cast of his thought regarding the natural environment: Nature is a commodity to be carefully exploited and ultimately used in order to satisfy human needs. In the book he claims:

Effective conservation requires in addition to public sentiment and laws, a deliberate and purposeful manipulation of the environment—the same kind of manipulation as is employed in forestry.[47]

Deer and quail he refers to as "crops" to be cultivated and harvested. Nature is a resource to be reorganized and managed to meet the needs of society. The aim of ecology here was to make the environment more productive and to use the latest scientific discoveries to do it.

But through all this battle with conservation, wolves, and deer, Leopold's own thinking about the community was slowly changing. That change is reflected in the essays written during this period of turmoil and controversy, some of which would be subsequently gathered together in Leopold's most famous work, A Sand County Almanac. It is in these essays that Leopold's views on ecoholism and the biotic community are most clearly and movingly expressed.

Holism, Webs, Pyramids, and the Biotic Community: A Professor Changes His Mind

Something was turning Leopold away from the view that he had held in 1909, 1920, and 1933 that advocated the strict manipulation of the ecosystem. Something was transforming him into an holistic ecologist as he began to seek a philosophy of balance for the biosphere. The change to this holistic ecological view, as with most of Leopold's views, was very slow in coming. The meaning of the green fire in the dying wolf's eyes was left to roil in his unconscious as he wrestled with other environmental problems.

One possible influence on Leopold's thinking at this time may have come from the Russian seer and mystic P. D. Ouspensky (1878–1947), who would write about "the mind of a mountain," and whom Leopold cites approvingly in an essay in 1923. Ouspensky, using the language of holism, held that the earth was organic, that it was greater than the sum of its parts, indivisible, and "any thing indivisible is a living being," a living superorganism with a nominal essence that was hidden from humans.[48]

In an essay of 1923, "Some Fundamentals of Conservation in the Southwest," Leopold, using the poetic language of the ecomystic, gives signs of a change of mind. He left no doubt that the biotic community, as he then conceived it, could be viewed holistically, that is, as a living, indivisible organism. In such a living, coordinated whole each part carried out its own function to the ultimate benefit of the entire community:

> Possibly, in our intuitive perceptions, which may be truer than our science and less impeded by words than our philosophies, we realize the *indivisibility* of the earth—its soil,

mountains, rivers, forests, climate, plants, and animals, and respect it collectively not only as a useful servent but as *a living being*, vastly less alive than ourselves in degree, but vastly *greater than ourselves* in time and space—a being that was old when the morning stars sang together, and, when the last of us has been gathered unto his fathers, will still be young.[49]

In the posthumously published "Round River," he stated his environmental holism even more memorably and succinctly:

Harmony with land is like harmony with a friend; you cannot cherish his right hand and chop off his left. That is to say, you cannot love game and hate predators; you cannot conserve the waters and waste the ranges; you cannot build the forest and mine and farm. The land is one organism.

Furthermore, "predators are members of the community and no special interest has the right to exterminate them for the sake of a benefit, real or fancied, to itself."[50] But seeing the biotic community as an organism, as a holism, will lead to significant problems, as we shall see below.

Throughout the 1920s and 1930s the view of what a true community is was then slowly forming as he moved away from the ecosystem utilitarian approach to land as an exploitable resource to a "universal symbiosis," an environmental holism. This new view will be given its clearest expression in 1939 as the concept of the biotic community, a web or net of interdependent parts, takes shape. In such a web, any ignorant interference with any part of the web (such as, the elimination of all wolves) could produce disastrous and violent consequences for the entire community. Here is Leopold in 1939 writing about "the land," another new concept synonymous with the biotic community:

Land, then, is not merely soil; it is a fountain of energy flowing through a circuit of soils, plants and animals. Food chains are the living channels which conduct energy upward; death and decay return it to the soil.

Leopold's famous "biotic pyramid" (fig. 2.1) graphically defines the biotic community, the web of life, the land. The biotic view of land as seen through the biotic pyramid emphasizes, again, the interdependence of the parts of a holistic biotic community:

This *interdependence* between the complex structure of land and its smooth functioning as an energy circuit is one of its basic attributes. When a change occurs in one part of the circuit, many other parts must adjust themselves to it. Change does not necessarily obstruct the flow of energy; evolution is a long series of self-induced changes, the net result of which has been probably to accelerate the flow; certainly to lengthen the circuit.

Up-circuit (Food Chains)   Down-circuit (Death-Decay)

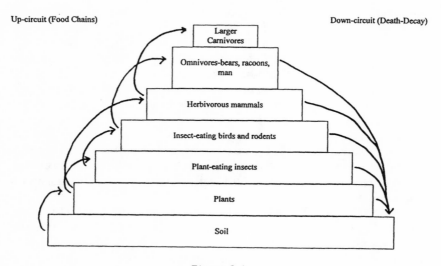

Figure 2.1
A rendering of Leopold's drawing of the biotic pyramid that appeared in the Journal of Forestry. The drawing depicts the plant and animal community as an energy circuit.[51]

Difficulties develop in the natural flow, the balance of energy, however, when humans with their utilitarian needs step in to redirect that energy; the result is violence:

> Evolutionary changes, however, are usually slow and local. Man's invention of tools [e.g., tractors, guns, and the legislative tool for the extermination of the large carnivores] has enabled him to make changes of unprecedented violence, rapidity, and scope.[52]

That description of violence to the land is given further range in Leopold's classic essay, "Thinking Like a Mountain" (1944):

Since then I have lived to see state after state extirpate its wolves. I have watched the face of many a newly wolfless mountain and seen the south-facing slopes wrinkle with a maze of new deer trails. I have seen every edible bush and seedling browsed, first to anemic desuetude, and then to death. I have seen every edible tree defoliated to the height of a saddlehorn. . . . In the end the starved bones of the hoped-for deer herd, dead of its own too-much, bleach with the bones of the dead sage, or molder under the high-lined junipers.[53]

Leopold was by this time professor in, and chairman of, the newly created (Summer 1939) Department of Wildlife Management, housed in the College of Agriculture at the University of Wisconsin in Madison. Leopold's years of thinking about deer and wolves and forests had finally changed his mind from the earlier view that too many deer was God's blessing to the new discovery that God's blessing would be an ecological disaster. In March 1941 the professor, mindful of the natural calamity of the overpopulated Wisconsin deer community, and the human catastrophe in Europe rapidly overtaking the entire world community, spoke movingly in the opening lecture to his Wildlife Ecology 181 class. The lecture contained the theme and language of the biotic community, its rise and fall, its health and its sickness, and the balance of give and take that defines that health and balance. It was a theme that was to dominate the remainder of his philosophic life:

Ecology tries to understand the interactions of living things and their environment. Every living thing represents an equation of give and take. Man or mouse, oak or orchid, we take a livelihood from our land and our fellows, and give in return an endless succession of acts and thoughts, each of which changes us, our fellows, our land, and its capacity to yield us a further living. *Ultimately we give ourselves.* That this collective account between earth and its creatures ultimately balances is implicit in the fact that both continue to live. It does not follow, however, that each species continues to live. Paleontology is a book of obsequies for defunct species.

That's the problem, of course, when the imbalance in the ecosystem goes critical. And going critical is the result of human intervention not nature's. Leopold was convinced that nature for the most part and in her own way was capable of rebalancing herself before untoward extinctions occurred:

> One of the most emphatic lessons of ecology is that animal populations are usually self-limiting; that the mechanisms for limitation are diverse, even for a single species; and that they often shift inexplicably from one kind to another; that the usual sequence is for some limitation to act before the end of the current food supply is in sight.

This admission, that there is in nature a cure for nature's own ills, represents another turn-about for Leopold. To acknowledge that humans might not have to step in at all and kill any of the wolves, for example, in order to keep the deer herds healthy, represents a change of mind of monumental proportions:

> Such self-limiting mechanisms are an integral part of nature, and are as immutable as the color, form, and habits of the individual creature.

Leopold then identifies the chief cause of the imbalances in nature and, of course, it is man:

> Return now to man: having suspended the laws of carrying capacity by inventing tools [digging wells that lower the water tables or building dams that destroy natural habitats], he next suspended the laws of predation by inventing ethics [exterminate the wolves who prey upon the helpless deer].[54]

The ironical conclusion from all of this is, of course, that the chief job of the environmentalist, whether Forest Service officer or Fish and Wildlife Service warden or even ecologically minded professor, must simply be to get out of nature's way, that is, to let nature alone, precisely the thing that salaried bureaucrats and crusading intellectuals by training and temperament cannot do. But Leopold was so convinced by his discovery that we must let nature go her own way that by 1945 he was able to express his new view in a blistering review of a recently published book ("intensely disappointing"), *The Wolves of North America*. It was a book that reflected "the naturalist of the past, rather than the wildlife ecologist of today":

Entirely unmentioned in this book is the modern curse [*sic*] of excess deer and elk, which certainly stems, at least in part, from the excessive decimation of wolves and cougars under the aegis of the present authors [intellectuals] and of the Fish and Wildlife Service [bureaucrats].

And then he confesses his own error:

None of us foresaw this penalty. I personally believed, at least in 1914 when predator control began, that there could not be too much horned game, and that the extirpation of predators was a reasonable price to pay for better big game hunting. Some of us have learned since the tragic error of such a view, and acknowledge our mistake.[55]

Leopold's thinking like a mountain and the change of mind that accompanied it were parallel to the thinking of other naturalists during the decades in which he was writing. It was American environmentalism and Aldo Leopold maturing and coming of age together, it was learning to focus more on the environment than on the species. The idea that a healthy community could be obtained by letting the community go its own way was new; and that, together with the idea that at critical times the ecologist might have to step in and modestly recommend limited methods of species control, must have seemed downright wrong and inconsistent, if not outright insane, to the naturalists of the time. But Leopold would argue, quite rightly, that where nature's balance has been upset by human tools and human greed, only human wisdom and human compassion could set the balance right again.

The key lessons that Leopold had learned from the previous two major incidents in his life were, of course, lessons about community. First, from "Deer and Community," there is a lesson about the human community and the recalcitrance of the elements in it that regard nature as a commodity separate from us, one to be used at our discretion. Second, from "Wolves and Community," there is a lesson about the biotic community to which we all, wolves and deer included, belong. That lesson is that what happens to them also happens to us. It is that sense of belonging that will define the biotic community for Aldo Leopold. Both of these incidents helped to shape Leopold's views on community and, subsequently, on the rules for belonging to it, namely, the land ethic.

The Land Ethic

The land ethic of Aldo Leopold is a synthesis of the moral views of David Hume, the evolutionary theory of Charles Darwin, the ecological thought of Charles Elton, and the philosophic genius and transformative experiences of Leopold himself. As ecologist Michael Nelson has stated, through the efforts of philosophers such as J. Baird Callicott, the land ethic "has been crafted into a philosophically respectable contemporary environmental ethic" over the last twenty years. As a consequence, those efforts have turned the land ethic, because of the popularity of Leopold's writings, into what has become "the most well-known environmental ethic to date," making it "one of the only (if not the only) genuine and proper environmental ethic so far formulated."[56]

Aldo Leopold had written in *A Sand County Almanac* that man's instincts prompt him to compete but his ethics prompt him to cooperate. Realizing that cooperation and not competition define community, Leopold's ecologic mission lay in explaining both the arena in which this cooperation is to take place, in what he refers to as "the land," and the rules by which members of the land community are to cooperate, in what he refers to as "the land ethic":

> The land ethic simply enlarges the boundaries of the community to include soils, waters, plants, and animals, or collectively: the land.

Up to the present time, Leopold points out, we have given only hypocritical lip service to our regard for the land. But our uncontrolled polluting and exterminating actions toward that land, toward its soil, waters, plants, and animals, betray us everywhere. The land ethic, when adopted, promises to change both our attitudes and our actions:

> In short, a land ethic changes the role of *Homo sapiens* from conqueror of the land-community to plain member and citizen of it. It implies respect for his fellow-members, and also respect for the community as such.[57]

Leopold's concept of community is what we would refer to nontechnically as an "ecology" (from the Greek *oikos*, "house"), that is, a house with living and nonliving things interacting with one another, all sharing a physical environment. That shared environment includes the house's solar energy, air, water, soil, heat, and wind, together with certain essential chemicals. The organic members of the ecosystem include the plants and animals sharing the house and sharing one another in various "eating" relationships. This community is called the "biotic community."

The biotic community contains properties that define it as a "community." We know that the human members must be cooperators and not competitors; that they exist interdependently, and not independently, with each other and with other nonhuman members; that they have fellow members, as well as the community, itself, to whom respect and loyalty are owed; finally, that they are not exploiters of the community or its members but persons who have an obligation to the entire community to employ its resources carefully and wisely because they recognize it as *their* community, even as an extension of themselves. But the land can be used:

> A land ethic of course cannot prevent the alteration, management, and use of these resources, but it does affirm their right to continued existence, and, at least in spots, their continued existence in a natural state.[58]

The land, therefore, can be used for survival, for hunting, mining, recreation, and the hundreds of other nonexploitative purposes to which members of a community can be responsibly and respectfully employed by other members. This responsible and respectful use is laid out by Leopold in his now famous definition of what constitutes a responsible and respectful action towards the biotic community:

> A thing is right when it tends to preserve the integrity, stability, and beauty of the biotic community. It is wrong when it tends otherwise.[59]

If the biotic community's happiness lies in the promotion of this rightness then we might inquire just how one goes about becoming a member of such a community? How does one go about obeying the land ethic and recognizing an obligation to engage in ecologically right actions as a citizen of the biotic community? Leopold has been quite clear on what the requirements are for anyone to qualify as a morally responsible and respectful member. What he seeks is nothing short of a total conversion of the self. This metanoia, reminiscent of Leopold's own transformation from an environmental ecosystemist to a holist, takes place as one's *ordinary* conscience becomes transformed into an *ecological* conscience wherein one comes to see the community as oneself. He begins:

> Obligations have no meaning without conscience, and the problem we face is the extension of the social conscience from people to land.[60]

This extension is really a psychological alteration that is brought about without benefit of supernatural grace or the aid of a divine Savior or a Bodhisattva; the transformation is wholly within naturalistic boundaries:

> No important change in ethics was ever accomplished without an internal change in our intellectual emphasis, loyalties, affections and convictions.[61]

The consequence is that the transformed members of the biotic community begin to express "love, respect and admiration for the land."[62] The land ethic comes into play only after self-transformation:

> A land ethic, then, reflects the existence of an ecological conscience, and this in turn reflects a conviction of individual responsibility for the health of the land.[63]

The land includes every living member as parts of the everflowing energy of the interconnected, interdependent organism that constitutes the biosphere. The land is the whole and its parts as well as the mysterious energy interconnecting those parts. Recall Leopold's words:

> Land, then, is not merely soil; it is a fountain of energy flowing through a circuit of soils, plants, and animals. Food chains are the living channels which conduct energy upward; death and decay return it to the soil.[64]

In other words, the feeling of ecological responsibility, and the sense that one has a duty to the biotic community, is the result of an intellectual intuition of the interconnectedness of all things, an intuition that also leads to the transformation of the self. One dis-

covers this interconnectedness and it is this discovery that transforms one's ordinary conscience into an ecological conscience.
Human members of a community have become members through
some kind of intuition leading to self-transformation by virtue of
which they become loyal, affectionate, loving, and admiring citizens of the community; these members now recognize that they
have an obligation to love, admire, and respect that community and
all of its members, and to preserve its integrity, stability, and
beauty. It is through this intellectual intuition and self-transformation that the good, the happiness, of this community is apparently
found and through it, finally, that one becomes identified with, is
at-one with, and loses oneself in, the biotic community. The logic
(rules) governing the relation between metaphysical sameness,
physical interdependence, and ethical mutuality is challenging (see
chapter 6 for a discussion of *identity*). But one thing seems quite
clear from all this: Aldo Leopold was an ecomystic.

Let's summarize our investigation thus far of Leopold's biotic
community using our four-stage Prescription for Community from
chapter 1.

Aldo Leopold's Prescription for Community: The Biotic Community

The Problems

The central problems are suffering and survival in the twenty-
first century in a world dominated by the violence of environmental pollution and ecological degradation.

The Causes

The causes of our environmental problems lie primarily with
the dangerous and outdated beliefs stemming from three sources:
First, a woeful *indifference* to the environment; second, inherent
human *selfishness* with respect to other members of the biotic
community; and third, an adamantine *ignorance* of where this
indifference and selfishness are carrying us.

The Solution

The solution to these three causes of suffering and survival,
and to the problems of enviornmental pollution and ecological

degradation, can only be found, Leopold argues, when we realize what the biotic community is and where our place within it lies.

The Way

The way to the solution of the problem of ecological violence is to be found in removing the selfishness, together with the indifference and the ignorance that accompany it. Leopold is calling for nothing less than a moral conversion, a self-transformation, through the development of love, respect, and admiration for all of the members, organic and inorganic, of the biotic community. This metanoia occurs when one begins to feel or intuit that one belongs to a biotic community of interrelated living and nonliving members. This intuition is a kind of ecomystical experience of precisely the sort that Leopold had in 1909 when he peered into the green eyes of that dying wolf.

But how does one get this experience in the twenty-first century? What is there that we can do now that will turn us around and transform our ordinary conscience into an ecological conscience? The opening line of Aldo Leopold's foreword to *A Sand County Almanac* leads to the answer that the way to self-transformation lies in opening oneself to the biotic community: "There are some who can live without wild things and some who cannot." And he closes this foreword by suggesting that it is living with wild things that culminates in the realization that "land is a community . . . to be loved and respected":

> Perhaps such a shift of values can be achieved by reappraising things unnatural, tame, and confined in terms of things natural, wild and free.[65]

For example, here is Leopold reflecting on an intuition made from living with wild things. In September 1936 he went on a pack trip into the wild Chihuahua Sierra in Northern Mexico. There, along the Rio Gavilan, he came upon a deer herd in total balance with its natural surroundings. "It was here that I first clearly recognized that land is an organism, that all my life I had seen only sick land."[66] In other words, the way to membership in the biotic community lies, quite simply, in living in that community.

We turn next to three problems that Leopold's Prescription for Community would seem to raise.

Problems with the Biotic Community

There are probably three difficulties that the implementation of the biotic community presents for anyone searching there for solutions to the problems of violence and peace in the twenty-first century.

The Problem of the Transformation of the Ordinary Conscience

We have answered the first question that we set out to answer for Leopold: What is a community? The second question—How does one become a member of a community?—has also been answered, that is, it is through self-transformation that one acquires membership in the biotic community and learns to behave in a communal, that is, dutiful, loving, and respectful, way. But a part of this second question and Leopold's answer to it need to be pursued further. How does Leopold propose to bring about this conversion from an ordinary conscience to an ecologic conscience? In other words, how does one come to see the land as one's community and as oneself?

Well, the obvious answer, as we suggested above, is, Go out there and live with the land! "There are some who can live without wild things, and some who cannot," Leopold says. And "living with wild things" means, it seems, precisely what it says. Like a Taoist mystic sage, Leopold invites the reader to leave the glass, the concrete, and the steel of the city and to seek contacts with nature. It all seems so simple. But Leopold warns:

> Perhaps the most serious obstacle impeding the evolution of a land ethic is the fact that our educational and economic system is headed away from, rather than toward, an intense consciousness of land. Your true modern is separated from the land by many middlemen, and by innumerable physical gadgets. He has no vital relation to it; to him it is the space between cities on which crops grow.[67]

The problem that faces us with respect to the problem of the transformation of the ordinary conscience into the ecological conscience is how to get to that intense consciousness of land. And now suddenly it's not as simple as it first appeared. Many of us are bored by the land, we have synthetic and expedient substitutes for the land, and we have "outgrown" the land. It seems that without some identifiable and practicable program of education, there will be more problems with the way of Leopold's biotic community than appeared at first reading.

But it may well be true, as Michael Nelson has reminded me, that it is wrong to assume "that the only way to gather this ecological worldview is by engaging in some sort of Thoreauian experiment." There may be other ways that even Leopold would have approved that did not involve "backpacking, canoeing, and bird-watching." The other ways to ecological understanding according to Nelson, and perhaps to Leopold, would include "reading books about wilderness experiences or ecology, taking academic courses that are biological or ecological in nature, simply thinking." There may be, in other words, many different environmental yogas to ecological self-transformation.

Rachel Carson, like Aldo Leopold, was aware of the frail balance that exists throughout the biotic community. And like Leopold she was aware of the repercussions that can explode throughout that community when the balance is upset. And she was also aware of the indifference that the general public felt toward that community:

> In some quarters it is fashionable to dismiss the balance of nature as a state of affairs that prevailed in an earlier, simpler world—a state that has now been so thoroughly upset that we might as well forget it.

She continues, speaking of that balance:

> The balance of nature is not the same today as in Pleistocene times but it is still there: a complex, precise, and highly integrated system of relationships between living things which cannot safely be ignored any more than the law of gravity can be defied with impunity by a man perched on the edge of a cliff.[68]

Carson's solution to the problem of violence to the biotic community was to write a book, believing that the solution to the problem of violence was education and public awareness. And Leopold would probably agree that the transformation of the ordinary conscience to the ecological conscience might be brought about by as simple a thing as reading a book. The optimism supporting such a transformation is captured in a remark made by Dr. Charles Elton and enthusiastically quoted by Carson: "We are hearing the early rumblings of what may become an avalanche in strength."[69] And with Carson and Elton the book, *Silent Spring*, led to that avalanche. Our consciences have been transformed: Today we are pesticide-aware and DDT has almost disappeared.

The Problems of Outrageous Rights and Confused Use

While Leopold admits that only humans can have moral obligations and responsibilities, he yet wants to extend moral rights from humans to other members of the biotic community. One consequence of this extension is that while animals, trees, and mountains have no moral responsibilities, they do have rights, rights as members of the biotic community. As a consequence, humans have moral obligations to them. These two implications, that nonhuman members have rights and that I am obliged to respect those rights, must seem patently absurd to the ordinary person. How, he or she might well ask, can trees and ponds have rights? And we're not talking about subsidiary rights that trees and ponds might possess in virtue of belonging as property to someone else, but rights in and for themselves in virtue of belonging, as full, nonhuman members-in-good-standing to the biotic community.

Finally, how can I have a moral obligation to a tree or a pond? If all members of the biotic community are to have equal consideration, and if none is to count as more morally worthy than another, then I might well owe as much moral consideration to a tree as to you. Hence, I am morally obliged not to injure a tree or pollute a pond, not because to do so would violate the rights of the owners of these objects, but because these objects have moral standing in the biotic community. The ordinary person, once again, must be struck by the sheer quaintness of the two implications of Leopold's proposal regarding these fellow members of the biotic community. I think that Leopold has an answer to the problem of outrageous rights but since that answer might also apply to a second and related part of this problem, we'll reserve that answer for the moment.

While Leopold admits that some members of the biotic community can be used by other members, for example he accepts eating, hunting, land-clearing, mining, and so on, he fails to mention that that use can easily become an exploitation; but he gives us no guidelines for determining the difference between legitimate use and exploitation nor how to avoid slipping over from the former to the latter. Neither does he, a critic might add, recognize that most use is already a form of exploitation, the taking advantage of another for one's own purposes and ends. So, when does my fair use of the land become unfair, when have I taken advantage? Is it when I possess or own too much? But what is "too much"? Is it when I refuse to share the land I have? With whom *must* I share? How am I to tell when I am being selfish and misusing something for my own purposes? Doesn't it follow that *any use* of any thing entails treating that thing as a means and not as an end; but then that treatment would be in danger of being selfish and immoral.

If the problem of outrageous rights led to something that affronts common sense, this problem of confused use would seem to lead to an outright contradiction since logically nothing can be *used* as an end in itself.

Leopold's answer to both of these problems probably lies in the development of the ecological conscience. Each problem can only be solved through the responsible use of the biotic community's resources. And that means developing a sense of responsibility, which brings us back, however circular the route appears to be, to ecological awareness and the self-transformation that led to it. A commonsense attitude to the rights of trees and ponds as well as a commonsense use of other usable members of the community call for sanity and maturity on the user's part. Recall that Leopold did say that the land ethic, while making *Homo sapiens* plain members and citizens of the biotic community, implied "*respect* for his fellow-members, and also respect for the community as such." But from this claim, that individual animals, plants, ponds, and dirt *deserve* esteem and high regard, it does not necessarily follow that each of these fellow-members deserves equal moral consideration. While all are intrinsically valuable, some may be more morally valuable than others.

As a solution to the problem of outrageous rights it might seem odd to hold that all members of a class deserve equal respect but not all deserve equal moral consideration. But historically Jeremy Bentham extended moral consideration to all sentient creatures; Albert Schweitzer's reverence-for-life extended it to all living things; both believing, possibly, that if something deserves respect then it also deserves moral consideration. But Leopold leaves himself open to siding with those who believe that some members of the biotic community are not deserving of equal moral consideration with other members. Leopold is no help really in resolving this matter. His unfortunate model of the biotic *pyramid*, hierarchical in shape, gives the impression of a power pyramid. The result of all of this, of course, is that we are probably left back where we started, where all are intrinsically valuable and none are worth more moral consideration than others.[70]

The Problem of Ecofascism

This final difficulty, the problem of ecofascism, is part of another puzzle that we have met before and called "the dilemma of community." That dilemma simply said that if community is too weak then we have violence and chaos; and if community is too strong then, while we may have peace, we may also have fascism, that is, an aggressively regimented, totalitarian dictatorship by and for the superior few. The goal, of course, in solving the dilemma of community is to find some middle way that will avoid anarchism on the one hand and fascism on the other.

The critic says that Leopold's holistic biotic community is too communally powerful to ever avoid fascism, for where everyone is equal and where no one, not even humans, counts as more equal than others, the way is open for the more powerful members to dominate and claim that the weaker members are expendable for the good of the organic whole: after all, what ultimately matters is the survival, "the integrity and stability," of the biotic community, and not its weaker expendable members. Ecofascism is the logical result of the suppression of individual rights for the good of the whole, where the whole is more valuable than any individual part.

Another consequence of this holistic and organic theory of the community is this: if it could be shown that one species was harmful to the whole, and that the whole would benefit from the extermination of that species, then presumably it would be right, in order to preserve the community, to exterminate that species—and it could be us![71]

Consider, again, Leopold's claim that the land ethic, in making *Homo sapiens* a plain member and citizen of the biotic community, implies "respect for his fellow members and also *respect* for the *community* as such."[72] The "holistic cast," as J. Baird Callicott has indicated, is plain enough:

> Indeed, as "The Land Ethic" develops, the focus of moral concern shifts gradually away from plants, animals, soils, and waters severally to the biotic community collectively.

This move toward reifying the abstract community climaxes, finally, in Leopold's grand moral maxim of the land ethic:

> A thing is right when it tends to preserve the integrity, stability, and beauty of the *biotic community*. It is wrong when it tends otherwise.[73]

Callicott, before launching into his own defense of Leopold against what seems *prima facie* to be ecofascism, gives an example followed by a warning:

> By this measure of right and wrong, not only would it be wrong for a farmer, in the interest of higher profits, to clear the woods off a 75 percent slope, turn his cows into the clearing and dump its rainfall, rocks, and soil into the community creek . . .

but, and more to the political point made by the problem of ecofascism,

> it would also be wrong for the federal fish and wildlife agency [or the community] in the interest of individual animal welfare [or individual human welfare], to permit populations of deer, rabbits, feral burrows, or whatever to increase unchecked and thus to threaten the integrity, stability, and beauty of the biotic community.

Callicott continues,

> The land ethic not only provides moral considerability for the biotic community per se, but ethical consideration of its individual members is preempted by concern for the preservation of the integrity, stability, and beauty of the biotic community.

And concludes with a warning:

> The land ethic, thus, not only has a holistic aspect; it is holistic with a vengeance.[74]

And if the charge stands, as I suspect it does, then so also stands the charge of ecofascism against the land ethic and the biotic community over which it reigns: holism is fascism, as both Plato and Huxley have already taught us, and the defenders of Leopold indeed have their work cut out for themselves.

Having said all of this regarding the Problems with Leopold's Biotic Community, where do we stand now with respect to answering our three central questions posed in the opening chapter of this book?

Conclusion: Three Central Questions

What is it that is shared that makes the biotic community into a community? What is shared, of course, is, first, the feeling of being a member of, or of really being, that community and, second, the responsibility for the community that that sharing entails.

Second, how does one become a member of the biotic community? It is sufficient to say that membership is achieved when the ordinary conscience is transformed into the ecological conscience and the feeling of sharing in, or of actually being, the community results. It is then that ethical altruism enters and with it the realization that one has duties first to the biotic community.

Third, and finally, we might ask, can the problems of violence and peace in the twenty-first century be solved through the biotic community? The answer is, Yes, of course, provided that everyone would agree to abide by the rules of the land ethic, that is, live by the rules of the altruistic ethic that Leopold seems to be persuasively promoting. It is here that the two community arguments from chapter 1 become joined to holism and the land ethic to provide Leopold's solution to these problems. Recall the community violence argument:

1. No one would intentionally do violence to oneself.
2. Oneself is one's community.
3. Therefore, no one would intentionally do violence to one's community.

Leopold's biotic community, of course, instantiates the second premise and the conclusion:

1. No one would intentionally do violence to oneself.
2. Oneself is the biotic community.
3. Therefore, no one would intentionally do violence to the biotic community.

The biotic community is a holism, an organism of interdependent parts or members, which is an unsubdividable whole such that removing, injuring, or doing violence to one part or member changes, and thereby injures, the whole. Each of those parts or members *is* the whole in this sense. Thus when one violates the parts or members, one is only violating oneself. Transforming the ordinary conscience into the ecological conscience makes this conclusion obvious and since no one wants to violate oneself, the problem of violence is solved.

The problem of peace can be solved in a similar fashion. The community peace argument from chapter 1 instantiated for Leopold would look like this:

1. Everyone would intentionally do peace to oneself.
2. Oneself is the biotic community.
3. Therefore, everyone would intentionally do peace to the biotic community.

The justification of the premises parallels the justification of the premises in the community violence argument. Again, the language is clumsy but the concepts should be clear. It is not enough to reduce the violence to the land, but acts aimed at promoting consideration and respect for other members of the community and directed at preserving the integrity, stability, and beauty of the community itself ought to be encouraged. Finally, both the community violence argument and the community peace argument focus attention on one of the chief causes of violence and peace to the community. As with Plato earlier, that cause is ignorance; and the solution to ignorance, as Leopold has repeatedly stressed, is education, environmental education. As with Plato, the aim of education is the transformation of the soul.

But beyond solving the central problems of violence and peace in the twenty-first century, the biotic community solution has problems of its own that must be addressed. What is needed is a transformative commitment to community that does not entail holism with its attendant threats to individual autonomy: We're back to our old problem, the dilemma of community. Finally, the biotic community solution leads to two further questions that Leopold has still not dealt with satisfactorily, it seems to me: How, and under what circumstances, does this self-transformation occur? And, secondly, if it is self-transformation that leads to a kind of "biotic altruism," the heart of the experience of community and the view that others, the community, have a value greater than one-self, then what does that mean? That is, how can biotic altruism be defended? We shall take up these questions together with an analy-sis of the *is* of identity in those second premises in chapter 6.

From the biotic community of Aldo Leopold, we turn next to the ashramic community of Mohandas Gandhi.

Chapter 3

❦

Mohandas Karamchand Gandhi
and the Ashramic Community

Mohandas Karamchand Gandhi (1869–1948), the Mahatma, the "great-souled one," of Hinduism and the statesman-pacifist guru of India's struggle for political liberation, developed an intriguing and far-reaching philosophy of community. That philosophy, put into practice as all the world watched, was uniquely bound up with his views about the ashram, a communal retreat, and his commitment to *satyagraha*, nonviolent disobedience to unjust laws and unfair social and political practices. Both satyagraha and the ashram are united in Gandhi's concept of the ashramic community.

Mohandas Gandhi's Life

Mohandas Karamchand Gandhi was born in Gujarat, a province on India's Western coast. He came from the Vaishya class, the merchant class, of the Indian social system, though both his father and grandfather had been prime ministers in the governments of local, princely states. In his famous *An Autobiography*, which he subtitled *The Story of My Experiments with Truth*, Gandhi tells of his early life and marriage in India. He tells of his adventures as a student in London where he went for study at the age of eighteen and where he obtained his degree in law three years later. He also tells of his early life in South Africa, where he prac-

ticed law, and of his later life in India, where he had his most popular success as both a political and a spiritual leader of millions of
his countrymen.

But it was Gandhi's experiences in South Africa that shaped
him for his later work of social reform and active political resistance against the British occupation of India. And it was these early
experiences in South Africa, applied subsequently in India, that
were to lead in no small measure to the eventual freedom of his
country from British rule in 1947.

Gandhi had returned to India from London with his new law
degree in 1891 but he was unable to earn a living as an attorney. It
was, actually, his uncontrollable shyness that cost him his professional career in the law courts of India. As he tells it, his first case
was typical and a disaster:

> This was my *debut* in the Small Causes Court. I appeared for
> the defendant and had thus to cross-examine the plaintiff's
> witnesses. I stood up, but my heart sank into my boots. My
> head was reeling and I felt as though the whole court was
> doing likewise. I could think of no question to ask. . . . The
> judge must have laughed. . . . I sat down and told the agent
> that I could not conduct the case.[75]

The adversarial method of arguing cases in courts, a method first
introduced in the West by the Sophists in fifth century B.C.E.
Athens, was a technique that Gandhi was psychologically incapable of using. So, in place of the adversarial approach to legal dis-
putes, Gandhi introduced in its place a new technique in which he
was eventually to become a master: The method of compromise. In
the adversarial method there are winners and there are losers, and
the stage is thereby set for future adjudication, future appeals,
hatred, and even violence. In the *method of compromise* there are
no losers for, ideally, everyone wins as both parties sit down and
talk out their differences.

But, after two years of trying to make winners of everyone and
unable to earn a living for himself and his family in India, Gandhi
accepted an invitation from some overseas Indians in South Africa
to represent their company in certain legal matters. Totally unpre-
pared for the prejudice and hatred in South Africa, Gandhi arrived
in that country in 1893 with his shyness, his relatively new degree,
his splendid English clothes, looking very much the British gentle-
man that he thought he had become. But in attempting to ride in a

first-class railway compartment, for which he held a first-class ticket, he was, because of his skin color and his refusal to vacate his seat, thrown off the train by the conductor. Gandhi tells the story of his first encounter with racism:

> The train reached Maritzburg, the capital of Natal, at about 9 p.m. Beddings used to be provided at this station. A railway servant came in and asked me if I wanted one. "No," said I, "I have one with me." He went away. But a passenger came next, and looked me up and down. He saw that I was a "colored" man. This disturbed him. Out he went and came in again with one or two officials. They all kept quiet, when another official came to me and said, "Come along, you must go to the van compartment."
> "But I have a first class ticket," said I.
> "That doesn't matter," rejoined the other. "I tell you, you must go to the van compartment."
> "I tell you, I was permitted to travel in this compartment at Durban, and I insist on going on in it."
> "No you won't," said the official. "You must leave this compartment, or else I shall have to call a police constable to push you out."
> "Yes, you may. I refuse to get out voluntarily."
> The constable came. He took me by the hand and pushed me out. My luggage was also taken out. I refused to go to the other compartment and the train steamed away.[76]

Gandhi had learned the hard way about racial prejudice in South Africa.

He spent nearly twenty years in that country with his wife and growing family, during which time both he and the unjust racial laws that he fought against slowly changed. He gave up his English clothes and aristocratic ways in exchange for simple Indian peasant dress; he disciplined himself after the manner of the traditional Indian holy man with prayer, fasting, celibacy, and an increasingly ascetic life. During this time he developed his way of community and his philosophy of political and social action, which may be summed up in one word: Satyagraha.

Satyagraha in South Africa

The practice of satyagraha was first used successfully by Gandhi in South Africa. On September 11, 1906, a mass meeting of over 3,000 British Indians was called in Johannesburg in the Transvaal. The Indians had been brought together in order to protest a proposed bill being offered by the colonial government called the "Asiatic Law Amendment Ordinance." Gandhi, one of the leaders of the meeting, had referred to the bill as a "crime against humanity," and had urged the people to refuse to comply with it if it were adopted. In effect the ordinance would require all Indians eight years of age and over to register and be fingerprinted by the government; further, all Indians could be forced to produce the required registration certificate on demand, on any occasion, for any reason; finally, their houses and their persons could be searched without warrant and without cause. Failure to comply with any of the above orders, and failure to carry the certificate at all times could mean a fine, or imprisonment, or deportation from the Transvaal province of South Africa, or all three. The Indians at the mass meeting made a solemn vow among themselves, Hindus, Muslims, and Christians, to stand together as one people and to resist the ordinance should it become law.

On December 6, 1906, the Transvaal was granted self-government, and despite the protests and warnings of over 13,000 of her Indian citizens, the new government passed the Transvaal Asiatic Registration Act (the old "Asiatic Law Amendment Ordinance") on March 22, 1907. On March 29 the Transvaal Indians met again in a mass protest, but under Gandhi's tutelage they offered a compromise to the government, which was to agree to register voluntarily if the act were repealed. Gandhi called on the colonial secretary, General Jan Christian Smuts, the great hero of the Boer War, and submitted to him this compromise plan—voluntary registration for repeal of the act. Nothing came of the offer, for on July 1, 1907, the act was enforced in Pretoria and the Indians were told to register within a month. The campaign to resist began on the same day with Gandhi offering to defend anyone arrested under the law. General strikes were organized throughout the Transvaal, public meetings were called to arouse the citizens to support the resisters, letters and telegrams were sent to London, and a newspaper letter writing campaign was begun to the papers in South Africa, England, and India. The whole mass effort turned out to be a great success for the Indians. On the last official day of registration, November 30, 1907, only 511 out of 13,000 eligible British Indians had registered under the new law.

The government made arrests throughout the summer and Gandhi represented the arrested until December 27, 1907, when he himself was finally jailed. He defended himself in court, and, while he was told on December 28 to leave the Transvaal within forty-eight hours, nothing ever came of his arrest and trial. Again it was a victory of sorts against the government.

The protest continued into January of 1908, with Gandhi again offering to compromise: Voluntary registration in exchange for repeal of the law. The alternative again, he told the Transvaal government, was that Indians would go to prison, or be deported, 10,000 strong, but they would never comply with the unjust law and accept forcible registration. On January 10, Gandhi was arrested, tried, and sentenced to two months in jail. On January 28, a representative of the government came to Gandhi in jail to discuss the compromise offer, and a tentative agreement regarding it was reached at that time. Two days later, Gandhi was escorted to Pretoria to meet with General Smuts. In their interview Smuts promised to rescind the law, if all Asiatics would register voluntarily. Both Gandhi and Smuts agreed on the compromise, and the former called off the disobedience to the law and the resistance to the government. All protesters were released from jail in a general amnesty, and on February 10, 1908, voluntary registration began. By May 9, the last day of registration, well over 8,700 Indians had voluntarily registered with the Transvaal government.

But the law was not repealed. General Smuts went back on his word, and the "Black Law," as the Indians called it, remained in force. Gandhi accused Smuts of "foul play" and on May 30 the campaign of nonviolent civil disobedience, now called *satyagraha*, was resumed. What followed, the public burning of registration cards by the Indians, their working in violation of the law, which said that only card holders could hawk or vend or sell in the cities, a new refusal to register, the mailing back of old cards, and so forth, became part of the new satyagraha campaign. This, then, was the history of the struggle by the Indian community for Indian rights in South Africa from September 1906 until July 1908, a struggle in which a new philosophy of nonviolent civil resistance was used.

The practice of satyagraha, or truth, *satya*, firmness in, *āgraha*, was to become the most potent weapon used by the Gandhians against the British in India, from its first use in Bihar in 1917 until 1947, when Indian independence was finally granted.

Satyagraha, as developed by Gandhi, is composed of four essential elements: First, civil disobedience must be offered to unjust laws. The Gandhians believe that if the law injures human dignity or causes unwarranted suffering to the human community, then one must choose to disobey the law by intentionally courting ridicule, jail, physical injury, imprisonment or death. The *satyagrahi*, as the Gandhian follower of satyagraha came to be called, must be prepared for the physical, the legal, and the moral consequences of the act of civil disobedience. Civil disobedience to unjust laws is important because it attracts and marshals public attention, that is, the attention of those who support the unjust law, those who are against it, as well as those who are indifferent to it.

Second, the disobedience must be carried out with an attitude of nonviolence and love. The satyagrahis, after fasting and prayer, must conduct themselves in a morally exemplary fashion so as not to hurt or harm those who would attempt to prevent their disobedience.

Third, Gandhi exhorted his satragrahis to look upon the act of disobedience as an offering of their bodies, souls and lives to God. Thus an element of what Hindus call *bhakti yoga*, the way of loving devotion to God, enters into satyagraha. The business of disobedience becomes a sacrifice, a spiritual act, a religious rite within a social or political environment, where the consequences of the act, through what Hindus call *karma yoga*, the way of selfless action, are renounced by the satyagrahi.

The fourth and final element of satyagraha followed hard upon the second and third. Gandhi felt that it was more important to change people than to change laws, hence, the aim of satyagraha ought to be to change the hearts and minds of the oppressor rather than the laws through which they oppressed. Only when those who had previously supported and defended the unjust law had been turned around, only then could one say that satyagraha had been successful: even the oppressor can be a member of the community. These four elements of satyagraha were to become the essential ingredients of Gandhi's later philosophy, a philosophy that he used in solving the day-to-day problems of human existence within, as well as outside, the community.

Gandhi's Death

Gandhi believed deeply in his instrument for liberation and used satyagraha dozens of times in his struggle for independence and community in India. On January 30, 1948, a half year after that independence was granted, and while on his way to public prayers in New Delhi, he was shot and killed by an assassin.

With his simple habits of food and dress, with his unadorned doctrines of love and forgiveness, Gandhi was to become an inspiration to millions of people all over the world (including the late Dr. Martin Luther King Jr.), who watched admiringly as one man's philosophy seemed to move the mighty British empire. It is out of this tumultuous and strife-ridden worldly activity that Gandhi's way of community was born.[77]

The Ashrams

In his lifetime Mohandas Gandhi established four major ashrams (*āśrama*, from the Sanskrit root *śram*, "to be weary or tired," hence, with the long "*ā*" prefix, a place *away from* exertion, that is, a communal retreat or hermitage). The model for Gandhi's ashram was the Indian village. His faith and trust in, and his hope for, the honest peasant and the life that the peasant lived in the village was extraordinary. In the village, Gandhi found his paradigm community citizen, who "overflowed with faith," "whose wisdom was boundless."[78] If satyagraha was to liberate a nation and the people who lived within it then it was important to recruit and train those future liberators. The people of India will respond to the call for satyagrahis because "people in general always follow in the footsteps of the noble";[79] and no one, Gandhi felt, follows more humbly and willingly than the village peasant, Gandhi's ideal satyagrahi. Further, he believed that "in order to restore India to its pristine condition, we have to return to the village," a belief that he maintained up to the final years of his life. Alluding to the traditional violence between Hindus and Muslims, Gandhi stated one year before his death:

> The new basis has to be built here in the villages where the Hindus and the Muslims have lived and suffered together on the land of their forefathers and must live together in the future. I ask all Hindus and Muslims to devote themselves to the noble task of reorganizing village life and in improving economic conditions. Through cottage industries they will find themselves working together in the common task, and unity will thereby grow among them.[80]

Returning to the village, finding unity through constructive work, meant retreating from the modern city, with its glass, concrete, and steel, and from the modern world, with its science, medicine, technology, and slick labor-saving inventions; after all, the village was where over 80 percent of India's population resided. Gandhi spoke repeatedly and fervently of these "village communities as ideal states,"[81] as perfect ashramic communities.

In what follows, we examine very briefly the four chief ashrams, four ideal village-communities, that Gandhi established from 1904 to 1933, the first two in South Africa and last two in India.

The Phoenix settlement (1904). In 1904 Gandhi was living in Johannesburg with his family and enjoying a fairly lucrative legal practice. One of the educational ventures that he had begun, one shared by the Indian community both inside and outside South Africa, was his weekly newspaper, *Indian Opinion.* But the paper had fallen into debt and was becoming more expensive to publish. Compelled to seek outside financial help, Gandhi decided to travel by train to Durban in Natal province. As he was departing the station, a friend gave him a book to read on the twenty-four hour journey. The book was John Ruskins's *Unto This Last.* Gandhi opened the work and was so enthralled that he was unable to put it down. Reading it made him determined to change his life "in accordance with the ideals of the book." *Unto This Last* was to become the sacred text of Gandhi's early communal movement.

According to Gandhi, *Unto This Last* establishes and defends three essential community principles: First, "that the good of the individual is contained in the good of all"; this was to become Gandhi's dogma of communal altruism and the foundation of the ashramic community, the peasant's village. Second, "that a lawyer's work has the same value as the barber's, inasmuch as all have the same right of earning their livelihood from their work"; this was to become Gandhi's dogma of social-vocational egalitarianism, a view that will later buttress his campaign for the political-economic rights of India's classless untouchables, the "*harijans,*" Gandhi's name for these "children of God." The principle was also to inspire his fight against the hereditary stigma of untouchability together with his conviction that the peasants' rights are as strong as the rights of any others in the community. Third, "that a life of labour, i.e., the life of the tiller of the soil and the handicraftsman, is the life worth living"; this will become Gandhi's dogma of the dignity of manual labor, now idealized in the life of the peasant. Gandhi's commitment to the belief in the necessity of everyone's working with his or her hands will reinforce the two previous dogmas, since the ashramic community, as well as social-vocational egalitarianism, cannot exist unless all acknowledge the value and the necessity of such work, from cooking, gardening, and latrine cleaning, to clothes washing, field work, and child-rearing.[82] Ruskin's book brought about "an instantaneous and practical transformation" of Gandhi. He was to translate it into his native language, Gujarati, and give it the revealing title *Sarvodaya*, "the welfare of all." Resolving to put Ruskin's principles into practice and to find a cheap place for his printing press, Gandhi set about creating Phoenix Settlement.

The Phoenix Settlement, or Farm, was established in South Africa in 1904. In his *Autobiography*, Gandhi tells us that he advertised for a piece of land near Durban. Within a week he had purchased twenty acres with a spring and fruit trees, to which he subsequently added eighty more acres with a cottage. The total cost was one thousand pounds. Here, fourteen miles from Durban and three hundred miles from Johannesburg, Gandhi set up a printing press for *Indian Opinion*; it was from that press that the first satyagraha campaign was announced, and it was from Phoenix Farm that the concept of the ashramic community began to take shape. Huts of corrugated iron were erected and the settlement members began to practice subsistence farming:

> In order to enable every one of us to make a living by manual labor, we parcelled out the land round the press in pieces of three acres each.[83]

Even Gandhi, when he could get away from his law practice and other public duties, was to keep and till a small plot of land on the site. By 1906, he was to recall, the importance of Phoenix as a retreat for contemplation and a place for making important decisions was already evident:

> The vow [of brahmacarya, i.e., sexual celibacy] was taken when I was in Phoenix. As soon as I was free from ambulance work [in the Zulu rebellion of 1906], I went to Phoenix, whence I had to return to Johannesburg. In about a month of my returning there, the foundation of Satyagraha was laid. . . . [It] had not been a preconceived plan. It came on spontaneously, without my having willed it.[84]

The Tolstoy farm (1910). As the satyagraha campaign throughout South Africa began to heat up, Gandhi needed a headquarters that was closer to the action. Phoenix had become more a retreat than the headquarters that the political circumstances now called for. He then accepted the offer of 1,100 acres of land twenty-one miles from Johannesburg and named the new ashram after his friend, the Russian Christian anarchist, pacifist, and novelist, Leo Tolstoy (1828–1910). Tolstoy Farm was soon populated by satyagrahi refugee families, those "passive resistors" dedicated to the principles of satyagraha. From the *Autobiography* we catch a glimpse of what it was that the tightly intertwined satyagrahis shared that transformed Tolstoy Farm from a mere settlement into a community:

> I did not think it necessary to import teachers from outside the Farm. I did not believe in the existing system of education . . . true education could be imparted only by the parents, and . . . Tolstoy Farm was a family, in which I occupied the place of a father.[85]

Tolstoy Farm was simply an enlarged family with Bapu, Gandhi, at the head. Whatever transformative experience makes the family a community was now turning Tolstoi Farm into an ashramic community. And we catch a hint that all had not been completely well at Phoenix Settlement.

Gandhi was intent on making sure that the problems that had arisen at Phoenix would not be repeated at Tolstoy Farm (or "Satyagrahi Farm" or "Passive Resistance Farm," as it was variously called). Gandhi's own words on the matter are revealing as the net of communalism closes around the new ashram:

> I am constantly trying to keep away the shortcomings of Phoenix from this [Tolstoy] Farm. That is why a different standard of living has been laid down. If instead of each cultivating his own plot separately all cultivate the entire land together, we can produce a larger crop more quickly. . . . [I]t would be good if those who could cooperate cultivated their plots together.[86]

The comment reveals early on a problem with which Gandhi was to wrestle, the dilemma of the individual and the community, a problem that we met in our discussion of Socrates and Aldo Leopold. We'll return to this dilemma shortly.

If a community exists in virtue of what is common and shared among its members then Phoenix Settlement as well as Tolstoy Farm were not only communities but something special that we are calling "ashramic communities." What did they share that made the difference? Education in the native languages of the community members; common meals; manual labor, including ditch digging, land clearing, and tree planting; gardening with cultivating, seeding, weeding, and harvesting; kitchen work, latrine cleaning, and house construction; intellectual, moral, and spiritual training, and from these latter, three other yogas especially close to the future Mahatma's heart, namely, fasting, self-denial, and self-restraint. It was the practice of these Hindu yogas, "ways," that transformed the satyagrahis; and it was the sharing of all of these activities that made that transformation possible and turned an ordinary settlement, as we suggested, into an ashramic community. The core of all of this sharing and these practices was the training in selflessness and service to others; a sort of ashramic altruism, a synthesis of Hinduism and John Ruskin, lay at the center of the ashramic community and made that community possible.

The two ashrams that were created in South Africa continue in existence to this day. They exemplify the nucleus of a concept that Gandhi will carry to India as the way of the ashramic community continues to grow.

The Sabarmati Ashram (1915). Gandhi returned to India in 1915 because that was where the new action was and that was where the principal goal of political satyagraha was to be achieved: The liberation of British India from British rule. The Sabarmati, or Satyagraha, Ashram was founded on May 15, 1915, in Ahmedabad, the capital of Gujarat, Gandhi's native state. On May 20, 1915, he drew up a draft constitution describing the nature of the new action and the rules for engagement directing the new community. "The object of the Ashram is to learn how to serve the motherland one's whole life and [then] to serve it."[87] There followed a list of the commitments that the Sabarmati satyagrahis were to make, including the vows of truth, nonviolence, celibacy, nonstealing, nonpossession, that is, taking or using no more than is needful for living, followed by an overall vow, consistent with nonpossession, to "simplify your life." The draft constitution of May 20, with some exceptions for the celibacy vow, was to become the foundation for all future satyagraha campaigns in India. The ashram began with twenty-five men and women who "had their meals in a common kitchen and strove to live as one family."[88]

The Sabarmati Ashram was inspired by a new hero in Gandhi's life, a man that he referred to as "my political guru," G. K. Gokale. The latter had been the founder of the Servants of India Society, whose avowed aim was "to spiritualize the political life of India." The Sabarmati Ashram had as its communal goal to give character to the satyagrahis by awakening in them their "religious instinct." Gandhi firmly believed, as "the maxim of life," that "no work done by any man, no matter how great he is, will really prosper unless he has a religious backing," where "religion" is not a grasp of the brain but a "heart-grasp" that is always with us but needs awakening.[89]

Following this period of the spiritualization of the satyagraha campaigns and the Ashram's stress on the liberation of India as a religious awakening, another issue had come to concern Gandhi. With such powerful emotional and spiritual forces now bonding the community, what happens to the rights and freedoms of the individuals caught in those bonds? Gandhi is aware of the problem and writes in 1924, "The individual is the one supreme consideration,"[90] and "If the individual ceases to count, what is left of society?"[91] In an interview in 1935 Gandhi comments on "the dilemma of the individual and the community," as we have called it above:

> I look upon an increase in the power of the State with the greatest fear, because, while apparently doing good by minimizing exploitation, it does the greatest harm to mankind by destroying individuality, which lies at the root of all progress.[92]

And the proof of that latter assertion is, of course, Gandhi's own rather spectacular individuality in his own rather spectacular life. All well and good, to be sure. But this problem, which, as we have seen, arose in Plato's *Apology* (a work that so impressed Gandhi that he had it translated into English, thereby honoring Socrates, "that greatest of satyagrahis"), had now come to haunt Gandhi: the power of the ashram can be just as much a threat to the individual as the power of the state. This haunting is all the more apparent when we find the champion of individualism asserting that "[life] will be [not a pyramid but] an oceanic circle whose center will be the individual always ready to perish for the village, the latter ready to perish for the circle of villages, 'til at last the whole becomes one life composed of individuals."[93] But individuals, their freedom and their energy, can drown in such circles.

Gandhi's model for the ashram has come farther away from the model of the Indian village after which he had patterned it in 1904. The ashram is now a theocratic state that, unlike the village, has a purpose beyond itself—the liberation of the motherland. Unlike the village, it runs into debt, needs expansion and funds and publicity. Unlike the village, the ashram runs the risk, with its monolithic purpose, of riding roughly over the members who compose it. Unlike the village with its many huts and houses, the Gandhi ashram has become one house dominated by sacred vows with one admitted aim. No wonder Gandhi is concerned about the plight of the individual in such a community.

But perhaps matters are not as bleak as the dilemma of individualism and the community would have us believe. To see how the inner workings of an ashram are carried out in an atmosphere of monolithic purposes we turn next to the fourth and last ashram founded by Gandhi.

The Sevagram Ashram (1933). After some sixteen years the Sabarmati Ashram at Ahmedabad was disbanded. The property was placed in trust for the uplift of the untouchables and it became known officially as the Harijan Ashram. In the last week of September 1933, Gandhi moved to the Sevagram Ashram at Wardha to better conduct his campaigns on behalf of the harijans.[94]

What follows is the recounting in dramatic form of an eye-witness incident at Gandhi's fourth Ashram in Wardha, India, in 1933. The reading, entitled *Salt*, shows the Ashram community in action, attempting to meet and solve problems using Gandhian techniques of satyagraha, that is, discussion, compromise, love, and mutual respect. The apparent lack of success of the technique in this particular instance will be discussed below in considering problems with Gandhi's concept of the ashramic community.

Among the issues, questions and problems raised by *Salt*—beyond asking, What is the ashramic community?—are the following: Does satyagraha provoke violence? Can a pacifism and an ashramic community be incentives to violence? What is "violence"? How does one recognize it? How does one prepare for voluntary suffering? What psychological or spiritual transformations in the members of the community seem to be necessary in order to qualify for ashramic membership? What must the ordinary citizen do in order to qualify? (Recall the same problem with Aldo Leopold in answering the question, How do I transform my ordinary conscience into an ecological conscience?) What duties does the satyagrahi owe to other communities? St. Paul, as we shall see below, states that one should be subject to the governing authorities, that is, the state—so, What does the satyagrahi do when the state tells him or her to become a soldier and protect with arms and violence the political state? When should one break the law? Should one "resist not evil" as Jesus of Nazareth counsels? Finally, What is "success" from the point of view of the ashramic community? Is going to jail a sign of success? Is being killed or martyred for one's beliefs such a sign? These are a few of the questions raised by the following encounter with Gandhi's ashramic community. Many of them will not be satisfactorily answered until we have finished our discussion of Martin Luther King Jr. in chapter 4.

SALT: The Ashramic Community in Action

The setting and the text of this reading are based upon and drawn from the 1933–34 Asian travel diaries of Professor George P. Conger (1884–1960), the longtime chairman of the Department of Philosophy at the University of Minnesota (1937–52). Following Conger's death, and while I was serving as his literary executor, the diaries were found in his attic. The reading, on the whole, follows with some philosophic license the incidents that Conger witnessed while staying at Gandhi's Ashram at Wardha in November and December 1933. For the rest, the reading is designed to present Gandhi as Conger saw him and as the world knew him, and at the same time to be as criticial of his views as philosophic good taste allows.[95]

CAST

Professor George Perigo ("Perry") Conger—Conger is about 65, conservatively suited, a full professor.
Mohandas K. Gandhi—About 65, dressed in dhoti and shawl.
A Jewish Girl—About 18, dressed in a flowery summer print.
Nazi Boy—About 18, dressed in lederhosen and boots.
An Australian Hairdresser—About 45, dressed for tea.
Mrs. George P. (Agnes) Conger—About 35, sensibly dressed for sitting on the floor.
Jamnalal Bajaj—About 50, dressed in smart Indian clothes.
Two Ashram Attendants—Both about 18, dressed in colorful saris.
Two American Students—Both about 18, dressed in jeans.

SETTING

The time is the recent past in an American college classroom in the Midwest; a blackboard, a lectern, and movie screen are on a stage. Professor Conger begins a classroom lecture on Indian philosophy, lapses into reminiscences of a time in India in 1933 when he met Mohandas Gandhi and lived in Gandhi's ashram in Wardha, India. The eight flashback characters and the two American students are scattered throughout the audience. They speak from where they are seated.

CONGER: (*Comes from stage right carrying books and notes. He is dressed in a conservative dark suit, has a vigorous powerful voice. As he crosses to his lectern-table a class-bell rings.*) Good morning. Thank you for coming. (*He puts his books and notes on the table.*) The topic for the day's lecture is going to be Mohandas Gandhi and as I mentioned. . . . (*Conger takes out his glasses, puts them on, adjusts them and notices a hand raised in the audience*) . . . Yes, a question?

FIRST STUDENT: Is this going to be on the final? Today's stuff?

CONGER: Yes, . . . alright . . . there will be questions on the final on Gandhi. And on these pages. (*He turns to the board and writes.*) "An Autobiography, The Story of My Experiments with Truth, pp. 575 to 577," and composed in 1927 and 1929 while Gandhi was in prison. Is that clear? Are there any other questions?

SECOND STUDENT: Will we have to know dates, again?

CONGER: "Dates?" Yes, you will. Dates, after all, are the pegs on which to hang events. (*Good-humored throughout, Conger looks about again and points to the first student.*)

FIRST STUDENT: Will it be essay or multiple choice? The final, I mean.

CONGER: The final will be all essay . . . about two hours. Any more? Alright, we're off to Mohandas Karamchand Gandhi (*He writes the name on the blackboard*) and, as I mentioned last time, I have some slides for you. The topics for the day are Gandhi and "SATYAGRAHA" (*He writes it on the blackboard*). Gandhi and nonviolent civil disobedience. Let's have the first slide, please. (*A picture of Gandhi, upside down, comes on the screen*). As I mentioned last time . . . Oh sorry (*noticing the mistake*) . . . turn it . . . (*calling back*) . . . would you turn it (*the screen goes blank*) . . . well, that's Gandhi upside down, anyway. As I mentioned last time I want to tell you about my own visit to Gandhi's ashram in Wardha, India, in 1933, and use that occasion to discuss his philosophy of satyagraha, the technique of nonviolent civil disobedience that he invented. And to hear from his own lips (*he taps the books*) about the most brilliant use of satyagraha ever conceived. I refer to the great Salt March of March 1930. (*The slide of Gandhi comes on the screen and remains there throughout the reading*). There, that's Gandhi. When I met him he was just as you see him, about 65 years of age, his greatest accomplishments behind him, but honors from the world and affection from his countrymen ahead of him. (*He pauses*) I recall now, and rather clearly, that my wife and I had written and telegraphed ahead to Wardha and then traveled by railroad and cart to confront the great man in the flesh. "Mahatma," as the world called him then, means "the great soul." (*He writes "Mahatma" on the blackboard.*) "Mahatma" is like our word "saint." . . . My first recollected impression was that he looked just like his photograph (*he points to the picture above*); but much darker; so brown, in fact, that he had been denied admittance to Christian churches in South Africa; a round head, partially bald, keen eyes with spectacles perched on the end of his nose; prominent lips, two or three front teeth missing; a trimmed moustache; a broad smile (*Conger then lapses into present tense*). His English is fluent and grammatically faultless, but because of the missing teeth there is a little difficulty with the "th" sound. The small room my wife and I enter is crowded, but the room, itself, is simple and uncluttered. Gandhi is sitting on a low cushion near a table with an alarm clock, a bottle of water and papers and books that flow onto the floor. All of these things symbolize something to me: The clock symbolizes his punctuality, the water his strict cleanliness; and the books and papers his devotion to hard work. . . . The first impression still stays with me (*Conger removes his glasses*) and that was a long time ago. . . .

GANDHI: (*Speaking from the audience, startling Conger*) Oh, do come in.

CONGER: What? Who's that please (*Peering out into the classroom and putting his glasses back on*).

GANDHI: Oh, do come in. And your wife, as well.

AGNES: Perry, we're being invited in. (*From the audience Agnes Conger holds out her hand to Conger. She is thirty years younger than he, energetic and also good-humored*).

CONGER: Agnes, is that you?

AGNES: Come along, Perry.

CONGER: But my class and my students.

GANDHI: Oh, do come in. I am going to make sure first of all that you can squat on the floor.

CONGER: I want to thank you for receiving us this way. Agnes, what's happening?

GANDHI: I am compelled, Professor Conger, to make room for you in an already overcrowded day. Please sit by me here. Your wife just there. What may I do for you then, please?

CONGER: (*To the audience*) This is the Gandhian honesty and truthfulness that I had heard so much about. No white lies or polite social fibs for him, but always the simple and direct truth at all costs. I noticed that other guests were all gathered in the crowded room, watching and listening, as a secretary, Chandrashankar Shukla, wrote down every word the master spoke. As I readied my questions, I observed that in addition to two female attendants there was a matronly hairdresser who had come all the way from Australia with an urgent message from God for the "Mahatma," as she called him. She was most insistent and rather "pushy," as I recall.

HAIRDRESSER: What I have to say, Mahatma, will take up very little of your time.

CONGER: She found the floor uncomfortable and constantly fidgeted while she talked.

HAIRDRESSER: It is a most important message, I assure you.

GANDHI: Perhaps, Madam, you will be so kind as to wait until the American professor has had his turn.

BOY: It would be unfair for you to use the time that has been allotted to someone else.

CONGER: There was a young German boy, Herr Buto, from one of the former German colonies in Africa. A red Swastika on his arm, he was a Nazi and a healthy specimen of the type of young Teuton who sets out to make his *Weltreise*, or pilgrimage around the world.

BOY: To interrupt at this time would throw the entire schedule off and make it exceedingly difficult for the rest of us, who also have their interview times approaching, to ask questions.

GANDHI: Perhaps our young friend is correct. Madam, if you could wait.

HAIRDRESSER: My message for you, Mahatma, is from God. He has sent me all the way from Australia. . . .

GANDHI: I am aware Madam. . . . Professor, if you would care to begin, perhaps God can wait a bit on us. We can save valuable time, if you will just start with your most important questions and "fire away," as they say.

CONGER: Of course. Thank you. I have three questions, if I may. First, the matter of Hindu and Moslem unity has always been a thorny issue for India and for the British. Why can't Hindus and Moslems get along and live in peace? And what can be done about this mutual hatred and violence?

GANDHI: That is a question that calls for a very technical answer. It relates to individuals getting along, loving one another and living peacefully together in community. I believe that all people can live in peace and love.

GIRL: (*Testily*) Perhaps there are some people who are incapable of love. Then what happens?

Conger: (*To the audience*) In the company at the Ashram was a young Jewish girl from Berlin. She had refused to share in the work of sweeping the latrines, saying that she had been educated for theoretical work and not for manual labor. The only discordant notes heard in the Ashram were the recurrent and heated arguments between her and the young Nazi. You must remember that Hitler had come into power earlier that same year in Germany.

GIRL: Sometimes they just cannot.

BOY: Some people are not worthy of love or respect.

GIRL: And I know who you mean.

BOY: Yes, you do. The Jews. Our Fuehrer, Adolf Hitler, has written,

> If the Jews were alone in this world, they would suffocate as much in dirt and filth, as they would carry on a detestable struggle to cheat and to ruin each other. . . .

How can such beings be worthy of love?

GIRL: Who could want to be loved by Adolf Hitler? And he talks about garbage!

SECOND STUDENT: A question, please?

CONGER: (*Stepping forward to audience*) What? . . . Yes, speak up a bit, would you?

SECOND STUDENT: What is the book he's reading from?

CONGER: (*Looking through the books in front of him, he picks up one and turns to the title page*) It's from Adolph Hitler's autobiography, *Mein Kampf*, first translated officially into English in 1933 from the German edition of 1925, volume one, and

1927, volume two, and composed while Hitler was in prison. (*He crosses to the blackboard and writes* "Mein Kampf, *p. 416.*") Is that alright? . . . Any other comment?

GIRL: Well, I have a comment . . .

CONGER: Yes, go ahead.

GIRL: Why does Herr Gandhi permit this Nazi to stay here when he continues to provoke everyone this way? Does he approve of such beliefs . . . ? such people?

AGNES: I'm sure he has his reasons.

CONGER: Yes, the Ashram is open to everyone, after all. We are all one community here.

AGNES: Perhaps if you tried a little harder to get along with the young man he would like you better.

CONGER: Yes, you haven't really tried, you know.

GIRL: I have tried. What do you mean I have not tried? Have you ever listened to him, Professor? Have you ever heard what he says?

GANDHI: You have another question, Professor?

AGNES: What are you going to ask him next, Perry?

CONGER: I had another question. But it's gone clean out of my head.

HAIRDRESSER: Mahatma, how much longer must I wait? I should think that what God has to say to you would be rather important.

GANDHI: Yes, Madam, I am waiting for the American Professor to finish.

CONGER: Yes, I recall now and I will be very brief. My second question is, Has Christianity made any significant contribution to your life and thought?

GANDHI: Yes. . . . Years ago, when I was a law student in London I promised a Christian friend that I would read the *Bible*, I tried and tried but I would always fall asleep over the *Old Testament* and nothing in the *New Testament* really interested me.

CONGER: Until? . . .

GANDHI: Yes, until I came to the Sermon on the Mount. Suddenly the teachings of Jesus came alive for me. I have written in my autobiography the very answer that you seek:

> But the *New Testament* produced a different impression, especially the Sermon on the Mount which went straight to my heart. I compared it with the *Bhagavad Gītā*.

(*Looking up*) That, as you know, is the sacred book of Hinduism; it is our own *New Testament*.

CONGER: Yes, I am aware of the *Gītā* and its influence on you as well.

GANDHI: *(Continuing)* The verses of the Sermon on the Mount, "But I say unto you, that ye resist not evil: but whosoever shall smite thee on thy right cheek, turn to him the other also. And if any man take away thy coat, let him have thy cloak, too," these delighted me beyond measure. So Christianity, with its stress on nonviolence, helped me to form many of my own ideas.

CONGER: And nonviolence lies at the heart of your entire philosophy.

GANDHI: Nonviolence is the only way to change the world and to form community. This is my strongest belief.

BOY: But what if the world refuses to change nonviolently? What if there is violence and oppression being done to you already? Can't you use force to stop that violence and oppression?

GIRL: But just see now who is speaking about violence and oppression.

BOY: *(Angrily)* I was thinking of the persecution of the German people by international Jewry and the Jewish bankers. Everyone knows that the wealthy classes have been behind the worldwide financial depression that brought Germany to disaster. Adolf Hitler has rescued us from those bankers.

GIRL: *(Angrily)* Whatever he has done he has done with violence.

BOY: "To make an omlette you must break eggs."

JAMNALAL: I must take exception to what our two German young people are saying.

CONGER: This is Seth Jamnalal Bajaj, a rich Indian banker who has dedicated his wealth and his talents to the good of India. In 1933 he was serving as Gandhi's timekeeper, secretary, and housekeeper. Everyone referred affectionately to this good-hearted man as "Jamnalalji."

JAMNALAL: And I take exception to remind them that here in the Ashram it is imprudent and unnecessary to always display such tempers at one another or at the other guests. Nonviolence must begin in one's own house, in one's own room. Secondly, it is possible for the wealthy to dedicate their wealth to the good of society and to do it nonviolently.

GANDHI: Our good Jamnalalji is being unnecessarily modest. For he is the living example of one of our wealthy bankers who has done just that. And nonviolence does indeed begin in one's own room, at the family center, in one's own heart.

GIRL: But what are we Jews to do when we are marked for oppression and possibly for extinction?

GANDHI: The Jews have been the Untouchables of Christianity. And we must come to see that we are all Untouchables, we are all Jews. Only then will the violence stop, only then will community be possible.

GIRL: But what can we do? What is the way to nonviolence?

GANDHI: Ah, but there is no *way* to nonviolence. Nonviolence *is* the way. If I were a Jew and were born in Germany and earned my livelihood there, I would claim Germany as my home even as the tallest gentile German might . . .

GIRL: Yes, I do. I am proud to be a German.

BOY: You're not a German, you're a Jew.

JAMNALAL: Let Mahatmaji finish, please.

GANDHI: . . . and challenge him to shoot me or cast me in the dungeon. I would refuse to be expelled or to submit to discriminating treatment. And for doing this I should not wait for my fellow Jews to join me in civil resistance, but would have confidence that in the end the rest were bound to follow my example.

GIRL: I do not understand what that would accomplish. I do not understand . . . it sounds . . . disgusting. Turn the other cheek to the Nazis? Why would Herr Gandhi say that? I do not understand.

GANDHI: For several reasons. First, using nonviolent resistance you could not be any worse off than you are now or than you are going to be. And, second, suffering voluntarily will bring you an inner strength and joy which no number of good wishes of sympathy passed in the world outside could possibly bring. The calculated violence of Hitler may even result in a general massacre of the Jews by way of his first answer to the declaration of such hostilities. But if the Jewish mind could be prepared for voluntary suffering, even the massacre I have imagined could be turned into a day of thanksgiving and joy that Jehovah had wrought deliverance of the race even at the hands of the tyrant.

GIRL: That is too much. Too much to expect. There must be another way.

HAIRDRESSER: I'll say. That's just going a little too far just to keep peace with that monkey in Berlin.

AGNES: Yes, what could be gained by such suicide?

GANDHI: I will tell you: To the God-fearing, death has no terror.

AGNES: Suppose you don't believe in God? Many people, good people, don't.

GANDHI: To the Jews of Germany I recommend satyagraha.

CONGER: *(To Gandhi)* What do you mean by satyagraha?

GANDHI: Yes. From its invention and first use in 1907 in South Africa I have believed that satyagraha is simple civil disobedience to an unjust law.

CONGER: Such as going to jail?

GANDHI: Yes, going to jail, or accepting abuse in any form. Further, the satyagrahi must cultivate an inner attitude of love, courage, and nonviolence toward his oppressor. Even while he is being beaten and tortured. Even while he is in jail.

GIRL: It does not seem possible.

BOY: With discipline and the proper training, anything is possible.

GANDHI: It is most difficult. To love your enemy. To do good to them that persecute you. However, the satyagrahi recognizes that satyagraha is a spiritual and holy undertaking and not merely an intellectual and physical activity.

CONGER: What do you mean?

GANDHI: I mean that we recognize that God is on our side. We are working and suffering in the name of God. That eases the burden.

AGNES: But then you do provoke those who beat you. I mean you forced the British lion to attack you.

JAMNALAL: He but twisted the lion's tail.

AGNES: But you did twist?

JAMNALAL: Oh, he did twist, indeed.

GANDHI: Finally, a successful satyagraha effort involves the conversion of one's opponent. That conversation brings the opponent into the community.

CONGER: Then I wonder if any satyagraha campaign has ever been or can ever be successful? Have any of your opponents ever changed or been converted?

GANDHI: Ah, Professor, you must understand that without the opponent's conversion or change of heart no success of any sort in the area of social justice is possible.

CONGER: Is that the only point of satyagraha?

GANDHI: That is the most important point. For just see here. If I win and my opponent loses then the stage is set for further unjust laws. If I lose and my opponent wins, the stage is set for further civil disobedience. Wherever there are winners and losers, everyone loses.

CONGER: And the conversion of the opponent . . . ?

GANDHI: Precisely. It turns the entire community into winners.

CONGER: Changing hearts is more important than changing unjust laws?

GANDHI: If you change laws, hearts might never change. If you change hearts, laws can always change. And then the violence disappears.

SECOND STUDENT: Question, Professor?

CONGER: A question? . . . Yes, alright. What is it?

SECOND STUDENT: What does "violence" mean? You never defined it. What is it?

CONGER: No, we didn't define it. Don't you know what it is?

SECOND STUDENT: No. . . . But I suppose it's causing pain. Making someone suffer?

FIRST STUDENT: Like my dentist?

CONGER: But we do need a definition.

FIRST STUDENT: Only my dentist isn't violent is he? Don't you have to *want* to hurt someone? That's violence. Wanting to hurt someone.

CONGER: But even the most violent Nazi could claim he never wanted to hurt anyone. Talking about intentions doesn't really clarify the definition of "violence." The murderer can always claim he didn't *intend* to cause pain when he killed. But murderers are violent, we would all have to agree.

SECOND STUDENT: Then how can we distinguish *his* dentist from a murderer?

CONGER: Try this: "Violence," let's say, means "imposing your will on the world." You are violent, this definition says, whenever you attempt to coerce the world or someone in it to be the way you want it or him or her to be. That's imposing your will on the world. And when you do it, you're being violent.

SECOND STUDENT: But then what about satyagraha?

CONGER: I'll ask you. What about it?

SECOND STUDENT: I suppose it means that satyagraha could lead to violence. It's imposing your will on the world. Isn't it? And Gandhi did twist tails.

CONGER: It would appear so.

SECOND STUDENT: But what if you're going to produce nonviolence by imposing your will. Can I use violence to produce non-violence?

AGNES: It would seem, then, that satyagraha may justify violence.

JAMNALAL: Not the way Gandhiji employs it. I'm not keen on your definition, Professor. And I think that a concrete example of satyagraha in action will clarify the nature of nonviolence and also answer the several questions that have been raised. I am thinking of the success of the great Salt March of 1930, just three years ago.

CONGER: Yes, and it was to be the subject of my third and final question. Just how successful was that march?

JAMNALAL: The British Crown had put a tax on salt in order to help support their colonial army which then, as even now, oppresses us. Remember, we are an occupied country. British troops and British administrators are everywhere. We live under a government, a bureaucracy and a Crown, that has been imposed on us. Our education, our literature, our economics, our politics, even our thoughts are dictated to us by a foreign invader.

HAIRDRESSER: Yes, but what happened?

JAMNALAL: The Crown put a tax on salt.

GIRL: Why salt?

JAMNALAL: Without salt you die.

GANDHI: It is the only condiment of the poor. Cattle cannot live without salt. It is a necessary article in many manufactures. Next to water and air, salt is the greatest necessity of life.

JAMNALAL: During the nineteenth century the British had ruthlessly repressed the manufacture of native salt in Bengal and elsewhere in order to dump their own cheap Liverpool salt on India.

GANDHI: Salt is the very essence of man—take away man's salt and he, too, becomes bland and lifeless.

JAMNALAL: The stage was set for one of the most spectacular displays of civil disobedience known to the civilized world.

ATTENDANT 1: On March 2, 1930, Mohandas Gandhi sent a letter to the British Viceroy of India. It began:

GANDHI: "Dear Friend." In my letter I described the Government as a curse, I blamed it for reducing India to servitude. I appealed to the Viceroy to remove the evil of the salt act, and to set up a conference between real equals. And I told him I would nonviolently disobey the law if it remained in effect.

ATTENDANT 2: And the Viceroy responded in a letter that began:

GANDHI: "Dear Mr. Gandhi." He regretted that I had set myself on a course that was in direct violation of the law. And that was all. It was a hard, unyielding letter. On bended knee I had asked for bread and in return I received a stone.

ATTENDANT 1: So on the morning of March 12, 1930, Gandhiji set out on the historic march that was to put satyagraha and India into the world's headlines. He intended to walk 241 miles with his followers from his Ashram at Sabarmati to Dandi at the sea.

ATTENDANT 2: There, at Dandi, Gandhiji would carry out an illegal act in dramatic defiance of the law: He would manufacture salt. Gandhiji was 61 years old at the time.

ATTENDANT 1: As we moved through the heat and dust from village to village the people came out to us with flowers and coconuts covering us like horses of sacrifice.

ATTENDANT 2: We youngsters had to run to keep pace with Gandhiji. He stopped on occasion to urge the people to give up alcohol and drugs, to abandon child marriage, to live virtuously and cleanly; finally, he urged them to join with him in breaking the Salt Law.

ATTENDANT 1: We walked ten miles a day and even though a pony and bullock cart had been provided for Gandhiji, he said:

GANDHI: God willing, I hope to do the entire march on foot. For me this is nothing less than a holy pilgrimage!

ATTENDANT 2: And he did it all on foot. All 241 blistering, parched miles; all on foot.

ATTENDANT 1: At times whole villages, men, women, and children, accompanied Bapu in this manner. The ranks of followers swelled by hundreds and then by thousands.

ATTENDANT 2: At first, the attention of the Western Indian villages was caught; then the Western Indian cities took notice, and than all of India itself was awakened by Gandhiji's intention to break an unjust British law with the entire world looking over his shoulder. Along the march Gandhiji would explain:

GANDHI: We are marching in the name of God.

ATTENDANT 2: On April 6, 1930, accompanied by over 2,000 people, Bapu bathed in the sea.

ATTENDANT 1: At 8:30 a.m., as he came back toward the shore, he swept some of the salt from a frothy, foaming wave with his hand. Then he returned to the shore.

ATTENDANT 2: He had manufactured salt. He had broken the Salt Law:

GANDHI: There is a deep-rooted superstition that a law cannot be disobeyed. This is nonsense. Every law can be broken. Unjust laws ought to be broken.

ATTENDANT 1: In Bombay 50,000 followers gathered to defy the Salt Law and hundreds were handcuffed and led off to jail:

GANDHI: Under a government which imprisons any person unjustly, the true place for a just man is also in prison.

ATTENDANT 2: In Ahmedabad where the Salt March had originated 10,000 people received illegal salt in the first week after the Dandi march.

ATTENDANT 1: In Patna thousands marched to make illegal salt. When their way was blocked by police they laid down in the road and stayed there for over forty hours:

GANDHI: "Satyagraha" is what I call this method of nonviolent *active*, not passive, resistance to injustice. Those who follow satyagraha must be actively prepared to lay down their lives as well as their bodies.

ATTENDANT 1: When the leaders of the crowd refused to move when ordered to do so by the police, they were told that the police would charge them with armed and mounted troopers. But, again, the satyagrahis refused to leave the battlefield:

GANDHI: "But I say unto you that you resist not evil: but whosoever shall smite thee on thy right cheek, turn to him the other also." That is my teaching, also.

ATTENDANT 2: As the troopers galloped toward them, the satya-grahis threw themselves on the ground and offered nonviolent resistance to the charging cavalry.

ATTENDANT 1: The horses stopped and the charge was broken by the Indians, who offered their bodies defenselessly to the armed and mounted policemen:

GANDHI: The aim of satyagraha is not to destroy or harass the opponent but to convert him or win him over by sympathy, patience, and self-suffering, and draw him into the community.

ATTENDANT 1: At Karachi the number of people disobeying the law by making salt was so enormous that the police could make no arrests.

ATTENDANT 2: Within a month following Dandi the entire country was acting as a single person in defiance of the law and the Government. Over 100,000 persons were sent to jail:

GANDHI: Only when we have demonstrated nonviolently that we are fit for independence, only then will we be free.

ATTENDANT 2: Finally, late on the night of May 4th, 1930, twenty armed Indian policemen, hands on their revolvers and led by a British magistrate came to Gandhi's camp near Dandi to arrest him. Going directly to Gandhiji's cot and shining a flashlight on his face, they woke him.

BOY: Are you Mohandas Karamchand Gandhi?

GANDHI: Yes . . . what . . . yes I am.

BOY: You are under arrest. Get up and get dressed.

GANDHI: Oh yes . . . yes I will . . .

ATTENDANT 2: While he dressed Gandhiji made a request.

GANDHI: Would you please be so kind as to read the warrant to me?

BOY: If you wish.

ATTENDANT 1: While the warrant was being read, Gandhi brushed his teeth.

BOY: "Whereas the Governor in Council views with alarm the activities of Mohandas Karamchand Gandhi, he directs that the said Mohandas Karamchand Gandhi should be placed under restraint under Regulation XXXV of 1827 . . ."

ATTENDANT 2: The regulation was drawn from a 100-year-old ordinance used to regulate the activities of the old East India Company and its minions.

BOY: ". . . and suffer imprisonment during the pleasure of the Government, and that he be immediately removed to the Yeravda Central Jail."

ATTENDANT 1: He said his prayers, the satyagrahis around the encampment sang a hymn, and, as the world watched, Mohandas Karamchand Gandhi was taken off to a waiting truck and to prison.

SECOND STUDENT: A question? Professor Conger?

CONGER: (*Recognizing a student's question*) Yes . . . (*Pause*) . . . Alright . . .

SECOND STUDENT: I don't understand. Was satyagraha a success or not? Gandhi's in jail. His followers are all in jail. The country's a mess. Where's the success?

CONGER: The "success?" . . . Well . . . the Salt Law was not repealed until a year later but the satyagraha salt campaign of 1930 accomplished three immediate things, nonetheless. Let me list them for you: First, it showed that satyagraha could be successful when used on a massive scale to draw public attention and world opinion to Indian social injustices and political persecution. Second, it demonstrated that . . .

GIRL: (*Interrupting*) Why do you call it "successful?" I do not think that it was successful.

CONGER: Perhaps not entirely. The independence of India is seventeen years in the future. And when it finally does come it will bring communal violence and a bloody, hate-filled partition.

GIRL: But then how can this 1930 march for independence be called a "success"? Herr Gandhi did not get what he wanted and he and everyone else went to jail. (*Turning to Gandhi*) And you want Jews to practice satyagraha in Germany?! Will it take us seventeen years, also? Can we wait until 1947, too, Herr Gandhi?

BOY: Satyagraha against established laws is illegal. The state should never tolerate such disobedience. Satyagraha did not work; it should never be allowed to work. It is insurrection and it leads to anarchy. Therefore, it is truly violent.

HAIRDRESSER: I hate to agree with him, but this time he's right. Which brings me to my message for you, Mahatma. My message from God.

BOY: Disobedience to lawful authority cannot be tolerated.

HAIRDRESSER: And it is this: St. Paul in the book of Romans in the *New Testament* of our *Bible* reminds us that we must all be subject to the governing authorities of the state. St. Paul tells us that their authority comes from God. "He who resists the lawful authorities will incur divine judgment and damnation." Mahatma, that is the message that I bring to you from God.

BOY: To legitimize resistance to the laws of the state in the name of satyagraha *now*, will legitimize insurrection and anarchy for your own republic in the *future*.

GIRL: Herr Gandhi, if you sow the seeds of satyagraha now, will you not reap a whirlwind of violence tomorrow?

CONGER: (*To Gandhi*) Yes, you seem to have contradicted your own pragmatism. If satyagraha was a success in 1930, and if it led to imprisonment and bloodshed in 1930, and if it somehow led to national bloodshed and failure in 1947, then it must have been a failure in 1930, as well. That's a paradox, surely: Satyagraha is a failure only if it's a success.

GIRL: But was it a success in 1930?

AGNES: You're all forgetting about world opinion. The British Government in India in 1930 now had to contend with world opinion.

BOY: "World opinion!" What is this world opinion? What the state says is right, that is all that matters.

AGNES: But what if the state makes an error,? What if it mistakes wrong for right? The state *can* make mistakes. And the Salt Law was one such mistake.

HAIRDRESSER: It's a sin to disobey the rulers that God has appointed.

BOY: What was immoral about the law? It is a way of raising taxes. Is that immoral?

GIRL: To deny salt to any human being is wrong.

BOY: She is speaking in riddles.

AGNES: She's speaking metaphorically.

HAIRDRESSER: That's no riddle to me. Salt is whatever you'd be willing to die for.

GIRL: Salt is what you're willing to live for; it's what keeps Jews alive.

HAIRDRESSER: Then the state has no right to take salt from you. But what about St. Paul and the Bible? I find all this now very confusing.

AGNES: But killing for salt is not satyagraha. Isn't that the point, Perry? But then dying for salt can't be satyagraha either. If you kill others, or let others kill you, it's still violence. Does satyagraha lead to violence, Perry?

CONGER: [*Ignoring her and continuing to lecture*] The second accomplishment of the Salt March was that it demonstrated that satyagraha as a nonviolent instrument of action could unite a community more securely, more unselfishly, than any violent campaign could ever hope to do. And that is the community, the ashramic community, of satyagraha.

GIRL: What is the point, Professor? Is nonviolence the only way to protect our lives? Will satyagraha save the Jews in Berlin? Will it save anyone anywhere?

CONGER: [*Ignoring the questions*] In meeting force, violence, and hatred with love, nonviolence, and active resistance, Gandhi and his satyagrahis demonstrated that the weapons used by the enemy could be blunted and deflected, once and for all.

GIRL: Herr Professor, *you* offer us only lectures and examinations. Herr Gandhi, *you* offer us only satyagraha and death. Is there no other way? Is the only response to evil to be found in ignoring it or in being devoured by it? Is there no other way?

CONGER: Third and finally, the Salt March of 1930 showed that common love, rather than common hatred, if it could defeat the British in India, could defeat any power on earth.

GIRL: Why will you not answer me?

CONGER: We have one item remaining. . . . [*The class bell rings. Conger waits for it to stop*]. Next time we turn to Sri Ramana Maharshi and Sri Aurobindo Ghose, the two greatest representatives of the contemplative life. . . .

FIRST STUDENT: [*Interrupting*] Professor, will satyagraha really be on the final?

CONGER: One moment. Hold . . . Yes, go ahead . . .

FIRST STUDENT: I said will all this stuff be on the final?

CONGER: The answer is "yes." *Salt* and satyagraha will both be on the final examination. And you'll be responsible for both. That's all. Thank you for your attention. (*Conger goes to erase the blackboard.*)

An analysis of *Salt* and the problems with the way of the ashramic community will follow our discussion of Gandhi's Prescription for Community and the four-stage summary of the ashramic community.

Mohandas Gandhi's Prescription for Community: The Ashramic Community

The Problem

For Gandhi the problem that he sought to solve was the problem of suffering, his own suffering as well as that of others. This suffering at the personal level had already been identified for him within his religion, Hinduism. As a Hindu, and as a devotee of the *Bhagavad Gītā*, Hinduism's most well-known sacred text, Gandhi recognized *saṃsāra*, the suffering of rebirth, as the major problem to be solved. But as a man sensitive to the poverty, ignorance, and chaos present in the plight of his fellow human beings, Gandhi was all too aware of the wider social dimension to *saṃsāra*. The problem of suffering, then, lay on two levels, personal and communal, and Gandhi sought to address both levels through the way of the ashramic community.

The Causes

For Gandhi the causes of the two kinds of suffering were distinct but related. The personal suffering that he experienced was, as the *Gītā* had explained, caused by both the ignorance of the true and real Self and its divine nature, as well as by the selfishness and desire that led to pain and bondage in actions. The communal suffering that he experienced was a compounding of these personal sufferings brought on by practices ranging from child marriage, untouchability, caste discrimination, and the presence of a foreign power on Indian soil to the poverty, disease, and appalling conditions of bare survival rife throughout the entire subcontinent of India. Removing one set of causes of suffering, Gandhi felt, would affect the existence of the other set of causes. Thus removing selfishness and desire in one's own life would have dramatic repercussions in the community in which one attempted to think and act. And altering the appalling social conditions would provide the arena in which self-realization, liberation from *saṃsāra*, could be developed and encouraged.

The Solutions

For Gandhi the two problems and the two causes needed two related solutions. The problem of personal suffering was solved by liberation from selfishness and uncontrolled desire, and the problem of community suffering was solved by the creation of the ashramic community. The solutions could be simply labeled "liberation for oneself" and "liberation for the community," the great world village.

The Ways

For Gandhi, the ways to the two solutions of the two problems were found by attacking the two causes of the problems. These two ways were to be found in the *Bhagavad Gītā*, and Gandhi used the concept of satyagraha to cover both of them. First, the problem of personal suffering was to be met by adopting *bhakti yoga* and *karma yoga*, the way of devotion to God and the way of non-attached, desireless action. By dedicating all of one's actions to God, the satyagrahi let go of the consequences of his or her actions and learned to act in a desireless, unselfish, altruistic manner. Second, the problem of societal suffering was to be met by adopting nonviolent, compassionate, and direct means to change the hearts and minds of those who follow the unjust laws and customs as well as of those who make them. Both ways lead ultimately to self-realization and release from *saṃsāra* as well as to communal liberation and release from communal suffering.

Both of these ways are clearly inseparable from one another because both problems, the personal and the communal dimensions of *saṃsāra*, are clearly inseparable. The way of satyagraha, that is, the way of the ashramic community, recognizes the dual nature of the problem, its causes and solutions, and it proposes the way of selfless service to the community to solve them.

This altruistic way is illustrated in the following story. Gandhi was once asked, Can a man or woman attain self-realization, that is, ultimate happiness or liberation, by mere recitation of Ramanama (repeating, or meditating on, the name of God, Rama) and without taking part in worldly actions, such as community service? The questioner (a woman) adds that her sisters have told her that one need not do anything "beyond attending to family requirements and occasionally showing kindness to the poor." The Mahatma answers:

> This question has puzzled not only women but many men and has taxed me to the utmost. I know that there is a school of philosophy which teaches complete inaction and futility of all effort. I have not been able to appreciate that teaching, unless in order to secure verbal agreement I were to put my own interpretation on it. In my humble opinion *effort* is necessary for one's own growth. It has to be irrespective of results. Ramanama or some equivalent is necessary not for the sake of repetition but for the sake of *purification*, as an aid to effort, for direct *guidance from above*. It is therefore never a substitute for effort. It is meant for intensifying and guiding it in a proper channel. If all effort is vain, why [engage in] family cares or an occasional help to the poor? In this very effort is contained the germ of national service. A national service, to me, means service of humanity, even as *disinterested service* of the family means the same thing. Disinterested service of the family necessarily leads one to national service. Ramanama gives one detachment and ballast and never throws one off one's balance at critical moments. *Self-realization* I hold to be impossible without service of and identification with the poorest.[96]

Mohandas Gandhi's beliefs about satyagraha and community are beautifully encapsulated in this brief answer quoted from a 1926 editorial column in *Young India*, his own weekly newspaper. That doctrine and that answer are both expressions of a philosophy of action that begins with self-*purification*, which, in turn, leads to *disinterested* or unselfish moral *effort*, which is, itself, *guided by God*. It is a commitment to a way of engaging in actions without which self-realization would be impossible. It is an altruism that makes the ashramic community possible.

We turn next to an analysis of three problems entailed by Gandhi's concept of the ashramic community. Our discussion will be directed to the issues raised in *Salt*.

Problems with the Ashramic Community

It is easy to criticize Gandhi's attempts at community and overlook the monumental problems and the Himalayan barriers that he encountered and tried to overcome. As Margaret Chatterjee has said, these experimental settlements, from a contemporary perspective, "seem to amount to a sharing in poverty" more than anything else. The two African ashrams, settled on a barely habitable frontier, were compelled, by the meager funds available, to be constructed on the poorest soil, in the most arid regions, at the most isolated sites. Because of his hostility to technology and mechanization, the crops raised by these subsistence peasants (farmers) were, of necessity, the lowest in both quality and yield. But Gandhi was driven by a vision of an alternative way of life that only the ashram could provide. A vision that was shared by a dozen like-minded souls at the beginning, then by hundreds and ultimately by thousands of persons looking for alternatives to their possessions-dominated lives. His ashramic community taught the educated classes a way of life that valued manual labor, and it taught the uneducated that the wealth of nations did not lie in the hands of the experts, the intelligentsia, and the purveyors of the new technologies, inventions, and gadgets; it resided, rather, "in the resources of ordinary men and women whose heroism had for centuries only been called upon in times of war but who had the capacity to transform their lives in times of peace."[97] Therein lay Gandhi's genius and his legacy to future generations. But the way of the ashram is not without problems.

There are at least three difficulties that the implementation of the ashramic community presents for anyone seeking solutions to the problems of violence and peace in the twenty-first century. In what follows I select three puzzles that would appear to arise from within the ashramic community, all of which have surfaced in *Salt*.

The Problem of the Meaning of "Violence"

The Second Student raised this first problem by asking, "What does 'violence' mean?" and it was also the Second Student who worried about a dentist's being violent under the definition that was offered. So what does "violence" mean and how does anyone know when he or she has suffered it? The matter is quite significant since people and nations are willing to kill and go to war when they feel they have been violenced. Here are several attempts to define the concept followed by various reasons for rejecting each definition:

First, "violence" could mean, as the Second Student suggested, causing pain and making someone suffer. But this won't work, as the First Student recognized, for it makes dentists into violent persons and everyone knows that is not necessarily the case. That is to say, the definition surely violates common sense since we don't ordinarily speak about "violent dentists."

Second, "violence" could mean causing *unnecessary* pain or suffering to anyone. While this may exonerate dentists, it introduces, as the Second Student and Conger both pointed out, human intentions into the search for a definition. Even the Nazis could argue that they didn't *intend* to cause unnecessary pain or suffering; they only intended to exterminate. Further, who knows what people actually *intend* anyway? The second definition of violence introduces more problems than it solves.

Third, "violence" could mean imposing your will on others. Conger introduced the definition, which is a variant of a definition proposed at one time by the modern Indian mystic and saint Jiddu Krishnamurti. But this won't work for two obvious reasons: Is the imposing of the will done nonviolently? But then the definition is logically circular, that is, "violence" means non-*violently* imposing your will on others, and we've defined the word by the word itself. Also, the definition violates not only logic but common sense, for it would mean that parents and teachers could be partners in violence in relation to their children ("Don't run in the street!") and pupils ("Open your books to page one!"), and we don't ordinarily say that such commands issue from violent parents or teachers (but the suggestion is intriguing, as is this third definition).

Fourth, "violence" could mean an attack on a community or, more inelegantly, an unwillingness to go to any lengths to restore community. This definition plays upon Martin Luther King Jr.'s definition of *agapē*, "love," as "the willingness to go to any lengths to restore the human community." In other words, "violence" is any action that tears apart the community. But this definition depends on our knowing what *community* means (which is not always extensionally clear, for instance, should "community" include animals and plants?), and raises the additional question whether it might not be right that some "communities" should be unrestored, for example, the KKK, Nazi communities, terrorist groups, and so on. Further, King's definition, as well as all the definitions we've explored thus far, exclude nonhuman communities. Isn't it possible that violence can occur in the biosphere and in the biotic community? Which brings us back to Aldo Leopold.

Fifth, "violence" could mean the destruction of the integrity, stability, or beauty of the biotic community; "violence," therefore, refers to the failure to preserve these features in the natural world. This definition comes, of course, from Aldo Leopold's definition of "ethical and aesthetical rightness" as tending to preserve the integrity, stability, and beauty of the biotic community. But such a definition is open to several obvious problems: The definition lends itself to a support of totalitarianism and a kind of ecofascism entailing a support for reactionary communities that resist change and improvement. As we have seen previously, organic theories of the state can easily lead to the attenuation of individual rights and freedoms. Also, there is the gnawing question of what takes rightful precedence when subcommunities within the biosphere clash with each other? For example, when Med flies threaten fruit trees in California, what do we save first? And why? And is the use of pesticides still violent? Common sense reels under the Leopoldian definition at this stage. Finally, suppose that I can preserve the beauty of the biotic community but only by destroying its stability or integrity. When the three criteria of integrity, stability, and beauty (supposing we know what these concepts really mean) clash, then which takes precedence? And why?

Sixth, and finally, "violence" could simply be indefinable and morally mature people know, they just *know*, when violence is present. To ask for or expect a verbal definition is useless and redundant since astute conscienceable adults know what the word means and they know what violence is even if they can't offer an analysis of it. But, the critic might say, isn't this just like giving up on the hunt for a definition of "violence"? And why give up? And who are these "morally mature people" you're talking about, anyway? Some of us are moral and mature and we don't go around claiming curious intuitive apprehensions, and, besides, we know the word can be defined. We just haven't tried hard enough. You make it all sound so mysterious, too mysterious. Thus the critic.

What all of this serves to emphasize, of course, is the difficulty of defining "violence." And that is precisely what the problem of the meaning of "violence" is all about.

The Problem That Nonviolence Provokes Violence

Agnes Conger raised this second problem by asking Gandhi, "But then you do provoke those who beat you. I mean you forced the British lion to attack you." And the Second Student said, "I suppose it means that satyagraha could lead to violence." And still later the Nazi Boy went to the heart of the problem when he stated, "Satyagraha against established laws is illegal. . . . It is insurrection and it leads to anarchy. Therefore, it is truly violent." This is the reason, of course, for maintaining the *status quo* in the state, that is, things could be far worse than they are now. It's what prompts the Australian Hairdresser to quote from St. Paul that he who resists the lawful authorities will incur divine judgment and damnation, allowing her to conclude, "It's a sin to disobey the rulers that God has appointed."

Martin Luther King Jr. mentioned a similar complaint registered against himself by eight white clergymen of Birmingham, Alabama, in April 1963. They had criticized King for coming to their city to implement a civil rights campaign, thereby, they felt, fomenting unrest and causing violence by his presence. King replied in his famous "Letter from Birmingham Jail" that he is in their city because injustice is there and he went on to say:

> In your statement you asserted that our actions, even though peaceful, must be condemned because they precipitate violence.

He then answered their charge:

> Isn't this like condemning the robbed man because his possession of money precipitated the evil of robbery? . . . Isn't this like condemning Jesus because His unique God-consciousness and never-ceasing devotion to His will precipitated the evil act of crucifixion?[98]

Whether King's answer ends the debate and solves this second problem is moot, of course, since "cause" is ambiguous in answering the question, Was King a cause of the violence? Marches, protests, and rallies where large volatile crowds are present can cause disturbances and violence at the same time that they focus local and national attention and legislation on civil rights violations. In a sense, the eight clergymen and King were both right: King's presence is a "cause" of the violence just as the wealthy man's purse is a "cause" of his being robbed, that is, without King and without the wealthy man there would be no violence and no robbery; each is a necessary condition to the physical cause of violence. But neither man is the *moral cause* of the violence, that is, each man is without moral blame in the violent events that followed and that's what we are seeking to focus on here, the claimed blamelessness of King and Gandhi in the matter of causing violence.

The Problem of the Way-to-Nonviolence

The Jewish Girl first asked the question on which this third and final problem rests, "But what can we do? What is the way to nonviolence?" When told by Gandhi that she must be prepared for voluntary suffering and even death, she became angry and rejected the idea of this passive martyrdom, "That is too much. Too much to expect. There must be another way." The reply, that there is no *way* to nonviolence because nonviolence is the way, really doesn't help here. The Girl's final hopeless and ironic cries serve to emphasize the significance of the question and the impotence of all of the responses to it, "Will satyagraha save the Jews in Berlin? Will it save anyone anywhere?" And Professor Conger's, and the world's, silent reaction to her final question, "Is the only response to evil to be found in ignoring it [the professor's response] or in being devoured by it [the world's response]? Is there no other way?"

Gandhi has a reply of sorts to the problem of What-is-the-Way-to-Nonviolence? It lies, of course, in community, in the ashram, making the world into a village, an ashramic community. But the problem of the way-to-nonviolence now recurs in a wider venue, What is the way to the ashramic community? Again, Gandhi's reply lies in demonstrating what it is that makes an ordinary person into a nonviolent person. And the peasant paradigm doesn't help one bit. What is it that must change in transforming a man or woman into a satyagrahi?

In response to Conger's question, "Have any of your opponents ever changed or been converted?"—which is the fourth stage of satyagraha—Gandhi stated, "Ah, Professor, you must understand that without the opponent's conversion or change of heart no success of any sort in the area of social justice is possible." This conversion of the opponent is synonymous with the transformation in the satyagrahi that makes the ashramic community possible. It is the same kind of transformation that Aldo Leopold has in mind when he talks about the transformation of the ordinary conscience into the ecological conscience. This is precisely what defines community; self-transformation is the essence of both the ashramic community as well as the biotic community. It was, certainly, the essence of community membership in the Republic, and, if one looks hard enough at that psychological conditioning, it may even define membership in the World State.

But what causes the transformation and how do I get it?

Prayer? Yoga? The grace of a higher power? Education? Is it what Sigmund Freud had in mind when discussing the naturalistic maturing of the adolescent male human, the dissolution of the Oedipus complex, and the formation of the superego or conscience? This internalization of the law, this transformation into adulthood, into moral maturity, issuing in responsible, caring, and loving behavior, does occur, and of that there is no doubt. So what makes it happen in some persons and not in others?

This mysterious transformation is an event in human development that made the ancients believe in Fate, Providence, Fortune, the mysterious workings of God's will, and the maturing of the soul's karma. Or maybe it is just an inexplicable accident, plain dumb luck.

Aristotle, I think, gives a grand answer to our question about human maturation in his answer to a similar question, What is it that makes happiness possible? or more to the point, Why are some people capable of being happy and others not? and, What are the conditions for happiness? After listing such necessities for happiness as having friends, riches and political power together with good birth, good health, having children, and beauty (the ugly, childless, sickly, lowly born, political outsiders, the poor, and the friendless, Aristotle claims, can never be happy), Aristotle finally mentions "luck," since all of the other necessary conditions can be present and one can still be unhappy: "As we said, then, happiness seems to require this sort of external prosperity for which reason some identify happiness with good luck (*eutychia*)."[99] Has Aristotle given up finding the necessary conditions for being happy by introducing this mysterious entity "luck"? Must we, too, surrender in finding the necessary conditions for self-transformed maturity? For what could be more mysterious than dumb luck or fate or fortune? There would be a surrender, I would suggest, if there was nothing one could do to get the luck. But what if it were possible to nudge fortune just a bit here?

Aldo Leopold felt that living with wild things made his own transformation possible. Living with wild things was a choice that he made, though it may have taken him over thirty years to produce the transformative effect in himself. Gandhi was ready for his transformation after he placed himself in the right place at the right time in South Africa in 1906. And King felt God's presence in his own kitchen at a crucial time in his life in Montgomery, Alabama, in 1956. Buddha, we shall see, put himself in transformation's way when he left his old life of wealth and luxury for a new life of poverty and denial. *Dumb* luck, indeed! We shall return to these matters again in the last chapter of this book.

We turn finally to our three central questions regarding community, violence, and peace.

Conclusion: Three Central Questions

What is it that is shared that makes Gandhi's ashramic community into a community? Very simply, and as with Leopold previously, it is the feeling among the members that the ashram is identical with oneself and that one is responsible for its maintenance and success. A community is, truly, the place when you go there, they have to take you in—because you are the community.

How does one become a member of the ashramic community? It is probably enough to say that membership is achieved through the way of selfless service, the *karma yoga* that the *Bhagavad Gītā* espouses. Gandhi's advice entails, as it does for Leopold, a self-realization or self-transformation, that makes altruistic action possible. His advice to the 1926 reader of *Young India* was, as it was in Leopold's slightly different context, to expend effort and to get involved! As Hamlet said to Ophelia, Assume a virtue if you have it not, that is, practice selfless action, and if you do it conscientiously, sufficiently, and well, it becomes spontaneous, easy, and natural. Whether you dedicate your actions to God or practice selfless service, the results will be the same, the gradual transformation from a selfish to an altruistic member of the ashramic, or the biotic, community.

Can the problems of violence and peace in the twenty-first century be solved through the ashramic community? Again, the answer is, Yes, provided that everyone can be brought into the ashramic community and share in the transformative experience that the community promises and expects. Again, the solution is best described through instantiating for Gandhi our two community arguments from chapter 1. First, the community violence argument:

1. No one would intentionally do violence to oneself.
2. Oneself is the ashramic community.
3. Therefore, no one would intentionally do violence to the ashramic community.

Second, the community peace argument:

1. Everyone would intentionally do peace to oneself.
2. Oneself is the ashramic community.
3. Therefore, everyone would intentionally do peace to the ashramic community.

Again, the language is clumsy, the justification of the premises of both community arguments follows from the previous discussions, and "education" remains the key to erasing the ignorance of who one is that creates violence and prevents peace.

There appear to be no objective, logical reasons for rejecting the ashramic community, that is, there are as yet no cited logical inconsistencies involved with its implementation. But as with Leopold, the problem of self-transformation, or self-realization, and the problem of altruism, or ashramic altruism, their implementation and their meaning, have appeared again. Both of these problems need to be explicated further and both will be with us throughout this book since "community," as our four authors and their traditions understand it, seems totally dependent on both self-transformation and altruism. These problems together with an analyses of the *is* of identity in those second premises will be taken up in chapter 6.

From the ashramic community of Mohandas Gandhi, we turn next to the beloved community of Martin Luther King Jr.

Chapter 4

Martin Luther King Jr.
and the Beloved Community

Martin Luther King Jr. (1929–68), the martyred Christian theologian and civil rights leader, has also left an intriguing description of community. King's "beloved community," like Gandhi's ashramic community and even Leopold's biotic community, is bound together by the sharing of vows, creeds, dogmas, and beliefs underlain by a transformative experience leading to a commitment of selfless service and a love of others. As with Gandhi and Leopold, the sharing makes it a community, but commitment and love make it a beloved community.

Martin Luther King Jr.'s Life

Martin Luther King Jr. was born on January 15, 1929, in Atlanta, Georgia. His father, Martin Luther King Sr. (1897–1984), was pastor at the Ebenezer Baptist Church in Atlanta. Martin senior, from a working-class background and dedicated to hard work, economic success, and personal independence, fully expected his namesake to follow in his ministerial footsteps. His mother, Alberta Christine Williams (1903–74), was the daughter of one of Atlanta's most aristocratic and prominent African-American ministers. The Williams family itself was dedicated to social and political reform, and to the arts and the culture of Atlanta.

These two families, the King family and the Williams family, opposites in many ways, would be synthesized in the life of Martin Luther King Jr.

Martin's People: Getting Things Right

There is an old saying that when you are introduced to people in the North the first thing that they ask you is, What do you do (for a living)? but in the South they ask you, Who are your people? The story probably drives home the challengeable point that in the North you are what you make of yourself, while in the South you are what your people have made you. Here are some of Martin's people.

On the Williams side, Martin's great-grandfather, a slave-preacher named Willis Williams (1810–?), had been active in an African-American church east of Atlanta since 1846. His owner and fifty whites and twenty-eight blacks also belonged to this church. Willis's son, Martin's grandfather, A. D. Williams (1863–1931), sharecropped the land with Willis after emancipation, and learned to read and write; in 1888, A. D. was converted to Christianity and earned his preaching license. In 1893, A. D. moved to Atlanta and in the following year was called as pastor to Atlanta's Ebenezer Baptist Church, the black church where both Martin and his father, Michael (later changed to "Martin") Luther King, were to become pastors.

A. D. Williams was in the forefront of the social gospel and civil rights activism throughout the early part of the twentieth century. He helped organize the Georgia Equal Rights League in 1906 and together with five hundred other African Americans from Georgia protested the treatment of blacks throughout the South. The league issued a proclamation that publicly and loudly "protested lynching, peonage, the convict lease system, inequitable treatment in the courts, inferior segregated public transportation, unequal distribution of funds for public education, and exclusion of black men from the electorate, juries, and the state militia."[100] A. D. Williams also served as branch president of the National Association for the Advancement of Colored People. During his presidency in 1919, he headed a drive to register black voters that successfully enrolled 2,500 black Atlantans. These in turn helped defeat referenda measures on the Atlanta ballot dealing with school taxes, in particular bond issues for public works that gave an unequal share of funds to white schools. His civic efforts included not only voter registration of blacks, but the passage of bond issues for more and better schools, the initiation and support of boycotts of office buildings where blacks were forbidden the use of elevators, the drive to improve park and recreational facilities for black Atlantans, and an aggressive drive to secure more and more members for the only national black civil rights organization in the South, the NAACP. All of these activities called for this comment from one of Atlanta's leading newspapers in 1924:

> It was the ballot that gave Atlanta Negroes modern . . . schoolhouses and facilities; and it was the inspiration that the race received from the local branch under the leadership of Dr. A. D. Williams that put the fight in their bones.[101]

On the King side, Martin's grandfather, James (Jim) Albert King (1864–1933) was a farmer-sharecropper whose life, and that of his son, Michael (Martin), and eight other children, was dominated by poverty and racism. It was a life that followed the dull and repetitious round of "spring sowing of cotton in fields fertilized with foul-smelling guano; summer weeding; fall picking and chopping; and winter turning of the resistant soil."[102] One time, when settling up with their landlord, Michael said that his father was due more money, whereupon the owner threatened them with physical harm and the King family was forced to move off the property. Aggressively pointing out injustices was to be part of the King inheritance. Abused, cheated, and cursed by their white landlords, their overseers and supervisors, another such incident of the King family is worth recounting in detail. It is a family story undoubtedly repeated many times to the young Martin:

> On one occasion, when he [Martin's father] was fetching milk for his mother, he was stopped by a sawmill owner who demanded that King get a bucket of water for the sawmill workmen. The youngster politely declined, whereupon the white man beat him and kicked over his milk. King ran home and explained what happened. His enraged mother returned with her son to the mill to confront the owner; when he acknowledged that he had hit the boy, she knocked him down and pummeled him. Jim King [Martin's grandfather], upon hearing of the incident, took his rifle to the mill and threatened to kill the man.[103]

There were repercussions, of course. Men on horseback showed up that night looking for Jim, who fled into the forest. He was to live there for months, returning only when everyone had cooled down.

If these stories from the Williams side and the King side of the family illustrate anything, they may say something about who Martin's people were and what they passed on to the future civil rights leader. Two qualities seem to emerge: from the Williams side, the preaching, ministerial, intellectual side, there will come love and patience; and from the King side, the working, muscular, aggressive side, there will emerge power and energy. As with all oversimplifications, there is a kernal of truth here and it probably lies in the balancing of these two ancestral elements. Martin speaks well to this balance in his last speech as president before the Southern Christian Leadership Conference in 1967, the year before his murder:

> Now we've got to get this thing right. What is needed is a realization that power without love is reckless and abusive, and love without power is sentimental and anemic.[104]

It will be King's task to take the legacy of the fragmented community from his people and synthesize love and power into the beloved community.

The Gandhi Influence on King

Martin was a bright, quick, perceptive child and early learned the hard fact that he was a black man in a world dominated by white racism, a world in which his inherited penchant for both action and intellect would be tested. Like Gandhi before him, he learned directly the insidious consequences of being "colored" in a white society through two experiences both involving public transportation. At the age of fourteen, King had traveled with a teacher, Mrs. Bradley, from Atlanta to Dublin, Georgia, to participate in an oratorical contest sponsored by the Negro Elks. He succeeded in winning the contest with his subject ironically entitled, "The Negro and the Constitution."

> Anyway, that night, Mrs. Bradley and I were on a bus returning to Atlanta, and at a small town along the way, some white passengers boarded the bus, and the white driver ordered us to get up and give the whites our seats. We didn't move quickly

enough to suit him, so he began cursing us, calling us "black sons of bitches." I intended to stay right in that seat, but Mrs. Bradley finally urged me up, saying we had to obey the law. And so we stood up in the aisle for the ninety miles to Atlanta. That night will never leave my memory. It was the angriest I have ever been in my life.[105]

A second incident involving bigotry and public transportation comes even closer to Gandhi's own first racist experience in South Africa. King had passed the entrance examination to Atlanta's prestigious Morehouse College, enrolling at the age of fifteen without graduating from high school. To earn money for his college tuition, he worked summers on a tobacco farm in Connecticut. He expressly enjoyed the personal and social freedom that the New England atmosphere provided, entering by the front doors and sitting wherever he wished in restaurants and theaters just like white folks. But the train trip back to Atlanta at the end of summer drove home to him once more the terrible reality of his situation as a Negro. On one such occasion as the train entered Virginia,

> King made his way to the dining car and started to sit down anywhere, as he had done on the way through New York and New Jersey. But the train was in Dixie now, and the waiter led him to a rear table and pulled a curtain down to shield the white passengers from his presence. He sat there, staring at that curtain, unable to believe that others could find him so offensive. "I felt," he said, "as though the curtain had dropped on my selfhood."[106]

On February 25, 1948, King was ordained to the Baptist ministry and in June he graduated from Morehouse with a B.A. in sociology. In September he entered Crozer Theological Seminary near Philadelphia intending to become a well-educated Christian minister. One Sunday in the spring of 1950 he heard Dr. Mordecai W. Johnson, the president of Howard University, give a lecture on the life and teachings of Mohandas Gandhi. Johnson talked of Gandhi's philosophy of soul force, satyagraha, the power of love and nonviolence as a way of social change. King was overwhelmed by Johnson's suggestion that the moral power of Gandhian nonviolence could revolutionize race relations in the United States: "I had heard of Gandhi . . . [but Johnson's] message was so profound and electrifying that I left the meeting and bought a half-dozen books on

Gandhi's life and works."[107] King was to become convinced that Gandhi's way was the only just and practical way for oppressed people everywhere to overcome social and political injustice. Some eight years later, and following the early success of the practice of his own Christian satyagraha, King wrote a paragraph that was to become the inspiration for the black nonviolent struggle for justice in the United States:

> American Negroes must come to the point where they can say to their white brothers, paraphrasing the words of Gandhi: "We will match your capacity to inflict suffering with our capacity to endure suffering. We will meet your physical force with soul force ["satya-graha"]. We will not hate you, but we cannot in all good conscience obey your unjust laws. Do to us what you will and we will still love you. Bomb our homes and threaten our children; send your hooded perpetrators of violence into our communities and drag us out on some wayside road, beating us and leaving us half dead, and we will still love you. But we will soon wear you down by our capacity to suffer. And in winning our freedom we will so appeal to your heart and conscience that we will win you in the process."[108]

King's March to Higher Education

In 1951 King graduated with honors from Crozer with a B.D. degree and in the fall he went to Boston University on a scholarship to pursue a Ph.D. in systematic theology. King intended to become a research scholar, find a quiet ivory tower somewhere, write inspiring books and articles, and let the rest of the troubled world roll by. He married Coretta Scott in June 1953 and, exams behind him, started work on his Ph.D. thesis that summer.

He chose as his topic for the dissertation the divergent twentieth-century theologies of Paul Tillich and Henry Nelson Wieman; and divergent they were, indeed. Tillich, a theological descendant of the Christian existentialist Søren Kierkegaard, had devoted his intellectual life to demonstrating and arguing that God was a transcendent pure Being, impersonal, and utterly beyond the world of particulars and sufferings. Wieman, on the other hand, a theological ancestor of current liberation theology, had held an equally supportable Christian position, maintaining that God was immanent in the world, ever present, and ever involved in that world. It was super-monist versus super-pluralist in Christian theology. King attempted a radical synthesis of the two views, and it was Mohandas Gandhi and satyagraha that gave him the insight into how the synthesis could be worked.

   The dissertation on Tillich and Wieman: A synthesis. Paul Tillich (1886–1965) and Henry Nelson Wieman (1889–1975) present a dichotomy in the development of American Christian theology in which one might see similarities to the dichotomy of the King and Williams families mentioned previously. If we can see Martin's *personal mission* as one synthesizing in his own life the latter family dichotomy, then it might be only natural that for his Ph.D. dissertation he would choose a topic offering the opportunity for a similar balance of opposites in his *academic mission.* Each synthesis leads to a kind of community, a balancing of opposites, in which what had formerly been opposed and separate now becomes integrated and whole.

   Both Tillich and Wieman, as Christian theologians, completely reject humanism, that is, making man supreme in the universe, a rejection that King applauds; but both reject the idea of a personal God, that is, a Creator-Father Who loves and cares, Who is jealous and vengeful, a rejection that King does not applaud. Both theologians warn against creating God in the human image. Wieman describes God as immanent in the world, but immanent as the process of "growth of meaning and value" in that world.[109] Tillich will have none of this; God is neither a being in, nor a process in, the world. Making God into a being with a lower case "b," an object, would make God just like other objects and not the supratranscendent *Being-in-itself,* the ground and source of all existence, that Tillich understands God to be. And Wieman's conception of God in the world, according to Tillich, is blasphemous. King was to write of them:

> Both overstress one side of the divine life while minimizing another basic aspect. Wieman stresses the goodness of God while minimizing His power. Tillich stresses the power of God while minimizing His goodness.[110]

In the dissertation King stated the following about Tillich and power:

> The one word that stands in the forefront of Tillich's God-concept is the word power. Power is that which makes God God. God is the underlying "ground" or "power" behind

everything that exists. God as power of being resists and con-
quers non-being. It is because of this power to resist non-being
that God warrants man's ultimate concern.[111]

And in the dissertation King said of Wieman and goodness:

> The question of the goodness of God is one that stands in the
> forefront of Wieman's thinking. Tillich, as we have seen, is
> more impressed with the power of God. . . . But, for Wieman,
> it is goodness or value that makes God God. These are the
> important words in Wieman's discussion of God. God is the
> "source of human good"; He is "supreme value."

King then used the language of community, language that would
emerge later again in discussing the beloved community:

> Wieman holds that God is supreme value because he brings
> lesser values into *relations of maximum mutual support* and
> *mutual enhancement*. This mutual support and enhancement
> is not only between contemporaries but also between succes-
> sive generations, ages and cultures.[112]

Thus Tillich and Wieman on God.

But therein lies the problem. For King now had to reconcile
these two views. He did it, first, by trimming and criticizing; second, by reconciling what is left into a grand synthesis in which he
expressed his own views about God. In doing so he laid the foundation for the beloved community. He began by attacking Wieman's
view of God:

> Wieman talks continually about the goodness of God. But one
> is forced to wonder whether Wieman's God is capable of bring-
> ing this goodness into being. As we stated above, value in
> itself is impotent. Hence a God devoid of power is ultimately
> incapable of actualizing the good. But if God is truly God and
> warrants man's ultimate devotion, he must have not only an
> infinite concern for the good but an infinite power to actual-
> ize the good.[113]

Next, he found Tillich's concept of God inadequate and for similar
reasons, namely, the one-sided incompleteness of the view that
God is an abstract and transcendent being-in-itself:

What one wants to know is whether the universe is good, bad or indifferent. It is the failure to grapple sufficiently with this question that seriously weakens Tillich's God-concept.

And King continued:

So in almost all of Tillich's references to God it is power that stands in the forefront. In a real sense, this emphasis is dangerous, because it leads toward a worship of power for its own sake. Divine power, like any other power, can become despotic power if it is not controlled by divine goodness.

And then concluded:

In short, neither Tillich's notion of being-itself, nor any other purely ontological notion is adequate for the Christian idea of God. The latter is a synthesis of the two independent concepts of value and being.[114]

Thus King on the attack against Wieman and Tillich.

It was King's task now to clarify and then implement the Christian "synthesis" in forming "the beloved community," a place where "both value *and* being are basic in the meaning of God, each blending with the other but neither being reduced to the other."[115]

Years later King would reflect, again, on the role that Gandhi's thought had played in that synthesizing and in a new problem then facing King, the problem of reconciling the old dichotomy of faith and works within the Christian church. Which takes precedence? And what is the place of works in an ethic of love and nonviolence when it is faced with the church's concern for strict Pauline, or Kierkegaardian, faith and the salvation of souls? The problem that he saw then in his seminary days was to haunt him even later:

Any religion that professes to be concerned about the souls of men and is not concerned about the slums that damn them, the economic conditions that strangle them and the social conditions that cripple them, is a spiritually moribund religion waiting burial.[116]

The problem of synthesizing the social gospel of works of Jesus of Nazareth as it is found in the Sermon on the Mount with the soul-saving faith of St. Paul and Paul's Danish apologist, Søren Kierkegaard, was nicely expressed when King later reflected on his student life at Boston University:

> During this period I had almost despaired of the power of love in solving social problems. The "turn the other cheek" philosophy and the "love your enemies" philosophy are only valid, I felt, when individuals are in conflict with other individuals; when racial groups and nations are in conflict, a more realistic approach is necessary.

But it was Gandhi who provided the way out:

> Then I came upon the life and teaching of Mahatma Gandhi. As I read his works I became deeply fascinated by his campaigns of nonviolent resistance. The whole Gandhian concept of *satyagraha* (*satya* is truth which equals love, and *graha* is force; *satyagraha* thus means truth-force or love-force) was profoundly significant to me.
> . . . I came to see for the first time that the Christian doctrine of love operating through the Gandhian method of non-violence was one of the most potent weapons available to oppressed people in their struggle for freedom.[117]

His dissertation gave him the opportunity to join together the two indispensable elements of Christianity, faith and works. In doing this he brought to the fore his own Christian beliefs grounded in the African-American religious tradition, where God is perceived as a loving, caring, personal force capable of interceding in history. In 1960 those beliefs would enable him to write:

> In recent months I have also become more and more convinced of the reality of a personal God. . . . I am convinced that the universe is under the control of a loving purpose and that in the struggle for righteousness man has cosmic companionship. Behind the harsh appearance of the world there is a benign power.

And he optimistically concluded:

> In a dark, confused world the spirit of God may yet reign supreme.[118]

And it is that God that will ultimately and triumphantly reign over the beloved community.

But before beginning a scholarly career King felt he owed the world and his father his talents as a working minister. He hoped that after finishing his doctoral dissertation and after spending a few years preaching, there would be time enough to find a teaching post and take up a life in academe. It was not to be.

Civil Rights in the United States

In April 1954 King accepted an offer to become pastor of the Dexter Avenue Baptist Church in Montgomery, Alabama. Reluctant at first to return to the deep South with all the racial problems that he had known as a child, the church made him an offer that he couldn't refuse. Together with an annual salary of $4,200, the highest salary of any Negro minister in the city, they gave him a parsonage and guaranteed him released time and expenses to complete his dissertation.

He preached his first sermon as pastor in May 1954. It was the same month that the U.S. Supreme Court handed down a landmark decision that was to change the life of Martin Luther King Jr. as well as the life of the entire country. The decision was in the case of *Brown v. Board of Education of Topeka* in which the Supreme Court ruled that racial segregation in the public schools of the country was unconstitutional. It immediately set aside the Court's previous decision of 1896 in the case of *Plessy v. Ferguson* that had ruled that segregation of the races was constitutional, hence legal, as long as equal facilities were provided for both races. In setting aside the "separate but equal" decision of fifty-eight years earlier, the Court under Chief Justice Earl Warren found that "in the field of public education the doctrine of 'separate but equal' has no place" because "separate educational facilities are inherently unequal." The reason then given by the Court for overturning *Plessy* was that segregation in schools on the basis of race "has a detrimental effect upon the colored children" by developing "a feeling of inferiority as to their status in the community" that may "affect their hearts and minds in a way unlikely ever to be undone."[119] With that decision and with that reasoning to substantiate the ruling, the legal path was now open to a plethora of legitimate challenges to *all* separate but equal public facilities, from lunch counters, restaurants, motels, and hotels, to theaters and housing, and, of course, to trains and buses.

In Boston on June 5, 1955, his dissertation completed, accepted, and successfully defended, Martin Luther King Jr. received his Ph.D. in Systematic Theology from Boston University.

The Montgomery Bus Boycott

In Montgomery on December 1, 1955, her work at the city's leading department store finished for the week, Mrs. Rosa Parks, a forty-two-year-old Negro seamstress, boarded a bus for home. She was tired, her feet hurt, and she sat down in the first seat in the Negro back section of Montgomery's segregated Cleveland Avenue bus. The law throughout the South's segregated bus systems was that of sitting segregation, and it was very simple: If you were black, you sat in the back half of the bus; if the white half of the front section filled, you could then be forced to surrender your seat in order that whites might sit in your seat even if it was in the black section.

Rosa Park's bus had filled and the bus operator ordered her to stand up and to move back in order that boarding white passengers might be seated. There were no other vacant seats that Friday; it was the Christmas shopping season. But Mrs. Parks was not about to surrender her seat so that a white male could sit while she stood all the way home. Like Gandhi decades before her in South Africa, but unlike King years earlier in Georgia, Rosa Parks quietly refused to give up her seat. The bus was stopped and she was subsequently arrested and jailed. Four days later on December 5, after lengthy discussion with other Negro leaders, the Montgomery bus boycott began. It was not the first such boycott. In 1953 the Reverend Theodore J. Jemison of Baton Rouge, Louisiana, a close friend of King's, had led a successful bus boycott in that city. Nor was Jemison the first to recommend nonviolent direct action in opposing segregation. The Congress of Racial Equality (CORE) had advocated its use as early as 1942.[120]

Events now moved swiftly for the young Dr. King. The Negroes of Montgomery were asked to stop riding city buses and to find alternate means of transportation. King was elected president of the Montgomery Improvement Association (MIA), which was to direct the strike against the buses and to find substitute transportation for 17,500 former bus riders. The strike had far broader implications, however, as other grievances were presented by King and the MIA to the city of Montgomery, grievances relating to the employment of Negroes in city jobs.

On February 2, 1956, the MIA went to Federal District Court to ask that segregated transportation be declared unconstitutional. The boycott in Montgomery became nearly 100 percent effective as the Negroes managed to stand together and find alternative transportation. The city fought back with injunctions and arrests, accusing those waiting for rides of loitering and of those riding in car pools of hitch-hiking. Standing together for the first time, and doing it without retaliation and without violence, refusing to be intimidated by beatings, arrests, and harassment from the racists, the city, and the police, the Negroes began to find what Gandhi and his South African satyagrahis had found fifty years earlier, a new sense of pride, worth, and dignity, a new sense of community.

On January 30, 1956, after days of receiving obscene phone calls, hate mail, and an arrest for driving 30 mph in a 25 mph zone, King's house was bombed. On February 21, King and one hundred other MIA members were indicted and later found guilty of not obeying an outdated antiboycott law. On June 4, 1956, the Federal District Court ruled that segregation on Montgomery's bus lines was unconstitutional. The city appealed but on November 13, 1956, almost a year after Rosa Parks refused to obey an unjust law, the U.S. Supreme Court affirmed that Alabama's state and local laws requiring segregation on buses violated the Constitution. A month later segregation on buses officially ended and on December 21, 1956, the MIA ended the boycott.

Christian Satyagraha

Now it was King's turn, like Gandhi fifty years earlier, to reflect on the success of his own nonviolent protest; and reflect he did, drawing up the necessary and sufficient elements of what we shall call "Christian satyagraha," the foundation of the beloved community.

On January 10, 1957, one hundred Negro clergy came to the Ebenezer Baptist Church in Atlanta and agreed to form what came to be called "the Southern Christian Leadership Conference" (SCLC). They elected Martin Luther King Jr. their president. In speaking to them, King outlined his philosophy and the philosophy that was to guide SCLC in the violent days ahead. It was a philosophy that would enable committed Christians everywhere to defeat the evils of segregation as well as, it turned out, to nonviolently confront the evils of poverty, hatred, and war. Christian satyagraha became Martin Luther King Jr.'s answer to the question, Can we solve the problems of violence and peace? King began by recognizing his indebtedness to Gandhi:

> The alternative to violence is nonviolent resistance. This method was made famous in our generation by Mohandas K. Gandhi.

And then he stated four of the five points for his program, points that included each of the four familiar elements of Gandhian satyagraha:

> Five points can be made concerning nonviolence as a method in bringing about better racial conditions.
> First, this is not a method for cowards; it *does* resist. . . . [The nonviolent resister] is not physically aggressive towards his opponent. But his mind and emotions are always active, constantly seeking to persuade the opponent that he is mistaken. . . .
> A second point is that nonviolent resistance does not seek to defeat or humiliate the opponent, but to win his friendship and understanding. . . . The end is redemption and reconciliation.
> A third characteristic of this method is that the attack is directed against forces of evil rather than against persons who are caught in those forces. . . . As I like to say to the people in Montgomery, Alabama: "The tension in this city is not between white people and Negro people. The tension is at bottom between justice and injustice, between the forces of light and the forces of darkness. . . ."
> A fourth point that must be brought out concerning nonviolent resistance is that it avoids not only external physical violence but also internal violence of spirit. At the center of nonviolence stands the principle of love.[121]

This principle was grounded in the *New Testament* and in particular in Jesus of Nazareth's *Sermon on the Mount*. This sermon lay at the heart of the nonviolent pacifist message preached by both Gandhi and King. The nonviolent core of Jesus' entire ministry was elegantly summarized for both Gandhi and King, when Jesus said, "The second commandment is this: 'You shall love your neighbor as yourself.' There is no other commandment greater than this."

The *New Testament* Greek word for love was *agapē*, which King defined as "a willingness to go to any length to restore community."[122] And that restoration became the ultimate goal of all of his Christian satyagraha efforts.

King concluded his reflections on his program with a fifth and final Gandhian characteristic of the new philosophy:

> Finally, the method of nonviolence is based on the conviction that the universe is on the side of justice. . . . [T]he nonviolent resistor has. . .cosmic companionship. This belief that God is on the side of truth and justice comes down to us from the long tradition of our Christian faith.[123]

Christian satyagraha is, consequently, the way wherein, as King put it, "Christ furnished the spirit and motivation while Gandhi furnished the method."[124] Later, in reflecting on the boycott victory in Montgomery, King was to state:

> From the beginning a basic philosophy guided the movement. . . . It was the Sermon on the Mount. . . . As the days unfolded, however, the inspiration of Mahatma Gandhi began to exert its influence. I had come to see early that the Christian doctrine of love operating through the Gandhian method of nonviolence was one of the most potent weapons available to the Negro in his struggle for freedom.[125]

Letter from Birmingham Jail. Following a visit to India in early 1959 to study directly Gandhi's techniques of nonviolence, King and his family moved to Atlanta, Georgia, in 1960 where King became co-pastor with his father of the Ebenezer Baptist Church. It is from here that he put his Christian satyagraha to the test over the next several years, traveling to speak, to preach, to confront, to challenge, to march, to go to jail, to commit himself again and again to the struggle to integrate lunch counters, interstate buses, and living facilities, to start the drive to register Negro voters, to nullify the poll tax and literacy tests as requirements for voter registration, and to protest the laws of racism that had made Negroes untouchable citizens for over 100 years. While publicly demonstrating against the segregation of eating facilities in downtown Birmingham, King was arrested. On April 16, 1963, he composed one of the most moving and famous moral and social documents in American history, the "Letter from Birmingham Jail."[126]

The letter, a rare defense to his critics of the philosophy and tactics of Christian satyagraha, was written in response to an open letter published in January by eight white clergy who called upon King to let the fight for integration be waged in the courts and not in the streets. King's reply is not only a reply to the eight clergy, but a reply to Christians anywhere who had ever asked the question, What is the best kind of life for a Christian to lead in a world filled with violence and injustice? It is King's credo of Christian satyagraha set into the context of that kind of world.

He begins, "My dear Fellow Clergymen," acknowledges their claim that his present protests are "unwise and untimely," and goes to the heart of the charge against him, that he is an "outsider," here in Birmingham, where he clearly does not belong. He responds, "I am in Birmingham because injustice is here," and like Christ's apostles before he has come in response to the Christian community's call for help. Likening himself to Socrates, who had spiritually molested the community of Athens, King explains his mission as a nonviolent gadfly seeking "to create the kind of tension in society that will help men to rise from the dark depths of prejudice and racism to the majestic heights of understanding and brotherhood."[127]

To the question, Why can't you wait until the law changes by the means provided by the Constitution? King answers that "justice delayed is justice denied." He then eloquently proclaims that over 340 years have passed since African slaves were first brought to the Americas and that that is too long to wait for the recognition of rights that God and the Constitution have already granted. Asia and Africa have moved ahead with lightning speed in reaching political independence, while many here wait in vain for a simple cup of coffee at a lunch counter. And to secure that cup of coffee is the reason for the marches and the sit-ins; it is the reason that King, followed by a worldwide press of reporters and journalists, and an army of photographers, radio broadcasters, and television crews, is now in Birmingham. He then recounts the centuries of degradation, fear, and slavery. These were years of white mob-rule where lynchings, drownings, and slayings of Negroes dominated the land; years when hate-filled policemen brutalized, tortured, and murdered in the name of the law; years when an economic stranglehold smothered the Negro in poverty and hopelessness. It is easy for those, he continues, who have never suffered in this fashion to say "Wait!" But, he concludes,

when your first name becomes "nigger" and your middle name becomes "boy" (however old you are) and your last name becomes "John," and when your wife and mother are never given the respected title "Mrs."; . . . when you are forever fighting a degenerating sense of "nobodyness"; then you will understand why we find it difficult to wait.

To the question, How can you advocate breaking some laws and obeying others? King responds that there are two kinds of laws, just and unjust, and agrees with Saint Augustine that "an unjust law is no law at all." He goes on to explain the difference in a fashion that would have pleased Gandhi: a just law is one consistent with the moral law and the law of God; an unjust law is one out of balance with the moral law. He concludes:

> Any law that uplifts human personality is just. Any law that degrades human personality is unjust. All segregation statutes are unjust because segregation distorts the soul and damages the personality.

To the questions, Doesn't your disobeying the law end up in the same way that the segregationist's disobeying ends up—in anarchy? So what's the difference between your illegal disobedience and theirs? King answers that the difference is great. First, unjust laws ought to be disobeyed in order that the searchlight of public attention might be drawn to them. Second, like Gandhi before him, but unlike the segregationist, the Christian *satyagrahi* must be willing to go to jail or to give up life itself, if necessary:

> In no sense do I advocate evading or defying the law as the rabid segregationist would do. This would lead to anarchy. One who breaks an unjust law must do it *openly, lovingly* (not hatefully as the white mothers did in New Orleans when they were seen on television screaming, "nigger, nigger, nigger"), and with a willingness to accept the penalty. I submit that an individual who breaks a law that conscience tells him is unjust, and willingly accepts the penalty by staying in jail to arouse the conscience of the community over its injustice, is in reality expressing the very highest respect for law.[128]

One of the last questions that King answers is the oft-repeated question, If your nonviolent action is going to precipitate violence, then ought it not be condemned? King's response is masterful. It is reminiscent of a remark he will make some months later when he is about to lead a demonstration in Danville, Virginia, the last capital of the old Confederacy. Someone told him that there was a local injunction against civil disobedience: "I have so many injunctions that I don't even look at them anymore. I was enjoined January 15, 1929, when I was born in the United States a Negro."[129] And so he was. Citing the clergy's condemnation of his actions because they lead to violence, King says this is like blaming the robbed man because he had the possessions that led to his being robbed, like condemning Socrates because of his devotion to truth and his philosophical questioning that led to the demand for his execution. King concludes:

> Isn't this like condemning Jesus because His unique God-consciousness and never-ceasing devotion to His will precipitated the evil act of crucifixion? We must come to see, as federal courts have consistently affirmed, that it is immoral to urge an individual to withdraw his efforts to gain his basic constitutional rights because the quest precipitates violence. Society must protect the robbed and punish the robber.[130]

The letter itself ends as King praises the nonviolent army that has demonstrated for justice in Birmingham:

> One day the South will know that when these disinherited children of God[131] sat down at lunch counters they were in reality standing up for the best in the American dream and the most sacred values in our Judeo-Christian heritage, and thusly, carrying our whole nation back to those great wells of democracy which were dug deep by the Founding Fathers in the formulation of the Constitution and the Declaration of Independence.[132]

It was probably the South's, and the nation's, finest hour.

Two weeks later, on May 3–5, Eugene "Bull" Connor, director of public safety of Birmingham, ordered the use of police dogs and fire hoses against the protesters. The world sat in witness to the brutal effects on the young, unarmed, and peaceful demonstrators. But by May 20, 1963, it was legally all over as the Supreme Court of the United States ruled Birmingham's segregation ordinances unconstitutional. The lunchrooms were desegregated, and restrooms, sitting rooms, and drinking fountains were similarly desegregated, during the days that followed.

The final years. Martin Luther King Jr. helped to launch what was to become the hardest campaign of his entire life: The drive to register Negro voters throughout the South. The effort began in earnest in 1964. Busloads of young men and women, black and white, from North and South, attempted to register Negroes as King and others realized the importance of political reform if there was to be economic and social reform. The fight for political rights was most bitter but again it was carried out nonviolently by the protesters and registrars.

On March 9, 1965, a white Unitarian minister, James Reeb, was beaten by four white segregationists in Selma, Alabama. Reeb had left his wife and four children and a job as director of a low-income housing project in Boston to come to Selma "to make a direct witness" for human freedom. He had come with some four hundred other ministers, rabbis, priests, nuns, students, lay leaders, black as well as white, in response to the violence in Selma, as King called for a dramatic "ministers' march" from Selma to Montgomery, the capital of Alabama. The marchers had been viciously attacked by state and local police and by mobs of whites. James Reeb died from his beating on March 11.

On March 21, as the nation watched, Martin Luther King Jr. led the march that Reeb had started, guarded this time by federal troops, and arrived in Montgomery four days later. Gandhi's 1930 satyagraha Salt March to Dandi that had captured worldwide attention had been duplicated with the same dramatic and spectacular results. The marchers sang "We shall overcome" and "Ain't no-one gonna turn us around" and everyone knew that they meant every word of it.

As dozens and then hundreds of protesters continued to be killed, maimed, and injured by the violence throughout the South, the federal government finally stepped in, first, with armed troops as at Selma and then with federal marshals. Gradually the situation began to change. The political results of Christian satyagraha were, first, the Civil Rights Act of 1964, which barred discrimination on grounds of race, color, religion, or national origin in restaurants, hotels, lunch counters, gasoline stations, movie theaters, stadiums, arenas, and lodging houses with more than five rooms, and which also authorized cutting off government funds from any federally assisted program in any state practicing discrimination; and, second, the Voting Rights Act of 1965, which sent federal registrars protected by federal marshals into the South to register at government expense all eligible voters in federal, state, and local elections. These two acts guaranteed voting rights to all Americans with heavy penalties for anyone convicted of interfering with those rights. The climax was the passage of the 24th Amendment to the Constitution in 1964, which effectively outlawed the poll tax as a criterion for the right to vote in federal elections.[133]

"I have a dream." The famous march on Washington, D.C. for civil rights on August 28, 1963, organized by King, the SCLC, and others, undoubtedly precipitated the passage of those civil rights bills in 1964 and 1965. King himself gave the keynote address in front of the Lincoln Memorial while hundreds of thousands stood and listened and cheered. It was another never-to-be-forgotten recounting of a vision of a community freed from prejudice, discrimination, hatred, and violence. Coretta King has said of the speech, "At that moment it seemed as if the Kingdom of God appeared. But it only lasted a moment." To the hundreds of thousands who heard King that day, or the millions that have heard this speech since, his vision of community seemed both permanent and real. He ended his speech:

> So I say to you, my friends, that even though we must face the difficulties of today and tomorrow, I still have a dream. It is a dream deeply rooted in the American dream that one day this nation will rise up and live out the true meaning of its creed— we hold these truths to be self-evident, that all men are created equal.
>
> I have a dream that one day, on the red hills of Georgia, sons of former slaves and sons of former slave-owners will be able to sit down together at the table of brotherhood.
>
> I have a dream that one day even the state of Mississippi, a state sweltering with the heat of injustice, sweltering with the heat of oppression, will be transformed into an oasis of freedom and justice. . . .
>
> I have a dream that one day in Alabama, with its vicious racists . . . little black boys and black girls will be able to join hands with little white boys and white girls as sisters and brothers. I have a dream today!

And King concluded:

> And when we allow freedom to ring, when we let it ring from every village and hamlet, from every state and city, we will be

able to speed up that day when all God's children—black men and white men, Jews and Gentiles, Catholics and Protestants—will be able to join hands and to sing in the words of the old Negro spiritual, "Free at last, free at last; thank God almighty, we are free at last."[134]

With the federal legislation of 1964 and 1965 about to be passed, King's dream seemed close to reality, indeed.

On December 10, 1964, Martin Luther King received the Nobel Peace Prize in Oslo, Norway.

The struggle continued as King carried the fight against discrimination to the North. He rented an apartment in a Chicago ghetto in early 1966 and led marches and protests against discrimination in housing and the workplace. When asked why he marched, he said, "I'm marching for something that should have been mine at birth," that is, the right to live and work anywhere I wish. He exhorted his fellow Chicago marchers,

> We're going to march with the force of our souls, we're going to move out.
> We're going to mobilize bodies in concern for justice.
> We're going to take the ammunition of determination, we're going to move out with the weapons of courage.
> We're going to put on the breastplate of righteousness and the whole armor of God and we're going to march.

He concluded, "I march because I must, because I'm a man, because I'm a child of God."[135] And march they did while vicious mobs jeered, threw stones, burned their cars, and beat them and spit at them. But his effort to integrate housing and to do something about the poverty and the ghettos of Chicago failed. King later described Chicago as the most hate-filled city he had ever encountered.

On May 16, 1966, King read an antiwar statement at another large rally in Washington, D.C. Now he was protesting the war in Vietnam. He was to remain until his death one of the most outspoken opponents of the U.S. military involvement in Vietnam and Southeast Asia. Speaking again on February 25, 1967, he prophetically described the war as "one of history's most cruel and senseless wars," referring to "our" tragedy and "our" guilt in Vietnam along with "our paranoid anti-communism, our failure to feel the ache and anguish of the have-nots," he concluded,

I speak out against it not in anger but with anxiety and sorrow in my heart, and above all with a passionate desire to see our beloved country stand as the moral example of the world. . . . We must combine the *fervor* of the civil rights movement with the peace movement. We must demonstrate, teach and preach, until *the very foundations of our nation are shaken.*[136]

And preach he did. The war hawks in the United States were furious, President Johnson, in particular. The White House and the FBI began a campaign of harassment against a man they considered treasonously unpatriotic. The country as a whole in 1967 opposed King and it supported the war in Vietnam. He was branded an extremist, a communist, and a traitor. His nonviolent international position on the Vietnam War, on all wars, for that matter, was consistent with his Christian satyagraha, but the mood of the nation on the war in 1967 was like that of the mood of much of the nation on segregation before Montgomery in December 1955.

The end. In February 1968, 1,300 black sanitation workers in Memphis, Tennessee went on strike, protesting working conditions and viciously low wages. They called King for help and he responded, bearing witness against the economic injustice in Memphis, just as he had witnessed against the military injustice in Vietnam and the racial injustice in the South. On March 28 he led six thousand strikers and their supporters on a march through Memphis. Violence broke out; one person was killed and fifty people were injured.

And then, on April 4, 1968, Martin Luther King Jr. was murdered at his motel in Memphis by a white racist.

He was laid to rest in South View Cemetery in Atlanta on April 9 and on his tombstone were carved the words from the old slave spiritual that his vision for the beloved community enshrined: "Free at last, free at last; thank God almighty, I'm free at last."

We turn next, and finally, to Martin Luther King Jr.'s concept of the beloved community.

The Beloved Community

The classic expression of King's attitude toward community lies in his definition and use of the Greek concept *agapē*, (pronounced "ah-ga-pay"), "love," defined by him in 1958, as we saw above, as "a willingness to go to any length to restore community."[137] The source for this interpretation of love is the Swedish theologian Anders Nygren who, in his classic work *Agapē and Eros* (1953), had said:

> *Agapē* does not recognize value, but creates it. *Agapē* loves and imparts value by loving. The man who is loved by God has not value in himself; what gives him value is precisely the fact that God loves Him.[138]

King attempts to show that man, as lover and thereby the creator of value, creates the beloved community. Thus, on King's interpretation of *agapē*, it is your being loved that gives you value; and it is your selflessly loving others that gives them value and makes the beloved community possible. *Agapē* is the altruistic glue that suffuses Christian satyagraha and that then binds together the beloved community in the same fashion that love and altruistic satyagraha bound together the ashramic community for Gandhi. The role that "love" will play in King's understanding of community should not be surprising since the concept of the beloved community arises out of the Christian tradition.[139]

The first appearance of "beloved community" in King's writings occurs in April 1957. The goal of the Montgomery boycott had been, "reconciliation; the end [was] redemption; the end [was] the creation of the beloved community."[140] Other words and phrases that King subsequently employed as synonyms for "beloved community" are "integrated society," "the solidarity of the human family," "an inescapable network of mutuality," "the Kingdom of God . . . a Kingdom controlled by the law of love," and "the fatherhood of God and the brotherhood of man,"

One American theologian who, more than others, may have influenced King's social gospel and the development of the concept of the beloved community was the American theologian Walter Rauschenbush (1861–1918). Arguing that the primary purpose of Christianity was "to transform human society into the kingdom of God," Rauschenbusch declared:

> The kingdom of God is still a collective conception, involving the whole social life of man. It is not a matter of saving human atoms, but of saving the social organism.[141]

King's "beloved community," an organic unity in precisely this sense, oftentimes sounds like what Rauschenbusch will variously call "kingdom of God," "true human community," and "righteous community." All three denote "humanity organized according to the will of God," expressing "a progressive reign of love in human affairs," which is best expressed as "service to others."[142] King knew of Rauschenbusch's work while a student at both Morehouse and Crozer. But, while influence may be there, King was to reject many of the theological implications of Rauschenbusch's social gospel theology and what was subsequently to evolve from it, Protestant liberation theology:

> I was immediatley influenced by the social gospel [at Crozer Theological Seminary in 1950] as a method to eliminate social evil. . . . I read Rauschenbusch's *Christianity and the Social Crisis.* . . . [But] I felt that he had fallen victim to the nine-teenth-century "cult of inevitable progress" which led to an unwarranted optimism concerning human nature. Moreover, he came perilously close to identifying the Kingdom of God with a particular social and economic system—a temptation which the church should never give in to.[143]

The "beloved community," while rooted in the Protestant tradition, remains King's own unique contribution to a new social gospel aimed at ridding the world of social evils.

In a speech before the National Press Club in Washington, D.C. in July 1962, King spoke of the relationship between violence and "the broken community":

> I feel that this way of nonviolence is vital because it is the only way to reestablish the broken community. It is the method which seeks to implement the just law by appealing to the conscience of the great decent majority who through blindness, fear, pride, or irrationality have allowed their consciences to sleep.[144]

One way of awakening that sleeping conscience of the community lay through acts of love. And those acts of love are nonviolent, direct, social actions, that is, Christian satyagraha:

> The nonviolent resisters can summarize their message in the following simple terms: We will take direct action against injustice without waiting for other agencies to act. We will not obey unjust laws or submit to unjust practices. We will do

this peacefully, openly, cheerfully because our aim is to persuade. We adopt the means of nonviolence because our end is a community at peace with itself.[145]

The concept of the beloved community gives a new meaning to that tired old word "integration." At a church conference in Nashville in December 1962, King argued that racial integration, and not desegregation, was the ultimate goal of the civil rights movement. He calls for a different kind of interrelatedness that transcends competitiveness. King's vision of an integrated community is that of an organically unified body:

> Integration is creative, and is therefore more profound and far-reaching than desegregation. Integration is the positive acceptance of desegregation and the welcomed participation of Negroes into the total range of human activities. Integration is genuine intergroup, interpersonal doing. . . . Integration is the ultimate goal of our national community.[146]

The essence of this organically integrated community is, of course, altruistic love:

> The universe is so structured that things do not quite work out rightly if men are not diligent in their concern for others. The self cannot be self without other selves. I cannot reach fulfillment without thou. Social psychologists tell us that we cannot truly be persons unless we interact with other persons. All life is interrelated. All men are caught in an inescapable network of mutuality, tied in a single garment of destiny. This is what John Donne meant.[147]

He then concluded by reminding his audience that selfless love is the creative way to establish community and that love is the way to "self-transformation":

> Those dark and demonic responses ["fear, prejudice, pride, and irrationality, which are the barriers to a truly integrated society"] will be removed only as men are possessed by the invisible, inner law which etches on their hearts the conviction that all men are brothers and that love is mankind's most potent weapon for personal and social transformation. True integration will be achieved by true neighbors who are willingly obedient to unenforceable obligations.[148]

Finally, in 1966 in an article in *Ebony*, King repeated the goal for the community that he had been seeking to identify and to implement:

> Only a refusal to hate or kill can put an end to the chain of violence in the world and lead us toward a community where men can live together without fear. Our goal is to create a beloved community and this will require a qualitative change in our souls as well as a qualitative change in our lives.[149]

King, like Gandhi, and, in part, like Leopold, has answered both of the questions that we previously set for our community designers. He has told us what a community is, namely, a holistic, integrated, interrelated, interdependent, interactive body of human members who assume responsibility for each other, and who, through mutual concern, cooperation, and love, share a common destiny; and he has also told us that with an awakened or transformed conscience or soul one can join the beloved community using thereafter selfless love and nonviolence to restore and maintain it.

Let's turn to our four-stage Prescription for Community and our summary of the beloved community.

Martin Luther King Jr.'s Prescription for Community: The Beloved Community

The Problem

As King came to see the problem facing blacks in the South and Christians in the United States and humans in the world, the issues seemed far more complex than were at first apparent. Let's treat that complexity under *"Causes"* below, and simply state here that the problem was a combination of untold misery, fear, bitterness, and hatred, and that these were felt as much by blacks as by whites, by Americans as much as by Europeans, Africans, and Asians.

The Causes

In the beginning the cause was seen simply as racial discrimination; but as time passed, King saw that racial discrimination was imbedded in a larger network of injustices that enclasped whites as much as blacks. The unjust laws were born in fear, hatred, greed, and selfishness, and these same laws bred, in turn, further psychological illnesses. Later in his career King added economic injustice and poverty to his list of causes of suffering, degradation, and human indignity. Finally, with his pacifist stand he realized that the net of injustices was not confined to one region, to one country, but was thrown around the world itself. His congregation became all the earth's suffering human beings, his church the world, his pulpit the national and international news media: the beloved community had to be all of mankind.

The Solution

The solution remained in the end what it had been in the beginning—the conversion of one's opponent. To turn around the racist, the murderer, the thug, the international terrorist, as well as to energize and convert those who sit silently on the sidelines, uncommitted and aloof, all that became part of the solution. Gandhi had taught him an important lesson about winning and losing—that where there are winners, there are losers, and that where there are losers, everyone loses. The aim was not merely then to change laws, for changed laws can't alter attitudes and hearts, as the 1990s are demonstrating all too clearly. That King got it right and got the segregation laws changed was not an empty victory by any means; but it never was the primary goal of all of his satyagraha efforts: the laws are not the beloved community.

The Way

The way to transform the heart and mind of oneself, first, and then the hearts and minds of one's oppressors and opponents, is through Christian satyagraha. This involved the five points of nonviolent direct action against the impersonal forces of injustice and evil, action to be carried out with nonviolence and love for one's opponent, with the aim of persuading the opponent that he or she is mistaken, thereby bringing about redemption, reconciliation, and community.

But problems and questions remain for any designer and builder of an altruistic community. We turn, therefore, to an analysis of three problems entailed by King's beloved community set into a general critique of the altruistic communities of Leopold, Gandhi, and King.

Problems with Altruistic Communities: An Overview

There are three familiar problems to consider in connection with the altruistic communities of Mohandas Gandhi and Martin Luther King Jr., and, in part, Aldo Leopold. The first two, the problem of communo-fascism and the problem of community limitation, are serious but not destructive of the end that altruism seeks, that is, peace. The third problem, the problem of the way to soul-transformation, will be raised but then dealt with more explicitly in our next chapter on the karmic community of Buddhism.

The Problem of Communo-Fascism

This problem, similar to the problem of ecofascism for Aldo Leopold, refers to the compelling tendency of strong communities to submerge their members in group-identity to the exclusion of self-identity. Gandhi's satyagrahis are lured into believing that unselfish acts will lead to solving the problems of violence and peace. They are encouraged, as we probably all are, to behave altruistically and immerse their personal and private aims, desires, and agendas into whatever will benefit the community. The problem, as we first saw with Plato, lies in the conformity of the individual to the group with the subsequent devouring of the individual by the group, which is made all the easier by the tendency here to discourage selfishness and personal freedom. In chapter 1 we called this supercontrol of the individual by the community "the problem of communo-fascism."

Gandhi, for one, was certainly aware of the problem. In *Harijan*, February 1, 1942, he says:

> If the individual ceases to count, what is left of society? Individual freedom alone can make a man voluntarily surrender himself completely to the service of society. If it is wrestled from him, he becomes an automaton and society is ruined. No society can possibly be built on a denial of individual freedom.[150]

Strong community leaders together with weak community followers can produce a disastrous result for both: if the community is too strong then individualism is lost, personal freedom is jeopardized, and we have fascism. Surrendering oneself entirely to the service of another, here to the community, is one of the more insidious forms of insanity often called "suicide."

If self-surrender leads to the death of the self and if altruism leads to self-surrender, then it surely follows that altruism leads to suicide. This problem, the problem of communal altruism, follows hard upon the logical heels of the problem of communo-fascism. The attempt to universalize or communalize altruism and turn it into an ethical standard for behavior, while benign and even psychologically useful at the individual level (everyone loves a selfless person up to a point and, besides, being temporarily humble and momentarily self-effacing never hurt anyone) can be both serious and destructive at the communal level. Removing the self entirely from any moral situation, becoming the servant of all or the slave of everyone, can lead to either insanity or suicide and in either case can lead, and has led, to untrammeled violence. We will return to this important problem of communal altruism in the final chapter of this book.

The Problem of Community Limitation

The problem of community limitation, touched on indirectly with Leopold, is the result of having a too narrow and restricted domain for what counts as community. This problem points to that narrowing and argues that leaving out as members of community the populations of animals and plants, alters the entire conception of what community in the twenty-first century ought to be. King, in discussing the integrated community, is aware of the problem of community limitation. Recall his words:

> The universe is so structured that things do not quite work out rightly if men are not diligent in their concern for others. . . . All life is interrelated. All men are caught in an inescapable network of mutuality, tied in a simple garment of destiny.[151]

All well and good. But, the critic feels, we can no longer afford the luxury of believing that *Homo sapiens* alone constitute the whole of the integrated body of interacting and interdependent individuals on the planet: we are not the only ones caught in the network of mutuality; to think otherwise is to encourage another form of insanity sometimes called "ecocide."

The problem of communo-fascism is the other side of the coin with the problem of community limitation. The latter problem results from making the community too narrow and too weak; the former problem results from making the community too wide and too strong. Both problems result from a moral myopia regarding what is necessary in avoiding violence and securing peace.

The Problem of the Way to Self-transformation

There is one final puzzle that we might mention very briefly. King appears to argue in a manner similar to Leopold that membership in the community is dependent upon, or the result of, a change in the person who becomes a member. Where Leopold calls for a transformation of the ordinary conscience into an ecological conscience as a condition for membership, King calls for an awakening of conscience as if from a sleep; it is a personal transformation, a qualitative change, in the soul and in one's life. The question we might raise is this: How is such transformation to be accomplished? That is, what must one do in order to be transformed? Leopold seemed to say, Get out into the natural world, while King and Gandhi appear to say, Get into loving relationships with everyone and witness the power that love has to transform the soul.

I don't want to appear mean-spirited about this business, but I feel very much like the Taoist sage Lao-tzu when he confronted his rival Confucius, a man who had made a similar claim about the power of love:

> "Tell me," said Lao-tzu, "in what consist charity and duty to one's community?"
> "They consist," answered Confucius, "in a capacity for rejoicing in all things; in universal love, without the element of self."

In other words, the duty to community lies in loving everyone selflessly. At this point, Lao-tzu cries out in exasperation:

> "What stuff and nonsense! Does not universal love contradict itself? Is not your elimination of self a positive manifestation of self? . . . Alas! Sir, you have brought much confusion into the mind of man."[152]

Lao-tzu then offers his own answer to the question, In what consist charity and duty to one's community? Sounding very much like

Aldo Leopold, he prescribes getting out into the natural world. He points to the unchanging regularity of nature, the sun and moon, the stars, the birds and beasts, trees and shrubs, all exist in their own rhythmical, unvarying constancy. Learn from them, he concludes, "Be like these: follow the way of the natural world (*Tao*) and you will be perfect."[153]

All well and good; but there's still the problem of the way to soul-transformation or self-transformation all over again. Both King and Leopold, and now Lao-tzu and possibly Confucius, depend on a change or transformation of the person as a necessary condition for belonging to their respective communities. But none is specific about the way in which such transformation is to be accomplished. Lacking that means or recipe or map or way or yoga, we must conclude that merely saying, Consider nature! or Love everyone selflessly! simply won't do as descriptions of what must be done. Thus the critic and the continuing problem of self-transformation.

We turn finally to our three central questions regarding community, violence, and peace.

Conclusion: Three Central Questions

What is it that is shared that makes King's beloved community into a community? Again, as with Leopold and Gandhi, it is the feeling that one is identified with a community and that one is responsible for its maintenance and success. One possible difference from Leopold and Gandhi, however, is that King is willing to speak more forcefully of the feeling of *love* within the beloved community that holds the community together more than any other human emotion. Love is the glue that does the binding and I'm not sure that Leopold and Gandhi might not agree. That this is the case might be seen from the response to the second question.

How does one become a member of, that is, identified with, the beloved community? As with our previous community builders, membership is achieved through the way of selfless service. And it is, of course, this regard for others, this love, that makes selfless service possible, and it is selfless service that makes that love possible. In other words, it is psychologically impossible to separate love in King's sense from the expression of that love. Both are really one, parts of a single whole, and it would seem that each is causally related to the other and also to that conversion experience of self-transformation where subject and object merge into that single whole, where member and community become indistinguishable in the beloved community. And Leopold and Gandhi seem to be saying something very much like this in their versions of the altruistic community as well. Certainly, if altruistic love entails making the self as insignificant and small as possible, then both Leopold (remember the biotic pyramid and man's place in it) and Gandhi (remember *karma yoga* and the selfless action that it inspires) would appear to be in complete agreement: all three are communal altruists.

Can the problems of violence and peace in the twenty-first century be solved through the beloved community? From what we've already suggested—that the ways of the biotic community and of the ashramic community are practically and significantly identical to the beloved community—if the former two communities can solve the problems of violence and peace in the twenty-first century, then so also, it would seem, can the beloved community solve those same problems. I say that these three communities are *practically* and *significantly* identical in places where identity matters, even though Leopold and Gandhi would probably not speak of love in precisely the same (Christian) terms that King speaks of it, neither, it seems to me, would they disagree with what he says about love, that one gives value in loving and that one receives value in being loved. Once again, the solution is best described through instantiating our two community arguments from chapter 1. First, the community violence argument:

1. No one would intentionally do violence to oneself.
2. Oneself is the beloved community.
3. Therefore, no one would intentionally do violence to the beloved community.

Second, the community peace argument:

1. Everyone would intentionally do peace to oneself.
2. Oneself is the beloved community.
3. Therefore, everyone would intentionally do peace to the beloved community.

Once more, the language is unwieldy, the justifications for both sets of premises follow from the previous discussion, and, finally, "education" remains the key to removing the unintentional ignorance of the one who creates violence and prevents peace.

There appear to be no logical inconsistencies with the solution of the beloved community to these problems. But as we have just seen, the problems of transformation, soul-conversion, and altruism, "beloved altruism," lead to further questions that await explanations and answers. What is the nature of this conversion and how is it effected? What do "love" and "beloved altruism" mean? How does it relate to Leopold's "biotic altruism" and Gandhi's "ashramic altruism"? These are all questions, together with an analysis of the *is* of identity in those second premises, above, to which we will return in our final chapter.

We turn next to our final community, the karmic community of Gautama the Buddha.

Chapter 5

◁◇▷

Gautama the Buddha
and the Karmic Community

G autama Siddhartha Shakyamuni (ca. 563–483 B.C.E.), who, following his enlightenment, became known as "the Buddha" ("the awakened one"), developed an especially exciting concept of community. In order to get to it, we must examine his life, the two major Buddhist traditions that he inspired, and then, using the tradition called "Mahāyāna Buddhism," go roundabout to the Buddha's concept of the karmic community. The chapter will conclude, once again, by pointing to several problems that the Buddha's karmic community engenders in attempting to solve the problems of violence and peace in the twenty-first century.

The Buddha's Life

The man known as "the Buddha" was born in Lumbini in northeastern India (modern Nepal). His father, Shuddhodana, most Buddhists believe, was a great king who had his palace-capital in Kapilavastu, and his son, the future Buddha, was therefore a highborn Hindu prince. After his birth a soothsayer had prophesied that the young Gautama, as he was called, would grow up to be either a great king and a world monarch, or he would become a great religious saint. King Shuddhodana was intent on keeping his son a prince and on straight monarchical paths and, being fearful that Gautama would turn to the religious life, devised a scheme to make sure that the child would remain innocent of any experiences that might turn his head away from royal politics. Hence, the king kept Prince Gautama a virtual prisoner in the royal residence and surrounded him with all possible sensual and distracting experiences. All sources of unhappiness, pain, and anxiety were forbidden in what finally became a palace of pleasures, an Indian version of Huxley's World State. At the age of sixteen the young prince was married and it seemed as if his future, however boring and pleasure-filled, was safe and secure. And so matters continued for the next thirteen years of Gautama's life.

The Four Signs of Suffering

Shuddhodana, fearful that his son would ever experience pain and grief, had left strict orders forbidding him to be taken from the sanitized precincts of the palace grounds. But one day during Gautama's twenty-ninth year, his charioteer, a man named "Channa," disobeys the king's orders and takes the prince outside the royal walls and into the "real" world. As the horses carry them down an altogether new and strange road, Gautama sees a man, his body covered with pus-running sores, his face flushed, and his limbs trembling with fever. Shocked, Gautama asks his charioteer what is happening. "Sire," the charioteer replies, "this is sickness. It is the condition to which all human beings must sooner or later come." "Even I?" the prince asks. "Yes, even you," Channa replies. Disturbed by this first sight of suffering and perplexed even more by his driver's explanation of it, Gautama asks to be driven back to the palace. He spends a sleepless night, consumed with the experience of human misery, the suffering of sickness.

The next day he goes out, once again, with the charioteer. As the vehicle leaves the palace grounds, Gautama sees an old man tottering along by the side of the road, his face wrinkled with age, his hair white, his bent and withered body tremblingly supported by a staff. Again, perplexed, Gautama asks Channa about this man. "Sire," the charioteer replies, "this is old age. It is the condition to which all human beings must sooner or later come." Deeply moved, once more, by what he hears and sees, Gautama asks to be driven back to the palace. Again, he spends a wearisome night considering this second sight, the suffering of old age.

The third day, undaunted by the sights of the previous two days, Gautama is outside the palace walls, once again. This time he encounters a funeral procession and a corpse being carried to the cremation grounds. Moved by the sight of the dead man and the sorrowing relatives, Gautama asks Channa what is happening. "Sire," the charioteer replies, "this is death. It is the condition to which all human beings will at last come." Disturbed, yet again, by the experience, Gautama is driven back to the palace and spends the night considering this third sight, the suffering of death.

The fourth day events proceed as before but this time Gautama encounters a man in the ochre robes of a religious ascetic, his face tranquil and peaceful, walking by the road. Channa informs Gautama that the man is a *sannyāsi*, a wandering mendicant, one who has renounced the world of temptations and pleasures in order to conquer the anguish and suffering of sickness, old age, and death. Brooding on this fourth experience, Prince Gautama is driven back to the palace where his wife has just given birth to a son. Hearing of the event Gautama promptly names the son Rāhula, "bondage," and resolves that he, too, like the *sannyāsi*, will give up the life of a householder, of a prince and husband and father, and follow the way of the religious saint. Late that night, he leaves the palace and the easy life of pleasure, taking with him only the clothes on his back. He has renounced the world in order to find the solution to human suffering.

Gautama's Teachers and Companions

Gautama is twenty-nine years old at the time of his renunciation. As he travels into his new life as a renunciate, he encounters two master yogis, each of whom will teach him the art of yoga meditation. Strenuously practicing the techniques of yoga with the first teacher, he soon reaches the deep trance of total nothingness, surpassing thereby his master. Realizing the yoga powers of his young pupil, the teacher invites Gautama to become a partner with him in directing his other disciples in the art of meditation. But Gautama refuses and travels on to another teacher.

Studying with this second yoga master, Gautama soon surpasses him as well in the depth and quality of his meditation. This second teacher, recognizing the superiority of Gautama's attainments, then offers to become Gautama's pupil. But Gautama is seeking neither disciples nor trance states of nothingness in meditation. He is searching for a positive and permanent state of mind, one of peace and tranquility that does not vanish when one ceases meditation. He is searching for liberation from suffering and liberation into permanent happiness. He is searching for what will come to be called *nirvāṇa*.

Leaving his second teacher behind, Gautama falls in with a group of five young ascetics. These men believe that the condition for which Gautama searches can be found only through the harsh physical disciplining of body and mind. Trustingly, he follows their example and for several years practices their way of the mortification of the body. He drinks only water, sleeps on the hard ground, eats sparingly of fruits and herbs, existing finally on one grain of hemp a day. His body wastes away until after two years he can push his hand through his emaciated abdomen and grasp his spinal cord. Weak and undernourished, he nearly dies, realizing only at the last moment that this way of pain, like the way of pleasure previously, is not the way to be liberated from suffering, for this ascetic way will lead only to death. There must be another way, a middle way, a path between the two harsh extremes of pleasure and pain. He now sets out to find that other way, a way that will forever after immortalize Buddhism as "the religion of the middle way."

Enlightenment

Recovering his strength and wits, and now rejected by his five ascetic friends for his apparent faint-heartedness, Gautama resolves to find the way to nirvana by his own means. Journeying to Gaya in modern Bihar, one day Gautama seats himself under a Bo or Bodhi tree ("the tree of wisdom"), a tree sacred to Hindus and, from this time forward, sacred to Buddhists as well. He resolves not to rise until he has achieved the goal for which all of his efforts over the last six years have been directed. During the night that follows he experiences four progressively deeper states of meditational trance. Finally, with the coming of the light of dawn, Gautama suddenly sees intuitively into the fundamental nature of all things. He becomes the Buddha, "the awakened one."

Following his enlightenment or nirvana, the Buddha journeys to Varanasi, the most sacred city of early Hinduism. His former five companions seek him out and become his disciples. At the Deer Park at Sārnāth near Varanasi, he preaches the first sermon of his ministry called "Setting in Motion the Wheel of the Law." The substance of that sermon, the Four Noble Truths, constitutes the Buddha's original and essential teaching and it will become the foundation of all future Buddhisms.

The Four Noble Truths

The Buddha is said to have summarized his teachings in one sentence: "I teach but one thing: Suffering and the release from suffering." Ultimately the matter is far more complicated than that, but penultimately it is precisely that to which the Buddha's doctrine comes. And the Four Noble Truths that he preached at Sārnāth are merely an extension of that one compact summary. The first three noble truths are about the essential nature of suffering; and the last noble truth is about how to be released from it. And yet upon the foundation of these four truths an enormous corpus of theological and philosophical literature has been erected, and dozens of separate sects, schisms, and individual interpretations have sprung from them, underscoring both their singular complexity and their extraordinary influence.

Here is the first of the Four Noble Truths that the tradition says were enunciated by the Buddha in the Deer Park at Sārnāth around 528 B.C.E.:

> Now this, O monks, is the noble truth of suffering: birth is suffering, old age is suffering, sickness is suffering, death is suffering, sorrow, lamentation, dejection, and despair are suffering. Contact with unpleasant things is suffering.[154]

The Buddha is mindful here of the three signs of suffering or anguish—sickness, old age, and death—that some six years previously had set him on his long search for peace and tranquility.

Here is the second noble truth:

> Now this, O monks, is the noble truth of the cause of suffering: that craving which leads to rebirth, combined with pleasure and lust, finding pleasure here and there, namely, the craving for passion, the craving for existence, the craving for non-existence.[155]

The Buddha follows the Hindu teaching that craving or desire is the cause of suffering. This is no commonplace utterance but a tremendously important discovery. The cause of suffering is existentially grounded in the individual; suffering is not the result of inherited metaphysical evil, like original sin, resulting from some ancestral Fall, as suggested by many Christians; nor is it simply due to actions performed by the individual in society and against God, as detailed in the Hebrew Decalogue and Pentateuch by Moses; nor is it one economic class in society exploiting another, as suggested by the Marxists. In fact, original sin, individual sin, and societal sin can all be neatly subsumed under the cause that all three sins have in common—they are all expressions of human craving or desire.

We turn next to the third noble truth:

> Now this, O monks, is the noble truth of the cessation of suffering: the cessation without a remainder of that craving, abandonment, forsaking, release, non-attachment.[156]

Buddha would have been a negligent religious guide, indeed, if he had identified both the problem of suffering and its cause but had said nothing about the fact that there is a solution such that suffering can be stopped.

We turn, finally, to the fourth noble truth:

> Now this, O monks, is the noble truth of the way that leads to the cessation of suffering: this is the noble eightfold Path, namely, right views, right intentions, right speech, right action, right livelihood, right effort, right mindfulness, right concentration.[157]

Buddha ends his first sermon at Sarnath with this description of the way to the cessation of pain and suffering. It must appear as both simple and disappointing at first glance. We might have expected something more complicated, something more esoteric and mystical, than this list of eight appears to offer. But the simplicity and the disappointment are assuaged when one realizes that there is a great deal that is practical and common sensical packed into each one of these "rights." For the listener is told that there is something that he or she can do, must do, and is able to do, *here and now*, in order to overcome craving and thereby permanently end pain and suffering.

The noble eightfold path. The eight "rights" are easily divisible into three quite distinct categories. The first category we might label "the internal path"; it comprises the first two rights—right views about the nature of suffering, and right intentions not to increase the suffering in the community. The internal path is concerned with mental activities in relation to the community of suffering beings, where those mental activities can be seen as necessary preliminaries to action or inaction in that community: For as your mind is, so are your actions.

The second category we might label "the external path"; it comprises the next three rights—right speech in relation to others in the community, right acts toward others in the community, and right livelihood or vocation while living in the community. The external path is concerned with the actions that one performs and that directly concern other human beings and not merely oneself. Consequently, Buddhists respect truth, life, and property; they refrain from occupations in the military and other businesses that involve killing in any form—the occupations of herdsman, tanner, leather worker, butcher, and the like.

The third and final category of the paths we might label "the meditation path"; it comprises the last three rights—right endeavor to control the qualities of the mind through meditation, right mindfulness achieved again through meditation in which one rises above the wants, lusts, and desires of the body and mind, and finally, right concentration, the deepest stage of yogic meditation or penetration where one advances by further levels to the highest stage of realization, nirvana. Yoga meditation is then the *sine qua non* of the Noble Eightfold Path and it is the cornerstone not only of Buddhism but of all the *major* philosophies and religions of India, China, and Japan.

Building a Community

Following the first sermon at Sārnāth, where the Four Noble Truths were preached, Buddha set about gathering converts to the new doctrine. The tradition tells us that at first a few, and then hundreds, and finally thousands, flocked to his religion's standard as he preached and traveled (up to twenty miles a day!) throughout northeastern India, to the cities of Rājagriha, Śravāstī, the capital of Kosala, Pataliputra or Patna, Vaiśali and Kusināra, and elsewhere for the remaining forty-five years of his life.

Beginning with his five ascetic associates, other disciples soon joined him, including one Yasa, the dissolute son of a wealthy guildmaster of Varanasi. The tradition says that Yasa left his riches behind in disgust, sought out the Buddha in the Deer Park at Sārnāth and after hearing the Four Noble Truths from him became the sixth disciple of the new movement. Buddha accepted a meal at Yasa's house and soon Yasa's mother and former wife became members of the lay or secular order. Then four of Yasa's companions entered the order as monks, and soon fifty other men of Varanasi became arhats or enlightened monks of the new community. As monks, they engaged in a ceremony still practiced today of shaving their heads fortnightly, wearing saffron robes, and reciting the vows by promising to take refuge, or have faith, in the Buddha, in the Doctrine or Dharma that he preached, and in the community or *saṅgha* of monks. The number of adherents eventually grew to such a number, we are told, that the Buddha ceased to direct the ceremony personally and left its performance to the monks, themselves.

Some idea of the nature of this first Buddhist community can be gleaned by looking to the rules of the order of monks (and, eventually, nuns) that governed its functioning. The community shared not only a high regard for the Buddha, an earnest hope for nirvana, and a desire to live together; they also shared the rules by which to pursue goals and they shared a tradition of stories and legends regarding the Buddha and his preaching. Here are some samples of the community's rules. First, permanent expulsion from the *saṅgha*[158] would result from sexual intercourse, from stealing, killing a human being, or attempting suicide, and from claiming to know the higher knowledge or complete knowledge when one does not know, and lying about it later.

In addition, there are other rules whose violation carries less stringent consequences than expulsion from the *saṅgha*. These are rules involving touching a woman (don't do it), the proper construction or building of a monk's cell (keep it plain and simple), prohibitions against causing problems within the order, disobedience of elders, rules regarding the begging for food, rules directing public confession before the *saṅgha* of one's sins, rules for dress and robes, what property may be owned by a monk, the use of money (don't touch gold or silver), association with nuns (don't touch them, either), the drinking of intoxicants (don't), travel to distant places, proper sleeping and meditation times, general rules of behavior in daily life, and the correct procedures for bringing charges against monks who violate any of these rules.

Here is one such rule, along with a story that demonstrates that the community about which the Buddha was concerned is considerably wider than the *saṅgha*. The story illustrates that the Buddha's compassion, for which he was so justifiably famous, extended to all sentient, that is, feeling and suffering, beings. It seems that a monk had been bitten by a snake and had died. The other monks tell the Buddha of the death and the Buddha says it was the monk's own fault, "For if, O monks, that monk had suffused the four royal communities of the snakes with his friendliness, that monk would not have been killed by the bite of the snake." Buddha then orders them to chant the following verses in order to infuse the communities of snakes and all creatures with their own compassion:

> Creatures without feet have my love,
> And likewise those that have two feet,
> And those that have four feet I love,
> And those, too, that have many feet.

> May those without feet harm me not,
> And those with two feet cause no hurt;
> May those with four feet harm me not,
> Nor those who many feet possess.

> Let creatures all, all things that live,
> All beings of whatever kind,
> See nothing that will abode them ill!
> May naught of evil come to them!

And the Buddha then concludes with this counsel:

> Infinite is the Buddha, infinite the Dharma, infinite the Community. Finite are creeping things: snakes, scorpions, centipedes, spiders, lizards and mice! I have now made my protection, and sung my song of defence [of them].[159]

Here is another story illustrative of that compassion that served, once again, to define the community and its commitment to an altruistic ethics. It is the very moving story of Buddha's moral injunction to tend the sick:

> Now at that time a certain brother was suffering from dysentry and lay where he had fallen down in his own excrements . . . [The Buddha with his chief disciple Ānanda comes to that brother's lodging]. Now the Exalted One saw that brother lying where he had fallen in his own excrements, and seeing him he went towards him, came to him and said:

> > "Brother, what ails you?"
> > "I have dysentery, Lord."
> > "But is there anyone taking care of you, brother?"

"No, Lord."

"Why is it, brother, that the brethren do not take care of you?"

"I am useless to the brethren, Lord; therefore the brethren do not care for me."

Then the Exalted One said to the venerable Ānanda: "Go you, Ānanda, and fetch water. We will wash this brother."

"Yes, Lord," replied the venerable Ānanda to the Exalted One. . . . [And the water is fetched and poured and they wash the brother and lay him on a bed. The Buddha leaves and calls the Order together.]

"Brethren, is there in such and such a lodging a brother who is sick?"

"There is, Lord."

"And what ails that brother?"

"Lord, that brother has dysentery."

"But, brethren, is there anyone taking care of him?"

"No, Lord."

"Why not? Why do not the brethren take care of him?"

"That brother is useless to the brethren, Lord. That is why the brethren do not take care of him."

"Brethren, you have no mother and no father to take care of you. If you will not take care of each other, who else, I ask, will do so? Brethren, he who would wait on me, let him wait on the sick."[160]

There is another legend, a powerful story, from the period of Buddha's forty-five years of preaching that is worthy of mention as well, illustrating as it does the practical nature of the Buddha's message and the absolute commitment to seeking the transworldly goal of liberation through nonattachment. Kisa Gotami's beloved son had died when he was just a toddler. In her anguish she carried the body of her dead child to the Buddha hoping for a miracle, for the tradition attributed many miraculous powers to the Buddha, such as, walking on water, flying through the air, knowing events before they happen, reading the hearts and minds of men, as well as raising the dead. Perhaps it was this reputation that brought her, sorrowing and in despair, to him. The Buddha tells her that she was wise in coming to him for medicine, and promises to help her. He tells her to return to the city and to seek for a mustard seed from a house in which no one has died. Full of hope for her innocent, dead babe she goes to the city enquiring from door to door for the mustard seed from a house that cannot, of course, be found. Realizing her own folly and the wisdom that the Buddha has shown her, that death touches everyone, she returns to the Buddha. The sorrowing mother takes up the body of her child and carries him to the cemetery. Gently laying him down and holding his tiny hand for the last time she says, "My little son, I thought that death had come to you alone; but it is not so; it happens to all people."[161] She leaves him there, returns to the Buddha and asks him for help in her despair.

The Death of the Buddha

In the twentieth year of his preaching he chooses Ānanda as his bowl-bearer and heir-apparent leader of the order. Converting kings, princes, and commoners, the wealthy and the poor, he travels about the northeastern parts of the subcontinent firmly establishing his reputation and the order.

One day, toward the end of his long ministry, the Buddha falls dangerously ill. Ānanda becomes concerned because the Buddha has made no official provision for the continuation of the order. He enquires of the Buddha what he has determined for the community. The Buddha, now in his eightieth and final year, replies rather sharply, we may suppose, saying, in effect, What more would you have from me? I have told you everything that there is to be told.

> Therefore, Ānanda, dwell as having refuges in yourselves, resorts in yourselves and not elsewhere, as having refuges in the Doctrine, resorts in the Doctrine and not elsewhere.[162]

That Buddha wished not to be revered as a god and that he desired not to fix attention on the Order as an institution seems clear from these remarks. The only source for enlightenment for future Buddhists is to be in the Doctrine or Dharma that he has preached, that is, in essentially, but not exclusively, the Four Noble Truths, and what each man and woman will make of this Doctrine within himself or herself; that, he seems to be saying, is where the real strength and power of Buddhism must rest. But his followers will have something else in mind as the Order evolves from this find-nirvana-by-yourself individualism into a secure and well-formed karmic community.

Moving on to Pāvā he stops at the mango grove of a blacksmith named Chunda. The latter provides a meal that brings on the Buddha's final sickness. He is taken ill with gushing blood and violent pains, but controls his mortal illness and sets off with Ānanda for Kusinārā. On the way he rests and speaks further about the Doctrine. He indicates that there are four places worthy to be visited by monks: the place where the Buddha was born; where he attained enlightenment; where he first turned the wheel of the law; and where he attained *parinirvāṇa*, or complete *nirvāṇa*, that is, where he died. Thus the way is prepared for the raising of future stupas (relic-chambers for Buddha's ashes) and temples at these holy places. Now dying, Buddha speaks to the sorrowing Ānanda,

> The Doctrine and Discipline, Ānanda, which I have taught and enjoined upon you, is to be your teacher when I am gone.

And then addressing all the monks gathered at the sacred spot at Kusinārā, he speaks to them for the last time:

> And now, O monks, I take my leave of you; all the constituents of being are transitory; work out your own salvation with diligence.[163]

And then, surrounded by his sorrowing disciples, Gautama Siddhartha Shakyamuni, he who was called "the Buddha," dies.

The Rise of Mahāyāna Buddhism

Following the death of the Buddha in 483 B.C.E., a series of Buddhist councils was called, with the first one instituted immediately following the Buddha's death. Their purpose was to establish the rituals, the dogmas, and the myths by which the followers of the Middle Way were to be identified. By the time of the Fourth Buddhist Council in Kashmir under the Emperor Kaniṣka in the first century C.E., a new movement in Buddhism had fully emerged that was hence forward to be known as Mahāyāna ("the large vehicle") Buddhism. It will also be called "Northern Buddhism," because of its geographical location, or "Sanskrit Buddhism," because of the language of its texts.

Mahāyāna exists today throughout China, Tibet, Korea, Mongolia, and Japan. Unlike its chief rival, Theravāda, or Hīnayāna ("the little vehicle") Buddhism, Mahāyāna was strongly influenced by Hinduism, and it came to accept a host of selves, deities, Saviors, and other supernatural entities already rejected by their Theravāda brethren. Among the beliefs that separate the two rival Buddhist religions is one that we shall refer to as "the karmic community," a concept that has its origin in Mahāyāna and that it attributes to the historical Buddha himself.

The Law of Karma and the Problems of Karma and Merit

The introduction of the Mahāyāna Buddhist concept of the karmic community may be related to the solving of two problems relating both to karma and to the law of karma. These two problems of karma resulted from an individualistic interpretation of karma and the law governing its distribution. The Mahāyāna solution to these problems will lead to a communal interpretation of the law of karma and to the concept of the karmic community. In what follows we shall briefly explore the history of the law of karma in Hinduism, the problems of karma or merit that resulted, and the Mahāyāna solution to these problems using the concept of the karmic community. Finally, we shall answer the three central questions with which this study began, concluding with, Can the problems of violence and peace in the twenty-first century be solved through the karmic community?

The Law of Karma in the Upanishads. The law of karma is the principle of cosmic justice that holds that all good actions will be rewarded and that all wicked actions will be punished, sometime, somehow, somewhere. This principle, Hindu in orgin, is probably related to the Vedic concept of *Ṛta* on the one hand (1000 B.C.E.) and to the later post-Vedic development of the concept of karma, "action, performance, business," on the other. The law of karma, as a principle of justice and action, probably receives its earliest Indian formulation in the oldest *Upanishad*, the *Bṛhadāraṇyaka* (about 700 B.C.E.), where it is said, "Truly, one becomes good by good action and bad by bad action."[164] And the principle is assumed in another classical statement regarding transmigration from the same Upanishad:

> This is what happens to the man who desires. To whatever his mind is attached, the self becomes that in the next life. Achieving that end, it returns again to this world.[165]

In a later *Upanishad*, the *Chāndogya* (about 650 B.C.E.), the principle receives a clearer formulation:

> Those whose conduct here has been good, they will enter a good womb in the next life, the womb of a Brahmin, a

Kṣatriya, or a Vaiśya. But those whose conduct here has been evil, they will enter an evil womb, the womb of a dog or a pig or a caṇḍāla.[166]

Finally, a still later *Upanishad*, the Śvetāśvatara (about 400 B.C.E.), states the doctrine of karma in the form in which it is roughly and popularly known to this day:

> He who has the *guṇas* [qualities] and is the agent of actions that will bring consequences, he is the recipient of the consequences of whatever he does.
>
> Taking on all possible forms . . . he, the *prāṇādhipa* ["the ruler of the vital breaths," i.e., the self], is reborn in bondage according to his actions.
>
> According to his actions, the embodied self chooses repeatedly the various forms in various conditions in the next life.
>
> According to his own qualities and acts, the embodied self chooses the kinds of forms, large and small, that it will take on.[167]

The Upanishadic law of karma is the traditional metaphysical principle of individual justice in Hinduism. It simply says that if *you* do the dharma ("right") or if *you* do the adharma ("wrong") then *you* get the karma, that is, sooner or later *you* will receive *your* due, for as *you* sow, so shall *you* reap. This metaphysical principle is directed primarily at the single, isolated, separate, existing *individual* and it guarantees that there will be moral fairness on a cosmic scale to every moral agent. It receives one of its clearest instantiations in the great Hindu text, the *Bhagavad Gītā*.

The law of Karma in the Bhagavad Gītā. Soteriological religions such as Hinduism provide Saviors who are able to share their merit or good karma with the faithful. In the *Bhagavad Gītā* (400–200 B.C.E.) a human incarnation of the Hindu preserver God, Vishnu, is born into the world as Lord Krishna. He now comes announcing to His friend-cousin-disciple Arjuna, as well as to all the world, the conditions—the origin, causes, and purpose—of His human incarnation as Savior:

> You and I have passed through many births, Arjuna; I know all of them but you do not.

Though unborn, for the Ātman [the sacred Self] is eternal, though Lord of all beings, yet using my own nature, I come into existence using my own māyā [magical power].

For whenever there is a decaying of dharma [rightness and justice] and a rising up of adharma [evil and injustice], then I send Myself forth.

I come into existence time after time to protect the good, to destroy the wicked, and to reestablish the holy Dharma.[168]

Subsequently, Krishna reveals to Arjuna one of the ways or yogas by following which he may attain the highest happiness:

Arjuna, you must see that my devotees never perish. . . . For those who take refuge in Me, whether of lowly birth, women, Vaiśyas and even Śūdras, they all go to the highest goal.

Fix your mind on Me; be dedicated to Me; sacrifice to Me; lay yourself devotedly before Me; discipline yourself and with Me as your Supreme goal, to Me you will truly come.[169]

The *Bhagavad Gītā* concludes with Krishna's promise to Arjuna and to all of His future devotees:

Listen once more to My supreme message, the highest secret of all. You are truly My beloved and so I will tell you what is best for you.

Merge your mind with Me, be devoted to Me, worship Me, revere Me, and you shall come to Me. I promise this to you truly for you are ever dear to Me.

Abandon all other duties, come to Me alone for refuge. Be not sorrowed for I shall give you liberation from all sins.[170]

Lord Krishna has laid out the conditions under which, it can be argued, any "Savior" must operate and under which any "soteriological game"[171] must be played. Thus Lord Krishna has the power to recognize sins, to forgive their consequences, to recognize the true repentance and devotion in His devotees that makes that forgiveness possible, to bring order and righteousness into a disordered and chaotic world, and to do all of this with perfect justice and fairness. In other words, from the beginning of His birth into the world of adharma until the saving of His beloved and worshipful devotees from sins and their consequences, to the gathering of those same liberated devotees into "the fair worlds of those of virtuous deeds,"[172] Krishna does what He does either in concert with, or under the aegis of, the law of karma. But it is here that the trouble begins for this very concerned and committed Savior in a universe dominated by the law of karma.[173]

Two Problems of Karma in the Bhagavad Gītā

Lord Krishna is able to dispense rewards to His devoted and loving disciples. His grace is operative in the created world where the law of karma also operates; and Krishna dispenses the former in accordance with His disciples' prayerful requests for liberation from sin and for help in reaching heaven:

> And while performing all actions, having taken refuge in Me, by My grace (*prasāda*) he reaches the eternal, indestructible goal.
> Focusing your thought on Me, you will overcome all difficulties by My grace. But if from egoism you will not heed this advice then you will be utterly destroyed.
> Flee to Me for shelter with your entire being, Arjuna. By My grace you shall attain the greatest peace and the eternal goal.

In the end, of course, Arjuna sees his way clearly as he cries out to his Savior:

> My delusion has been destroyed. I have come to my senses through your grace. With all my doubts gone I shall act according to your word.[174]

The route to enlightenment or liberation for the *Bhagavad Gītā*, as far as the yoga of devotion is concerned, would seem to be something like this: the disciple, Arjuna, first recognizes a problem he cannot solve by himself; he then begins the search for the solution to the problem and, on the advice of Lord Krishna, engages in *bhakti*, devotion, to Krishna; the latter on seeing His devotee's earnest and heartfelt yearning grants His disciple His *prasāda*; finally, armed with this grace the worshipful disciple is able to solve the problem with which the entire search began.

But what precisely is it that Arjuna seeks from Krishna? His favor or grace, to be sure; but what is this *prasāda*? It really is the power to overcome delusion, as he says, and it is the power to solve his problem, to reach the eternal goal of heaven or enlightenment. Why doesn't Arjuna have that power himself? Why does he need, as it were, outside help? The answer to all of these questions lies with the law of karma.

Lord Krishna, many Hindus believe, has "earned" his exalted position as Savior through eons of action that produced meritorious karmic consequences, consequences that have been stored and that are now available for dispensing as *prasāda*. In other words, Lord Krishna's power comes from His past actions and that power now operates as dispensed *prasāda* in accord with the law of universal cosmic justice. The good karma that produced that power has been *earned* by Krishna, it has been *stored* by Krishna, it lies waiting to be *used* by Krishna for those who commit *bhakti* to Krishna, and it will be dispensed by Krishna to deserving disciples such as Arjuna. All of this is made possible by the law of karma which simply says that everyone ought to get, and ultimately will get, precisely what's coming to him or her. It says, as we have seen, that sooner or later justice will be done, that the more good that is done, the greater the reward, and the more evil, the greater the punishment. Lord Krishna, because of the quality of His past lives, is on the receiving end of more good, more merit, and more rewards than one can possibly conceive.

But now consider two problems of karma that would appear to have arisen with our Savior Krishna and His attempts to dispense *prasāda*, that is, His own karma, within this universe dominated by the law of karma. Call these two problems of karma, first, "the problem of stored karma," and, second, "the problem of the transfer of karma." Both problems threaten the status of the law of karma as a dispenser (that's what it is because that's what it does!) of justice to individual agents in need of rewards.

The problem of stored karma. We have assumed that Krishna, over the millennia, through His actions and in accordance with the law of karma, has generated an enormous quantity of good karma. It is important to realize that He hasn't used this karma but has, as it were, stored it, banked it, waiting for opportunities to use it, to spend it. It is, after all, His karma, produced by him, now stored and waiting to reward him in accordance with the law of karma. But consider: the practice or possibility of the storage of good karma is quite inconsistent and threatening to the very law or principle that made the practice possible in the first place; to store the good and not reward the generator of the good is flatly contradictory to the law of karma. Now, however, Krishna as the Savior is in the business of needing none of the karma for Himself that has been stored for Himself. The Savior is now in the transfer business, clear and simple; hence, storage is necessary; hence, a store of karma is necessary; and that contradicts the law or principle by virtue of which the karma was made possible in the beginning. In other words, the Savior's karma account is not the Savior's karma account since it will not be used for Him but only by Him. In other words, His stored merit is no longer His stored merit.

Hand in hand with this problem goes another, and the two problems can be nicely considered together.

The problem of the transfer of karma. As we stated, to store the good without letting that store be used to reward the storer of the good is inconsistent with the law of karma . Thus to transfer Lord Krishna's good karma to you means that Lord Krishna's good karma is no longer His good karma; and, further, to say of Krishna's stored karma that it's not going to lead to a reward for Him because it's been transferred to you is, again, to say that Krishna's karma is not Krishna's karma.

Furthermore, even if you deserve Krishna's stored karma, the fact of your deserving it means that you, too, have done good actions that now demand to be rewarded. So what has happened to your deserved karma? To say that it has been topped off with someone else's stored karma entails either of two things: first, that someone else didn't get his reward, that is, he got less than he deserved, which is unjust; or, second, that you have gotten more than you deserved, which is also unjust.[175]

We might point out here that that stored karma is not ruled out *per se* by the law of karma; it is only necessary that it be stored and then used by the same one who stored it, that is, storer and user must be the same in some sense. For example, you might do many good works in this life but not be rewarded until the next life.[176] So in some sense your good karma has been "stored." However, if you reach the "eternal goal," and if your good karma is not used up or exhausted by rewarding you, then this dangling karma would be inconsistent with the law of karma.

We might point out, again, that transferred karma is not ruled out *per se* by the law of karma; it is only necessary that the person to whom it is transferred is the same person who made it, that is, transferer and transferee must be the same in some sense. For example, you might do many good works in this life, accumulate karma, but not be rewarded until the next life, but you are, nonetheless, the "same" person.

To repeat, if your stored karma is transferred to you then there is no problem; however, if you achieve liberation and your stored karma is transferred to some other person then there is a problem that we might call "the dilemma of stored karma": if that other person deserves stored karma, then, since that person has a reward of his or her own coming that doesn't involve your karma, their being deserving makes the transfer of your karma unnecessary. If that other person does not deserve stored karma, then such a transfer of karma would be unjust. Now, either that other person deserves stored karma or not. Therefore, either the transfer is unnecessary or it is unjust. Thus the dilemma of stored karma, the problems of karma, and the conclusion that the storage and transfer of karma for and to those other than the agent who produced it seems patently inconsistent with the ancient law of karma.

If the dilemma of stored karma is not solved then the theory of *bhakti* yoga is in trouble, since it is said to be efficacious in leading one to heaven only if the available karma is both stored and transferable to the *bhakta* (the devotee). And if the problems of karma that are generated from the karma being transferable are not solved then the law of karma is in trouble. On both counts, it must appear, *bhakti* yoga and the law of karma are in trouble.

Individualism, Saviorism, Communalism, and the Law of Karma

In the preceding sections we have attributed to the *Bhagavad Gītā* and possibly thereby to Hinduism a strictly individualistic interpretation of the law of karma. In this attribution, each individual earns karma or *prasāda* by personal effort and for very personal ends or goals. The interpretation led to the two problems of the storage and transfer of karma. But both problems may be solved by a new interpretation of the law of karma, an interpretation from Mahāyāna Buddhism.

There are probably three views that one could adopt with respect to the relationship between the person seeking the eternal goal of heaven or enlightenment and the law of karma. Let's denominate these three possible relationships: "Karmic Individualism," a *Upanishadic* and early Hindu view that we have briefly dealt with above; "Karmic Saviorism," the later Hindu view that we have been exploring in the *Gītā*; and "Karmic Communalism," a Mahāyāna Buddhist view that we shall take up presently. Let's speak quickly to each one.

Karmic individualism: "If you do the crime then you do the time." Karmic individualism is the most radical interpretation of the relation between a person and the law of karma. It rejects the possibility of the transfer of merit between one person and another either because there is no person as such or because there is nothing to pass over or because each individual is entirely "on his own" in matters of enlightenment. This rugged karmic individualism assumes that we each reach the goal we aim at on our own by each generating his or her own karmic chain with no outside help. The clearest example of radical karmic individualism is probably found in the early Upanishads and possibly in early Buddhism with the remarks of the Buddha, cited above, as he lay dying:

> The Doctrine and Discipline, Ānanda, which I have taught and enjoined upon you, is to be your teacher when I am gone.
> And now, O' monks, I take my leave of you; all the constituents of being are transitory; work out your own salvation with diligence.

There is no Savior here to share His or Her generated karma and the passage enjoins the listener/reader to start pulling himself up by his own karmic bootstraps. Gautama the Buddha's view of rugged karmic individualism was to remain a part of early Theravāda or Hīnayāna Buddhism with its attendant *anātman*, "non-self," and atheistic foundations, and its arhat-seeking monks. The view has been called "selfish" by the later Mahāyāna critics of "Hīnayāna" and in a sense selfishness defines the more rugged karmic individualists very nicely.

The law of karma, according to karmic individualism, applies only to persons wherein each generates his or her own karma through his or her present actions in splendid isolation from the karmic influences of others, whether those others be the living or the dead or Saviors or communities of karmic beings.

Karmic Saviorism: "If you do the crime then the Savior does (or has done) the time." A milder form of karmic individualism emerges with karmic Saviorism. It appears in the *Bhagavad Gītā*, as we have seen above. Here we meet with the notion of shared karma and, with that, the notion of an accumulated karma to be shared. The concepts of stored karma and transferred karma will emerge after 200 B.C.E. in early Mahāyāna Buddhism, perhaps as a consequence of the Hindu soteriological influence. That influence probably rested, as we have seen, above, on this milder form of karmic individualism wherein each person still pulls up on his or her own bootstraps to achieve desired goals but now there are the hands of the loving Savior, or the compassionate Bodhisattva, as we shall see below, in Mahāyāna Buddhism, that one can count on for some extra pulling and support.

The law of karma, according to karmic Saviorism, still applies to individuals but the action-generated karma is no longer entirely one's own but is constituted by a storehouse of karma or merit generated and accumulated by that Savior. This stored karma is then dispensed according to a soteriologic to deserving devotees or recipients. The law of karma, under karmic Saviorism, has been considerably broadened and expanded as we move from self-centered karmic individualism to Savior-centered or even God-centered karmic views.

But, as we have seen, this milder or mitigated karmic individualism introduces several problems that it cannot solve—the problems of stored karma and the transfer of karma. Which brings us to a new view, a Mahāyāna Buddhist view, about karma and the law that governs its dispersal.

Karmic communalism: "If you do the crime then the community does the time." Karmic communalism, our third and final view of the relationship between the individual and the law of karma, calls upon all members of a community of beings to share their merit, that is, their karma, with other members of the same community. Karmic communalism is found as early as the second century B.C.E. in evolving Mahāyāna[177] with the development of the concept of the Bodhisattva. Like the Avatar-God-Savior of the *Bhagavad Gītā*, the Bodhisattva comes declaring his love and compassion. But, unlike the Krishna of the *Gītā*, the Bodhisattva of Mahāyāna karmic communalism is a member of the community that he seeks to save; he has felt their pain, their terror, and he doesn't stand ontologically and majestically above and beyond it or them. The Bodhisattva remembers that he is yet a man; Krishna, though compassionate in His own way, gives no inkling that He remembers any such thing, even though He confesses that Arjuna, His cousin, is "truly My beloved": while both are "Saviors," the

Gītā-Hindu Avatar is not the Mahāyāna Buddhist Bodhisattva.

Here is the seventh century C.E. Bodhisattva, Shantideva, sounding very much like the historical Buddha, expressing this new way of shared or communal merit:

> Through the merit derived from all my good deeds I wish to appease the suffering of all creatures, to be the medicine, the physician, and the nurse of the sick as long as there is sickness. Through rains of food and drink I wish to extinguish the fire of hunger and thirst. I wish to be an inexhaustible treasure to the poor, a servant who furnishes them with all they lack. My life, and all my re-births, all my possessions, all the merit that I have acquired or will acquire, all that I abandon without hope of any gain for myself in order that the salvation of all beings might be promoted.[178]

In his *Śikṣāsamuccaya*, Shantideva summarizes the standard that has inspired all previous Bodhisattvas in their one endeavor in life—to put off their own liberation until everyone in the community of beings has been saved. This is ethical altruism and it supports Buddhist communal altruism, which in turn supports karmic communalism:

> A Bodhisattva resolves: I take upon myself the burden of all suffering, I am resolved to do so, I will endure it. I do not turn or run away, do not tremble, am not terrified, nor afraid, do not turn back or despond. . . . My endeavours do not merely aim at my own deliverance. For with the help of the boat of the thought of all-knowledge, I must rescue all these beings from the stream of Samsara, which is so difficult to cross, I must pull them back from the great precipice, I must free them from all calamities, I must ferry them across the stream of Samsara. I myself must grapple with the whole mass of suffering of all beings. To the limit of my endurance I will experience in all the states of woe, found in any world system, all the abodes of suffering. And I must not cheat all beings out of my store of merit.[179]

The Mahāyāna Buddhist who follows the way of karmic communalism is quick to point out that the law of karma need not be contradicted by the storage and transfer of merit. The latter two practices merely call for an extension of the law of karma. And that extension, far from being inconsistent with the original law is, rather, a logical deduction from it. The original formulation of the Hindu law of karma, whether interpreted as Upanishadic karmic individualism or Hindu karmic Saviorism, was merely too narrowly stated and too narrowly applied (to single individuals); what Mahāyāna did was to resist that narrow and personal interpretation of the law of karma and draw out its wider implications (to apply it to whole societies and communities).

Edward Conze gives a fine defense of karmic communalism as he speaks about the pristine and narrow belief in the law of karma:

> The original belief seems to have been that each one of us has his own series of karma, that the punishment for his misdeeds must be suffered by him, and that the rewards for his good deeds are enjoyed only by him. This excessive individualism was not essential to the karma doctrine, and just as historically the notion of collective responsibility preceded that of individual responsibility, so, in the *Vedas* it had been assumed that the members of a family or clan all share one common karma.

Conze concludes with this objection to that original belief about the law of karma:

> The individualistic interpretation of the law of karma throws each individual on his own resources, and seems to deny any solidarity between the different persons as regards the more essential things of life, that is, as regards merit and demerit.[180]

The Mahāyāna interpretation of the law of karma is, according to Conze, less individual-oriented, and more community-oriented: Merit is made to be shared in a community. As such, it would allow, according to Mahāyāna, the storage and the transfer of merit to other *bhaktas*, to other members of the *bhakta* community.

Under karmic communalism, it is permissible to store what you cannot use for the future benefit of all sentient beings and to have transferred to you what you may not strictly speaking deserve, having produced less merit in your lifetime than you're going to get back after it. But it's all quite fair and all because the answers to questions about what belongs to whom and who deserves what from whom have all changed radically. The law of karma, according to karmic communalism, more closely resembles a familiar communalist cry of the nineteenth century in the West: "From each according to his ability; to each according to his need." It is upon such a foundation that Mahāyāna communalism, karmic, moral, and social, will in the future be constructed.

Just as karmic communalism lies as a middle path between karmic individualism and karmic Saviorism, so also the way of the karmic community is a middle path between the too-much-ness of Aldo Leopold's way of the biotic community with its problem of outrageous rights and confused use (for now ponds, mountains, and plants don't have rights) and the not-enough-ness of Martin Luther King Jr.'s way of the beloved community with its problem of community limitation (for now all sentient creatures do have rights). The way of karmic communalism may also solve the problem of self-transformation that we met in Leopold and King for now there are the helping hands of the Bodhisattva to effect that change.

Further, karmic communalism has also solved two problems dealing with the storage and transfer of merit and as such it has considerably altered the traditional interpretation and scope of the law of karma. This has made possible the transfer of stored merit to anyone who belongs to the community and who, through bhakti, requests it. The community of those capable of making such requests could now theoretically include the entire world. This world community of potential merit receivers and merit generators we call "the karmic community."

Once again, the Bodhisattva turns to that store of merit for dispersal to those in the karmic community since the merit in it was generated for them, stored for them, and it is now dispersable to them. In the oldest Mahāyāna sutra, the *Aṣṭasāhasrikā Prajñāpāramitā Sūtra* of the second century B.C.E., Subhuti, a merit generator and disciple of the Buddha, lays out the details of the Bodhisattva's task:

> He considers the mass of morality, the mass of concentration, the mass of wisdom, the mass of emancipation, the mass of the vision and cognition of emancipation of those Buddhas and Lords.
>
> In addition he considers the store of merit associated with the six perfections, with the achievement of the qualities of a Buddha, and with the perfections of self-confidence and of the powers; and also those associated with the perfection of the superknowledges, of comprehension, of the vows; and the

store of merit associated with the accomplishment of the cognition of the all-knowing, with the solicitude for beings, the great friendliness and the great compassion, and the immeasurable and incalculable Buddha-qualities.[181]

That store of merit has many generators, we are reminded. It comes, Subhuti tells us, from all those who abide by the Dharma, that is, from Buddhas and Bodhisattvas at all levels of liberation; in addition, the store comes from monks and nuns of the order, lay persons who engage in meritorious works, gods, *nāgas, yakṣas,* men, ghosts, and so on, and all those who entered *parinirvāṇa* without using up their generated merit. Ordinarily this would produce the problems of karma mentioned above. But now we have members of the karmic community to consider as the generators, storers, and dispersers of all this merit and not the single individuals of traditional Hinduism.

The *Aṣṭasāhasrikā* is quite clear on what and who constitutes the karmic community. In addition to the gods, supernatural beings, men, and ghosts mentioned above, Subhuti also includes animals. The result is that this Mahāyāna karmic community is somewhat smaller than Leopold's biotic community, since it excludes plants and ponds, but larger than King's beloved community, since it includes animals. Is there an advantage to such an addition for the Buddhist karmic community as opposed to our other two communities? There is to the extent that it solves King's problem of community limitation; and with the law of karma now covering a community that includes all sentient creatures, Leopold's problem of outrageous rights and his problem of confused use also disappear; because if use slips over into exploitation the punishment to the offender is ordered and clear: Leopold had no law of karma to warn and guard against such slippage.

We turn next to Gautama the Buddha's Prescription for Community and our four-stage summary of the karmic community.

Mahāyāna Buddhism's Prescription for Community: The Karmic Community

The Problem

Since our Prescription for Community throughout this book is patterned on the Buddha's Four Noble Truths, it is not surprising that Mahāyāna Buddhism will incorporate the Buddha's description of each of the four truths at each stage of the Prescription for Community. But Mahāyāna will expand that description to include the concept of community at each of the four stages. Consequently, for Mahāyāna the problem is, as it was for Gandhi, and even Leopold, not only personal suffering but public, communal suffering as well. The problem is, and remains, *duḥkha*, anguish, anxiety, grief, and terror, at the individual and at the community levels.

The Cause

The cause of suffering is and remains, desire or craving. Once desire is controlled and eliminated, suffering will end. This craving or attachment to objects or views can occur, it must seem, at both the individual and the communal levels where both personal attachments and societal collective graspings can bring on *duḥkha*.

The Solution

The solution to the problem of anxiety and pain lies in stopping, eliminating, or controlling the cause of the suffering. That this is possible at both the individual as well as the communal level is the optimistic promise of the Buddha of Mahāyāna Buddhism.

The Way

The way to end the craving that leads to suffering is simply to follow the Noble Eightfold Path, the way of moral behavior and meditational practice. But now in that following one has the help of the Bodhisattva. Through the practice of *bhakti yoga* or the way of devotion and dedication to that Being who has dedicated his or her entire existence to helping the suffering world, individuals, and communities, suffering can be brought to an end. The Bodhisattva, the Buddha-to-be, has through compassion for the suffering world stretched out helping hands and promised salvation, transformation, and liberation from sin and attachment to all those who request it in an earnest and prayerful way. The devotee and the community can thereby share in the Bodhisattva's accumulated merit or good karma and in that sharing peace and tranquillity can come to both.

But all is not without difficulty. We turn next to three problems raised by adopting the Buddha's karmic community.

Problems with the Karmic Community

General Summary: Where Are We Now?

The central question that we set out to answer in this study was, Can the problems of violence and peace in the twenty-first century be solved through the way of community? The answer that we suggested entailed getting persons to see that they are members of a community and as such they are the community; and since no one would knowingly and voluntarily do violence to himself or herself, and since persons would help their community knowing it to be themselves, violence would be diminished and peace would prosper. The questions then became, What is it that is shared that makes a community? And how does one become a member of a community?

This then led to an investigation of three communities, the biotic community of Aldo Leopold, the ashramic community of Mohandas K. Gandhi, and the beloved community of Martin Luther King Jr., and the ways that each adopted for overcoming the problems of violence and peace. Each of these communities, good as they were, generated other problems that rendered their usefulness sometimes questionable in solving the problems of violence and peace.

We then turned to our fourth community, the karmic community. We discussed its history and its relation to the law of karma as a solution to the two problems of the storage and transfer of karma or merit in Hinduism. At this point we suggested that the karmic community was able to solve these two problems as well as several of the other problems that our two other ways of community generated but could not solve. However, the karmic community generates at least three problems of its own. Each of these problems relates to puzzles already raised and that seem to be indigenous to the kinds of communities discussed thus far, communities dominated by altruism, self-transformation, and the fear of a loss of personal freedom.

The Problem of Self-Transformation

Membership in Leopold's biotic community and in King's beloved community seemed dependent, as we saw, on a person being altered or changed in some way or other, as a condition for membership in those communities. Just how these rites of passage are to be implemented was not clear in either case. The question might now be asked with regard to the way of the karmic community: How does one become a member of the karmic community?

The question is readily answered since the law of karma has in a sense already determined membership for each participant in the community. Thus, you and I are here in the karmic community because of our past lives and the karma generated by each of us in those lives. That past karma and the law governing its dispersal has brought us into this community of sentient beings and it is the ground on which subsequent awareness of that community rests. Presumably, the awareness that I share karma with other sentient beings is the source of the realization that I belong to the karmic community. And that awareness transforms me from an outsider to an insider who knows that when I harm others I harm myself and when I help others I help myself. But how do I achieve that awareness? Must I reach nirvana or liberation, first? And if I do then who needs the community, since it's really all over for me? In other words, if I change too much, transform too profoundly (attain nirvana), then I don't need the community. And if I don't change at all, remaining mired deep in sin, then I can't use the community. So how much should I transform? Thus the dilemma of self-transformation, a problem solved, presumably, in the person of the Bodhisattva who found a middle way between the horns of too much change and no change at all.

The Problem of Karmic Fascism

Membership in both the biotic community and the beloved community seemed to lead, as we saw, to the individual being devoured by the community. But unless the community is strong there can never be peace; and if the community is weak there will always be violence. Recall that the dilemma of community demonstrated that if the community was not strong enough then violence and chaos resulted; and if the community was too strong then, while peace might result, eco- or communo-fascism was the price that one paid for it. Both ecofascism and communo-fascism waited to envelop the individual in the name of peace and security.

But the problem of what we might call "karmic fascism" is now easily solved, if we keep in mind that we are not talking about an isolated community, a *sangha* for example, dominated by central rulers or elders who lay down absolutes that guarantee the survival of the group no matter whom it devours. What binds the karmic community is not a common energy, life, or mystical spirit but karma, and karma is being generated afresh each moment by the individuals of the karmic community. They have as their goal the reduction of bad karma and violence, and the production of good karma and peace; as such, individual striving and personal initiative are most essential to community survival. Without such action, bad karma enters and the community is destroyed by its own violence. Far from devouring the individual, the karmic community depends on the triumphant survival of the individual.

The Problem of Karmic Altruism

Membership in the biotic community, the ashramic community, the beloved community and, now, the karmic community, is driven by a self-transformation that ends in communal altruism. This desire to place oneself last and to work for the good of the community takes an interesting turn in Mahāyāna Buddhism. For not only does the Bodhisattva exemplify this altruistic ideal, but all Buddhists are called upon to become Bodhisattvas themselves, and to emulate the Bodhisattva ideal in all of its forms. The Bodhisattva ideal includes delaying one's own final liberation until all creatures have been saved, showing heartfelt compassion for all sentient beings and engaging in acts of communal altruism. And therein lies the problem.

If karmic altruism is the practice of earning, storing, and then transferring one's own karma to others in the community, then the problem of karmic altruism points to three difficulties: First, it would seem to be logically impossible for everyone to practice karmic altruism (which needs both earners and receivers) since, if everyone were to become an earner, a storer, and a transferer, there would be no transferees and no community of receivers of the merit: and without receivers transfer would be impossible. For consider: just as there can be no salvation without sin, no nirvana without saṃsāra, so there can be no altruistic Bodhisattvas (the ideal of Mahāyāna) if everyone is an altruistic Bodhisattva. Second, it would seem to be empirically impossible for merit to be transferred to individual members of the community, if the community as a whole has received the merit. Part of the problem of karmic altruism lies in the opaqueness in the concept of transfer. Presumably, the karma has been earned by the altruistic behavior of the Bodhisattva(s). That merit is now available only to "the community," whatever that means. But the community is an abstract entity that can't receive anything, only individuals can do that. So then we're back with the concept of karmic individualism, again, a concept that led to problems of the storage and transfer of merit. Third, the practice of altruism needs more careful scrutiny aside from the difficulty of its consistency with, and its universalization in, the Bodhisattva ideal. Is it ever possible for persons to do anything for others without benefiting themselves? For if they benefit themselves, then the action is not ideally altruistic. Can anyone intentionally set out just to benefit someone else saying, "I now intend to benefit you alone"? Doesn't the fact of having *any* intention or motive signal the self-centeredness of the action? And if the action is self-centered, can it also be altruistic? Is it not the case that ideally altruistic actions are impossible and that actions may be only partly selfless, partially altruistic? But then what happens to the *ideal* of karmic altruism? And to the *ideal* of karmic communalism? We will return for further analysis of these three difficulties that form parts of the problem of karmic altruism in the last chapter of this book.

Assuming that satisfactory answers and solutions to the above problems can be found, we turn, finally and briefly, to the three central questions regarding community, violence and peace with which this book began.

Conclusion: Three Central Questions

What is it that is shared that makes the karmic community into a community? It is, of course, the shared karma of the Bodhisattva(s) and others that makes community possible. The community is bound by merit, merit that has been banked for the community by the Bodhisattva(s) and others and that remains to be drawn upon by the entire community.

How does one become a member of such a community? Membership is gained by participating in the merit-producing and merit-drawing activities under the good auspices of the Bodhisattva. Awareness that such merit exists, worshipfully approaching the great Banker, the Bodhisattva, begging for his or her grace, one draws upon the infinite guantity of good karma available while producing good karma oneself in order to add to the store of merit, all of this entitles one to community membership. Recall the words of the Bodhisattva Shantideva, calling his devotees to membership in the karmic community by reminding them of his soteriological mission:

My endeavours do not merely aim at my own deliverance. For with the help of the boat of the thought of all-knowledge, I must rescue all these beings from the stream of Samsara, which is so difficult to cross, I must pull them back from the great precipice, I must free them from all calamities, I must ferry them across the stream of Samsara.[182]

Once again, the first step toward such community participation is the result of an initial move on the part of the devotee who seeks the grace of the Bodhisattva. Such a move leads to a transformation from being an outsider to becoming an insider, a depositor and drawer in the merit bank. The penultimate goal for all such Mahāyāna debtors and creditors is to become a Bodhisattva themselves, the final transformative stage in the Buddhist banking community. It is by such stages that membership in the karma community is achieved. And each of these progressive self-transformations leads presumably to higher levels of altruistic behavior.

Can the problems of violence and peace in the twenty-first century be solved through the karmic community? Again, as with our previous ways of community, there appear to be no obvious logical inconsistencies in the implementation of such a community. If nonviolence and peace depend upon treating others as oneself, that is, in seeing the karmic community as oneself and vice versa, then, once again, by self-transformation and altruism, but now through the grace of the worshipped Bodhisattva, the problems of violence and peace would seem to be solvable within the karmic community. Once more, the solution is best described through instantiating for the karmic community our two community arguments from chapter 1. First the community violence argument:

1. No one would intentionally do violence to oneself.
2. Oneself is the karmic community.
3. Therefore, no one would intentionally do violence to the karmic community.

Second, the community peace argument:

1. Everyone would intentionally do peace to oneself.
2. Oneself is the karmic community.
3. Therefore, everyone would intentionally do peace to the karmic community.

Once more, the language is awkward, the justifications for the two sets of premises follow from the previous discussion, and, finally, even for the Buddha, "education" remains the key to removing the ignorance of who one is that creates violence and prevents peace.

Again, our two recurring problems—the problem of self-transformation or enlightenment for the Buddhists, and the problem of karmic altruism to which it appears to lead, where each of us becomes a Bodhisattva—remain to plague us. How does enlightenment occur? And, if enlightenment does lead to "karmic altruism," then what does that mean and how are these two concepts related? We shall return to these matters, together with an analyses of the *is* of identity in those second premises, above, in the final chapter of this book, to which we now turn.[183]

Chapter 6

❦

Conclusion: Community
and the Twenty-First Century

We have been at some pains throughout this study of community, violence, and peace in the twenty-first century to raise several questions and problems that were never satisfactorily answered or met. In what follows let me remind the reader of two such previously considered problems that stand in need of deeper analysis, major problems that cropped up in one way or another with our community creators. The first problem was considered directly in discussing the problems of the four historical and altruistic communities of Aldo Leopold, Mohandas Karamchand Gandhi, Martin Luther King Jr., and Gautama the Buddha, as opposed to the utopian and fictional communities of Plato and Aldous Huxley. Let's call it, again, "the problem of self-transformation" and identify it as the difficulty of explaining what "self-transformation" means and what makes self-transformation possible? The second problem was dealt with more indirectly and was related to a property or characteristic common to each of our historical community creators and to each of their communities, that is, altruism or ethical altruism, the view that an action is right if and only if it promotes the welfare of others. Let's call that problem, again, "the problem of communal altruism" and identify it as the difficulty of explaining what "communal altruism" means and what makes communal altruism possible. The two problems of self-transformation and communal altruism are related, as we shall see, since self-transformation, *inter alia*, seems to be a means for bringing about the sense of altruism upon which the formation of, and continuation of, our four communities depended.

In what follows we begin with the problem of self-transfor-mation by analyzing the concept of self-transformation and its appearance in the personal lives of each of our historical commu-nity creators. In this context we offer a solution to the problem by pointing to the role of self-transformation among our community creators. Next we take up the problem of communal altruism by analyzing the concept of altruism in a communal setting. In this context we offer a solution to the problem by pointing to its rela-tion to self-transformation. We continue with an analysis of, and the cure for, communal holism, the chief culprit behind the prob-lems that we have been meeting in our four altruistic communities. We conclude the chapter and this book by turning briefly to that cure, communal egoism, and to some advantages to, and some problems with, communal egoism as a solution to the problems of violence and peace in the twenty-first century.

The Problem of Self-Transformation

All four of our historical community creators have held that in order for community to be created some form of self-transfor-mation is necessary, some type of change must occur within those seeking community. This led to problems since none of our com-munity builders was altogether explicit as to what such change means or how this change in person, soul, or self is to take place.

In what follows we define "self-transformation," describe four transformative experiences, offer some additional insights into this phenomenon by examining other similar cases of transformation, and note, finally, how all of this seems to relate to the development of community and how its absence seems either to destroy commu-nity or to make community impossible. We will be identifying, in passing, some further questions and puzzles with the concept of self-transformation as it relates to our second problem, the problem of communal altruism. It will appear that self-transformation of the type to be illustrated by our four community creators is directly and causally related to communal altruism and to our second problem.

Peak Experiences as Self-Transforming Experiences

Self-transformation experiences are very varied and have been widely labeled as "nirvana," "*mokṣa*," "enlightenment," "libera-tion," "conversion," "being saved," "awakening," "opening," "*apatheia*, peace of mind," "*ataraxia*, tranquility, quietude," "pure happiness," "intense and lasting pleasure," and so on. Whether the experience be mystical and spiritual, "God and I are one," or neurological and psychological, "I saw myself as I'd never seen myself before," it is *generally* described as sudden and unexpected, overwhelming and impressive, more often pleasurable and tending to produce subsequent gratifying recollections: one is agreeably and surprisingly turned around and one never forgets it.

Abraham Maslow of Brandeis University reported on a set of similar experiences in a massive study of "the finest, healthiest people, the best specimens of mankind I could find." Maslow discovered something very curious about, and common to, their experiences that relate to our transformative experiences:

> I learned many lessons from these people. But one in particular is our concern now. I found that these individuals tended to report having had something like mystic experiences, moments of great awe, moments of the most intense happiness or even rapture, ecstacy or bliss (because the word happiness can be too weak to describe this experience).
>
> These moments were of pure, positive happiness when all doubts, all fears, all inhibitions, all tensions, all weaknesses, were left behind. Now self consciousness was lost. All separateness and distance from the world disappeared as they felt one with the world, fused with it, really belonging in it and to it, instead of being outside looking in. (One subject said, for instance, "I felt like a member of a family, not like an orphan.")[184]

Among the characteristics of these experiences, many of which would have been cited previously as "religious" or "supernatural," Maslow now called simply "psychological" and "natural." In fact, given Maslow's findings, the distinction between the supernatural and the natural experience tends to become blurred. From a subsequent study of the sheer ordinariness of these experiences among common people, experiences that Maslow called "peak experiences," we select the following twelve out of twenty-five properties, as of particular interest to those of us concerned with community and with communal altruism:

1. For instance it is quite characteristic in peak experiences that the whole universe is perceived as an integrated and unified whole. . . .

4. [P]erception in the peak-experiences can be relatively ego-transcending, self-forgetful, egoless and unselfish. . . .

8. The world in the peak experiences is seen only as beautiful, good, desirable, worthwhile, etc., and is never experienced as evil or undesirable. . . .

12. In the peak-experience, such emotions as wonder, awe, reverence, humility, surrender, and even worship before the greatness of the experience are often reported.

13. In peak-experiences, the dichotomies, polarities, and conflicts of life tend to be transcended or resolved. . . . The person himself tends to move toward fusion, integration and unity and away from splitting, conflicts, and opposition. . . .

15. Peak-experiences sometimes have immediate effects or aftereffects upon the person. Sometimes their aftereffects are so profound and so great as to remind us of the profound conversions which forever after changed the person.

17. In peak-experiences, there is a tendency to move . . . to his real self, to have become a more real person.

18. The person feels himself more than at other times to be responsible, active, the creative center of his own activities and of his own perceptions, more self-determined, more a free agent, with more "free will" than at other times. . . .

20. The peak-experiencer becomes more loving and more accepting, and so he becomes more spontaneous and honest and innocent.

22. Because he becomes more unmotivated, that is to say, closer to non-striving, non-needing, non-wishing, he asks less for himself in such moments. He is less selfish . . . (the unmotivated being becomes more god-like).

23. People during and after peak-experiences characteristically feel lucky, fortunate, graced. A common reaction is "I don't deserve this." A common consequence is a feeling of gratitude, in religious persons, to their God, in others, to fate, to nature or to just good fortune. . . .

25. What has been called the "unitive consciousness" is often given in peak-experiences, i.e., a sense of the sacred glimpsed *in* and *through* the particular instance of the momentary, the secular, the worldly.[185]

I have been at some pains to list the results of Maslow's research into "peak experiences" and for four reasons: First, that research gives us some important insights into an experience that is more common than we might realize; second, the experience leads to practical results, as well as pleasant effects, producing expressions, as well as feelings, of love, unity, and community; third, one of the most important feelings to which it leads is altruism, that is, a lessening of self-centeredness and a growing of other-centeredness; and, finally, the peak experience can be interpreted as having either spiritual and supernatural origins and repercussions or as having psychological and natural origins and results. But whatever it is, it forever transforms, in greater or lesser degrees, the person who has it. The peak experience, then, is self-transforming, and if that transformation leads to selflessness and altruism, and if the latter is necessary to communal altruism, then the relation between peak experiences and communal altruism ought to be identifiable. Given this hypothesis, we ought to be able to locate in our four historical and altruistic community creators their peak experiences of either a religious-spiritual character, for example, Gandhi and King, or a philosophic-psychological character, as in, Leopold and the Buddha, depending on the interpretation the reader or the devoted disciple cares to make of the experience.

The first part of our problem of self-transformation—What does "self-transformation" mean?—has been answered. Self-transformation has occurred, we might now tentatively say, whenever there is a substantial, that is, a permanent and significant, change in a person's ideas, attitudes, and behavior; it is often, but not always, sudden and unexpected. The second part of our problem of self-transformation—What makes self-transformation possible?—has also been answered. We know that under certain circumstances it can probably be brought about by a kind of peak experience. If all of this is the case, then we may also have answered the second part of our problem of communal altruism—What makes communal altruism possible? Communal altruism is brought about, we might now tentatively say, by self-transformation through peak experiences. However, one must be careful here in not imputing too strong a connection between communal altruism and self-transformation. I don't believe that the evidence will support the claim that self-transformation is a sufficient condition, that is, which alone and by itself will always lead to putting the interests of the community before the interests of oneself. It is historically the case that many instances of self-transformation have led to just the opposite, a search for solitude, isolation, and separation from the community, as the lives of the great mystics, saints, and anchorites, from the Christian Desert Fathers to the Hindu sannyāsis, might well attest. However, I do believe that the evidence will support the claim that self-transformation is a necessary condition for communal altruism, such that without some substantial change in the self, neither communal altruism nor community could result.

It remains now to examine the above hypothesis and provide the evidence for the relation between peak experiences and communal altruism. Finally, we will deal further with the central question, What makes self-transformation possible? and, at the same time, deal with the question, What does "communal altruism" mean?

Four Transformative Experiences

In what follows we focus on the "peak experience," the converting experience, for each of our four community creators, discuss self-transformation generally as a necessary prerequisite for altruism, communal altruism, and community building, and, finally, deal with some problems connected with peak, and transformative, claims generally.

Aldo Leopold and the transformation of conscience. Aldo Leopold's conversion from hunter to poet, from a person with an ordinary conscience to a man with an ecological conscience, is probably found in the incident that we've mentioned previously. Leopold recalls the killing of a she-wolf and her death:

> We reached the old wolf in time to watch a fierce green fire in her eyes. I realized *then*, and have known *ever since* that there was something new to me in those eyes—something known only to her and to the mountain.[186]

It is an experience Leopold had then in 1909 and that is now repeated in this recounting in 1944. If there can be a relived peak experience then this 1944 recounting is probably it. From it Leopold's life changes as the impact experienced *then* so long ago has grown *ever since* turning him from a trigger-itching hunter into the world's foremost exponent of eco-empathy and protector of the biotic community.

Consider two similar examples of purely psychological peak experiences, each from a tradition of naturalism and empiricism. Each is an expression of a never-to-be-forgotten emotion that led to identification with the biotic community as a consequence of an identification with a part of it. Each expresses a feeling of self-transformation as a result of the encounter. The first description is from the West, the second is from the East; each is concerned with nature and with flowers, solitude and inexpressible happiness.

The first peak experience is a recounting by the American naturalist and conservationist John Muir (1838–1914) of an incident in the Canadian wilderness in 1864. Muir had been traveling on foot for some six months "botanizing in glorious freedom around the Great Lakes," as he tells us. Avoiding human contacts, homeless and friendless, but feeling depressed and isolated at this moment in his solitary ramblings, at sundown one day in June he comes to the bank of a stream. He suddenly sees the rare orchid *Calypso borealis*, two white flowers shining on a background of green moss. The blossoms, hidden, unseen, and unremarkable, reminded him, there in the wilderness, of his own isolation:

> They were alone. I never before saw a plant so full of life, so perfectly spiritual, it seemed pure enough for the throne of the Creator. I felt as if I were in the presence of superior beings who loved me and beckoned me to come. I sat down beside them and wept for joy.

He tells us that his melancholia vanished, he continues on his journey and finds lodging for the night.[187]

The second peak experience has similar properties but with a more restrained expression of emotion. The Japanese Zen Buddhist poet Basho (1644–94) is on a solitary walk along a deserted path when he notices by the pathside an insignificant wild flower, the white flowering herb, nazuna or shepherd's purse. The poet is suddenly and overwhelmingly moved by the sight and composes a haiku, a three line poem, to express his indescribable joy:

> When I look carefully
> I see the nazuna blooming
> By the hedge!

The poem ends with the Japanese word *kana*, which signifies a strong feeling of admiration, praise, joy, or even sorrow. The word is untranslatable and the Zen Buddhist scholar D. T. Suzuki, who cites Basho's haiku, uses an exclamation point to render the poet's inexpressible passion.

Suzuki then juxtaposes Basho's poem and his peak experience with another poem, also involving an encounter with a flower but with far different consequences:

Flower in the crannied wall,
I pluck you out of the crannies;—
Hold you here, root and all, in my hand
Little flower—but if I could understand
What you are, root and all, and all in all,
I should know what God and man is.

The second poem is by the Victorian poet laureate, Alfred Lord Tennyson (1809–92). Instead of merely contemplating the flower *in situ*, the poet pulls it out of the wall, "root and all," and then, holding the withering, dying plant in his hand, he begins his lucubrations. Tennyson's poem, like much Western poetry, is dualistic, personal, probing, inquisitive, and full of bathos and sentiment as it appeals to the reader's feelings by letting the poet's spill out over the page.

The two poems call forth reflections of one's own, of course, and Suzuki's comments are most insightful on the essential differences between the poems, the poets, the traditions from which they came and the two peak-experiences that they aroused:

Basho does not pluck the flower. He just looks at it. He is absorbed in thought. He feels something in his mind, but he does not express it. He lets an exclamation mark [*kana*] say everything he wishes to say. For he has no words to utter; his feeling is too full, too deep, and he has no desire to conceptualize it.[188]

Tennyson, on the other hand, tears the flower from the cranny where it naturally belongs, so that it must surely wither and die. He then analyzes and dissects his feelings just as surely as he analyzes and dissects the flower.

Basho never touches the flower, preferring merely to look and to look with complete attention at the flower and not beyond it. The flower, for Basho, becomes neither a springboard into his own agonized feelings nor an excuse for a flight of philosophic fancy. Basho is not inquisitive and inquiring but silent and restrained. His experience is ineffable and that ineffability is eloquently communicated by his silence.

Suzuki continues, saying of Tennyson:

His appeal to the understanding is characteristically Western. Basho accepts, Tennyson resists. Tennyson's individuality stands away from the flower, from "God and man." He does not identify himself with either God or nature. He is always apart from them. His understanding is what people nowadays call "scientifically objective." Basho is thoroughly "subjective." . . . Basho sees the *nazuna* and the *nazuna* sees Basho.[189]

Basho and the *nazuna* at this moment become unified, inseparable; they form a biotic community.

One has the feeling, of course, if we can borrow Leopold's own terminology here, that the ecological conscience is already well in place for both Muir and Basho; it certainly is not in place for Tennyson. But that brings us back to our central question, once again, What makes self-transformation possible, that is, how does one develop this ecological conscience without going through Leopold's wolf-killing actions? Or, for that matter, without rambling alone for six months, as John Muir did, in the Canadian wilderness? Or by becoming a Zen Buddhist monk like Basho? Aldo Leopold has provided some evidence for our previous hypothesis regarding the relation between peak experiences and communal altruism by answering this central question and demonstrating in his own life that self-transformation is necessary to the sense of community.

On June 27, 1947, the year before his death, Aldo Leopold delivered one of the "most forcefully worded addresses of his career." It was given to the Conservation Committee at the annual meeting in Minneapolis of the Garden Club of America. The speech, "The Ecological Conscience," provides a clue to answering that central question, How does one develop an ecological conscience and the sense that I am a member of the biotic community? And, more importantly for us, it provides the evidence for the hypothesis that without ecological peak-experiences both self-transformation and biotic communal altruism would not be possible.

To the delegates Leopold stated the problem of developing the ecological conscience by citing four case histories that "show the futility of trying to improve the face of the land without improving ourselves."[190] He goes on to say further that the problem that we face is one of developing obligations to the land:

Obligations have no meaning without conscience, and the problem we face is the extension of the social conscience from people to land.[191]

This, of course, entails the development of the ecological conscience, which is "an affair of the mind as well as the heart."[192] But
how is this development to take place? The answer is both simple
and reasonable. The only defense against environmental depreda-
tion and degradation is "a widespread public awareness of the values at stake."[193] This was not done in the four case histories Leopold
cites. People simply did not realize what was at stake:

> The practice of conservation must spring from a *conviction* of
> what is ethically and esthetically right, as well as what is eco-
> nomically expedient.[194]

But what brings about that conviction that comes from both mind
and heart, and that depends on the creation of the ecological conscience? Leopold is not altogether sanguine about its creation in the
public at large:

> I have no illusions about the speed or accuracy with which an
> ecological conscience can become functional. It has required
> nineteen centuries to define decent man-to-man conduct and
> the process is only half done; it may take as long to evolve a
> code of decency for man-to-land conduct.

And here Leopold concludes his speech by identifying the way to
that conversion from a man-to-man ordinary conscience to a man-
to-land ecological conscience. The advice is commonplace, ordinary, obvious, even banal in the all-too-familiar cry of "Get
involved"—but I believe it's insightful and I believe he's right:

> In such matters we should not worry too much about any-
> thing except the direction in which we travel. The direction is
> clear, and the first step is to *throw your weight around* on
> matters of right and wrong in land-use. Cease being intimi-
> dated by the argument that a right action is impossible
> because it does not yield maximum profits or that a wrong
> action is to be considered because it pays. That philosophy is
> dead in human relations, and its funeral in land-relations is
> overdue.[195]

The change from economic conscience to ecological conscience
can come about, for Leopold, before or during or after environmental
involvement. The key to self-transformation and conscience-trans-

formation lies in immersing oneself in the environment, the biotic community, itself. Thus John Muir plunges into the aloneness of the wilderness and Basho goes for solitary monkish rambles where shy orchids and hidden shepherd's purses conceal themselves, lying in wait to emotionally ambush the unwary, inviting deep reflections and self-transformations. And if the conditions are right it is just then that convictions arise and the magical and mysterious psycho-spiritual conversions occur. And for Leopold the same thing happens in the wilderness where dying wolves watch you as they die or the same thing can mysteriously happen in public protest meetings where perhaps tempers fume, ideas clash, and even righteous indignation flares.

Aldo Leopold felt that living with wild things made his own conversion possible. And living with wild things was a choice that he made. Gandhi was ready for his transformation after he voluntarily placed himself in the right place at the right time in South Africa in 1906. And King knowingly placed himself in front of howling mobs and then felt God's presence at a crucial time in his own kitchen in Montgomery, Alabama, in 1956. It would seem that peak experiences that are maturing and self-transformative are possible in the wilderness, in kitchens, in public protest meetings, anywhere that humans open themselves to the experience.

A more recent peak experience involving such an opening that led to self-transformation is recorded by J. Baird Callicott, the brilliant philosopher-ecologist and, like Leopold, ecomystic:

> For me this realization took concrete form, as I stood two decades and an ecological education later, on the banks of the Mississippi River where I had roamed as a boy.

Callicott, near his home in Memphis, Tennessee, gazes at the sewage-choked Mississippi River. Suddenly he experiences "a palpable pain" at what he witnesses, followed by a self-transforming experience:

> My narrowly personal interests were not affected, and yet, somehow, I was personally injured. It occurred to me then, in a flash of self-discovery, that the river *was a part of me.*[196]

The experience was preceded by two decades of "ecological education," reading, writing, loving, and living the wilderness and nature. We'll have more to say on this self-transformative experience that solves the problem of self-transformation as we turn to Mohandas Gandhi.

Mohandas Gandhi and self-realization. From what we've said thus far about self-transformation experiences for Leopold, Muir, and Callicott, one might have gotten the impression that, first, they are sudden, overwhelming, and occur once in a lifetime; and, second, that without having had these monumental mystical boomers one can do nothing, or ought to do nothing, about the problems of community and the environment. But, first of all, as Maslow has made clear, peak experiences are far-ranging in quality as well as in quantity. That is to say, peak experiences leading to self-transformation can run the gamut from low-intensity aesthetic "aha" feelings of the solitary rambler to the high-energy ecstatic letting-go experiences of the religious mystic: they can be many and often or they can be once-in-a-lifetime and never again. Second of all, energetically immersing oneself in the milieu of life by protesting wrongs, as Leopold suggests, or by taking those solitary rambles, as Muir and Callicott did, or by dabbling in the medium with pencil and paper as many artists do in order to be inspired and be put into the creative mood, are all ways of overcoming the idea that one can do nothing for community until the spirit wallops your soul.

Mohandas Gandhi is a good example of a community creator whose life consisted of a number of transformative peak experiences. Each one led to his maturing as a community member and no single one could be pointed to as *the* occasion for self-realization or self-transformation.

The chief source for the descriptions of Gandhi's peak experiences is *An Autobiography*. The chapters were written in and out of prison beginning in 1925 and serialized for publication in English and Gujarati in his newspapers, *Young India* and *Navajivan*, before being published in book form in 1927 and 1929. Each chapter, therefore, contains an edifying story ending with a moral or a lesson. Almost every chapter-story makes a kind of peak-experience point as we observe Gandhi, the callowest of youths, full of energy and errors, stumbling and struggling to maturity and adulthood. But because Gandhi's experiences are in a sense so ordinary, one can recognize the gradual changes in his life as he goes, as it were, from peak to valley to peak solving the problems that life throws at him. And here's the point: Gandhi intentionally put himself in the way of life's problems; he went to England, he went to South Africa, he saw injustices, he immersed himself in the booming, buzzing, chaotic flow of life and in doing so that mysterious thing happened, he grew, he matured, he was transformed. I should mention two incidents not previously recounted in chapter 3.

As a student in London in 1890 Gandhi was converted from a conceptual vegetarian to an existential vegetarian. He had promised his mother, when he left India to study for the law at the University of London, that he would refrain from sex, liquor, and meat. His vegetarian vow was merely "conceptual" in the sense that he was committed to the vow but not to not eating meat. But then something happened that turned him from an intellectual to an ideologue, a zealous convert, of vegetarianism and his very existence became defined by the transformation. As Gandhi tells it, hungry and poor he had gone off in search of a place to eat and suddenly came upon a vegetarian restaurant. He is inexplicably moved by the encounter:

> The sight of it filled me with the same joy that a child feels on getting a thing after its own heart. Before I entered I noticed books for sale exhibited under a glass window near the door. I saw among them [Henry] Salt's *Plea for Vegetarianism*. This I purchased for a shilling and went straight to the dining room. This was my first hearty meal since my arrival in England. God had come to my aid.

But this was not all. Gandhi continues:

> I read Salt's book from cover to cover and was very much impressed by it. From the date of reading this book, I may claim to have become a vegetarian by choice. I blessed the day on which I had taken the vow before my mother. I had all along abstained from meat in the interests of truth and of the vow I had taken, but had wished at the same time that every Indian should be a meat-eater, and had looked forward to being one myself freely and openly one day, and to enlisting others in the cause.

And he concludes, transformed now by a restaurant and a book into an enthusiastic convert:

> The choice was now made in favor of vegetarianism, the spread of which henceforward became my mission.[197]

Years later Henry Salt wrote to Gandhi, remembering their first meeting in Portsmouth, England, in 1890. Salt's letter provides a nice summary of the relation between existential vegetarianism, as perceived now by both of them, and community:

> I feel as strongly as ever that food reform, like Socialism, has an essential part to play in the liberation of man-kind. I cannot see how there can be any real and full recognition of *Kinship*, as long as men continue either to *cheat*, or to *eat*, their fellow beings.[198]

A second transformative experience in Gandhi's early life will also make the point that ordinary peak experiences lead to significant self-transformations. The recounting comes from Gandhi's first encounter with racism, mentioned above in chapter 3. Gandhi has landed in Durban, Natal Province, in 1893, to "Try my luck in South Africa." He is to journey from there to Pretoria. He takes the train at Durban and at Maritzburg a white man boards the train, encounters Gandhi in the first-class compartment, and demands his expulsion. Gandhi protests that he has a first-class ticket and refuses to leave. A policeman is fetched and the future Mahatma is summarily throw off the train. Gandhi narrates the incident years later in his *Autobiography*, recalling the severe cold and his shivering isolation:

> I began to think of my duty. Should I fight for my rights or go back to India, or should I go on to Pretoria without minding the insults, and return to India after finishing the case? It would be cowardice to run back to India without fulfilling my obligation. The hardship to which I was subjected was superficial—only a symptom of the deep disease of colour prejudice.

And then comes the transformation and the resolve:

> I should try, if possible, to root out the disease and suffer hardships in the process. Redress for wrongs I should seek only to the extent that would be necessary for the removal of the colour prejudice. So I decided to take the next available train to Pretoria.[199]

Many years later when a Christian missionary in India asked Gandhi, "What have been the most creative experiences in your life?" Gandhi responded by repeating the story of his cold night in the Maritzburg station.[200]

Peak experiences and the self-transformations to which they lead can be many and varied. They can be instantaneous, overwhelming, and momentous as with the Buddha, as we shall see below, or they can be overwhelming but not recollected as such until years later, as with Leopold; or they can be quiet peak moments that viewed at the time may even seem dismissable, their true significance realized only years later, as with Gandhi. But whatever form they take, they signify a pattern of change that leads to maturity, to self-realization, and, for our purposes, to a commitment to community. Where exploitation exists, whether of animals or man, where racism exists, as Gandhi came to see, there can be no community, no peace and only violence. But it was by putting himself in harm's way, as it were, that Gandhi engaged in his own version of dabbling in the medium that made his own version of a transformation possible. Gandhi's reflections on racism, of course, were not lost on the third of our community creators. Martin Luther King Jr. will also recount a significant moment in his career after which there was no turning back.

Martin Luther King Jr. and conversion. In January 1956 a crisis occurred in the life of Martin Luther King Jr. The young minister had been elected president of the Montgomery Improvement Association a month earlier following the arrest on a segregated bus of Rosa Parks, a woman who had refused to surrender her bus seat to a white man. The bus boycott of Montgomery, Alabama, had begun with great success on December 5, 1955. The number of persons who stopped riding the city's segregated buses was growing daily. On the night of January 30, 1956, the anniversary of Mohandas Gandhi's murder in New Delhi some eight years earlier, a fact not lost on King, a mass meeting was called in Montgomery. King was speaking when he received the news that his home had been bombed, the first of many such attempts at intimidation and assassination. His wife and new baby were uninjured by the bomb that had been placed on the front porch, but its explosive force had shattered the porch and front windows. The bombing climaxed a month that saw hundreds of hate letters and dozens of death threats sent by telephone to King and his family.

One late night three days before the bombing, and at the height of the anxiety and terror that was slowly enveloping the entire city, King had received a telephone call from an angry voice crying, "Listen nigger, we've taken all we want from you. Before next week you'll be sorry you ever came to Montgomery." King then found himself unable to sleep. He got out of bed, paced the floor; deeply disturbed he went to the kitchen and heated some coffee:

> I was ready to give up. I tried to think of a way to move out of the picture without appearing to be a coward.

Head in his hands, he bowed over the kitchen table:

> The words I spoke to God that midnight are still vivid in my memory. "I am here taking a stand for what I believe is right. But now I am afraid. The people are looking to me for leadership and if I stand before them without strength and courage, they too will falter. I am at the end of my powers. I have nothing left. I've come to the point where I can't face it alone."

But then something happened to King that was to change his life ever after:

> At that moment I experienced the presence of the Divine as I had never before experienced him. It seemed as though I could hear the quiet assurance of an inner voice, saying, "Stand up for righteousness, stand up for truth. God will be at your side forever." Almost at once my fears began to pass from me. My uncertainty disappeared, I was ready to face anything. The outer situation remained the same, but God had given me inner calm.[201]

It was that presence that kept King calm when three nights later that bomb exploded at his house. In remarks redolent with the vision of the beloved community he was attempting to create, he then brought together the two incidents, the conversion in the kitchen and the bombing:

> Three nights later, our home was bombed. Strangely enough, I accepted the word of the bombing calmly. My experience with God had given me a new strength and trust. I knew now that God is able to give us the interior resources to face the storms and problems of life.[202]

Following the explosion at his home, he finds the strength to calm an angry and armed mob of blacks who had gathered around the shattered remains. Creating then and there a small community by his own presence and his calming words, he tells the hate-filled and frightened crowd:

> My wife and baby are alright. I want you to go home and put down your weapons. We cannot solve this problem through retaliatory violence. . . . We must love our white brothers, no matter what they do to us. We must make them know that we love them. Jesus still cries out across the centuries, "Love your enemies."

His voice trembling, he concluded:

> Remember, if I am stopped, this Movement will not stop, because God is with this Movement.[203]

The mob is calmed, the crowd disperses, and a white policeman later comments:

> I'll be honest with you. I was terrified. I owe my life to that nigger Preacher, and so do all the other white people who were there.[204]

Of such is the foundation of community.

We turn, finally, to the transformative experience of the Buddha and its effects on the creation of community.

Gautama the Buddha and enlightenment. One day in 528 B.C.E. and at the age of thirty-five Gautama the Buddha had sat beneath a tree near the city of Bodh Gaya in northern India. Shortly before dawn on that fateful day he had entered into enlightenment, nirvana, and changed not only his own life but the lives of millions of persons ever after. Following his transformation, Buddhists believe, he sat for forty days and nights beneath that tree and meditated upon what he had discovered. That discovery included two concepts and the two doctrines embodying those concepts that would form the foundation of the Buddha's notion of the karmic community. From a transformative peak experience will emerge the Buddha's commitment to ethical altruism and communal altruism. The evolution of the Buddhist concept of the karmic community from these several elements is worth the trouble that it will take to excavate them, so let's proceed with some care.

The doctrine of Anitya. The doctrine of *anitya* makes its appearance early in the history of Buddhist thought where we find the Buddha cited in an early third century B.C.E. text:

> Whether Buddhas arise, O monks, or whether Buddhas do not arise, it remains a fact and the fixed and necessary constitution of being, that all its constituents are transitory [*anitya*].[205]

Anitya means "impermanent, transient, or perishable." Its primary sense for the Buddhists is that of incessant flowing and changing. Buddha concludes:

> Impermanent, alas! are all compound things. Their nature is to rise and fall. When they have risen they cease.[206]

The doctrine of *anitya* is simply this: All existence is characterized by ceaseless change.

One doesn't have to search Buddhist texts to see the truth and force of this dogma. Trees and grass grow and die, the days turn into nights, the seasons wax and wane, the years, decades and centuries roll inexorably past. Things that seem permanent really only seem that way. The Buddhists have simply taken a rather ordinary, commonsense property of objects in the space-time world and by calling philosophical attention to that property's universality they have made it an essential dogma of their philosophy. Ceaseless change is driven by karma or desire and it manifests itself in the interconnectedness that yields the Buddha's second discovery.

The doctrine of Pratītyasamutpāda. The doctrine of dependent origination or *pratītyasamutpāda*[207] has been called the second greatest discovery made by the Buddha following his enlightenment peak experience. Essentially, the doctrine states that there is a chain of causes together with their effects that bind us to repeated births in the world. This chain of causes and their effects is made up of twelve links, or *nidānas*, "beginning" with the link labeled "ignorance" and "ending" with the link composed of old age, death, suffering, and despair, which then leads, cyclically, back to ignorance, which is the ultimate cause of rebirth, that is, ignorance of the Four Noble Truths and the Noble Eightfold Path. Briefly summarized the twelve causal links and the chain that they forge are:

1. *Ignorance* of the Four Noble Truths causes (or is the condition that leads to) karma (action) and the desire to live again.
2. *Karma* and *desire* in turn cause consciousness and life, the first characteristics of a newly formed human embryo.
3. *Consciousness* then causes name and form, the mental and physical self, in the developing embryo.
4. *Name and form* now cause the six organs of sense and the desire to use these organs (eyes, ears, nose, touch, taste, and *manas*, or mind, which is the organ of internal perception).
5. The *six organs of sense* in turn cause contact with objects and the desire to seek out objects in the infant of two to three years of age.
6. *Contact* then causes sensation or feelings of pleasure and pain in the child of four to ten years of age.
7. *Sensation* now causes craving or coveting in the youth of eleven to fifteen years of age.
8. *Craving* in turn causes attachment, the active seeking of sense objects, in the young adult.
9. *Attachment* then causes the desire for existence and continued life wherein the seeds of karma are sown all over again.
10. *Existence* in turn causes birth in the future as the desire for continued life extends beyond this existence into the next life.
11. *Birth* now causes old age, death, suffering, and despair, one's entire life in a future existence.
12. *Old age, death, suffering and despair* finally cause *ignorance*, which, again, is the real cause of rebirth, and we are back where we began at the first link of the chain.

It might be helpful to see the entire round of birth and death as a wheel made up of the causal links with arrows to represent the causal connections between the parts of the wheel. Let the arrows also be interpreted as the desire that causally and forcefully leads to the next state or link on the wheel, for it is desire that moves the "self" from one state to the next (fig. 6.1).

The path to liberation from the round of birth and death, using the links of the chain of bondage as a kind of map, entails finding the weakest links and then breaking the chain of *pratītyasamutpāda* at those points. For the Mahāyāna Buddhist bent on liberation there are two weakest links: (1) *ignorance*; and (2) *karma* (action) and *desire*. One breaks these two links by following either the way of knowledge, which breaks ignorance, or the way of desireless and selfless action, which breaks karma-desire. The map shows, thereby,

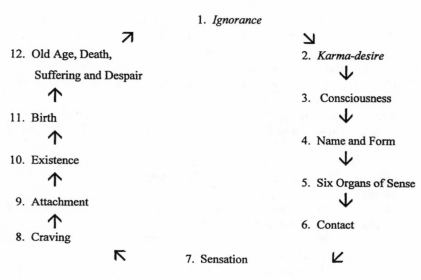

Figure 6.1
Pratītyasamutpāda as Dependent (Abandonment) and Interdependent
(Community) Origination.

two distinct ways of liberation. The first is the way of *dependent* origination, "an arising after getting," the second is the way of *independent* origination, "to come into dependent existence together." (See note 207.) Call the first way "the path of abandonment," wherein one seeks to break the chain of *pratītyasamutpāda* at the link of ignorance and reach liberation by the insight and mystical knowledge leading to world transcendence. Call the second way "the path of community," wherein one seeks to break the chain of *pratītyasamutpāda* at the link of karma (action) and desire, and reach liberation by selfless action and the communal life of world involvement. The path of community entails recognizing the fact of the interdependence of all parts of the chain of dependency and then trying to make the best of what is found. The path of *abandonment*, following the doctrine of *dependent* origination, leads out of the world and toward nirvana; the path of *community*, following the doctrine of *interdependent* origination, leads back into the world and toward altruism and the karmic community. How does the latter work?

Bringing together Anitya, Interdependence, and Altruism. With the concept of interdependence we have the essence of the ethical position that we have been calling "altruism," the view that all are responsible for all. The metaphysics that communal altruism rests upon is the view that all *are* all—that identity relates the interdependent members of the community, that no one is separate, isolated, or independent. And because nothing is separate, and this is the Buddha's reasoning gleaned from that nirvanic peak experience, anything that one member does, all of the others, in some sense, do as well.

Consider the famous imagery of Indra's jewel net of Hua-yen Buddhism as described by Francis H. Cook. The metaphysics of the net relates directly to *anitya*, *pratītyasamutpāda*, and altruism:

> Far away in the heavenly abode of the great god Indra, there is a wonderful net which has been hung by some cunning artificer in such a manner that it stretches out infinitely in all directions. In accordance with the extravagant tastes of deities, the artificer has hung a single glittering jewel in each "eye" of the net, and since the net is infinite in dimension, the jewels are infinite in number. There hang the jewels, glittering like stars of the first magnitude, a wonderful sight to behold.

But even more wonderful is what follows:

> If we now arbitrarily select one of these jewels for inspection and look closely at it, we will discover that in its polished surface there are reflected all the other jewels in the net infinite in number. Not only that, but each of the jewels reflected in this one jewel is also reflecting all the other jewels, so that there is an infinite reflecting process occurring.

And Cook concludes:

> The Hua-yen school has been fond of this image, mentioned many times in its literature, because it symbolizes a cosmos in which there is an infinitely repeated interrelationship among all members of the cosmos. This relationship is said to be one of simultaneous *mutual identity* and *mutual inter-causality*.[208]

This is interdependent origination in its most radical form and this intercausality lies at the heart of the way of community. As a concept of community, it flows from the Buddha's nirvanic insight, through *anitya* and *pratītyasamutpāda*, climaxing in the way of the karmic community, caught here in the vision of Indra's net and bound with ties of altruism and compassion. From the Buddha's enlightenment and epistemological insight came a metaphysical discovery about change and interdependence that ended with the knowledge that not only are we all responsible for our karmic brethren, not only do we share their karma, but in addition there is a real sense in which we are they and they are we.

We turn next to the second major problem that has been gnawing away beneath the previous discussions. Following its explication we'll try to clear the air by proposing a solution to this second problem.

The Problem of Communal Altruism

All four of our community creators have held that in order for community to be created some form of altruism is necessary. Altruism—the view that promoting the welfare of others is right and good and that, in some sense, all are responsible for all—is the glue that holds the altruistic community together. Without it, community must fail, they seemed to say. Further, altruism arose for our four community creators as a result of their self-transforming peak experiences. But now a rather devastating problem develops, the problem of communal altruism. In what follows, we begin with an explication of the problem of communal altruism; we then attempt to demonstrate that altruism is doomed to failure; finally, we continue with a modest proposal for solving the problem of communal altruism that entails giving up altruism altogether in favor of a more common sensical and defensible way of community—communal egoism. We conclude by pointing to three problems that might yet haunt communal egoism.

Communal altruism is serious and destructive of community and is traceable to a problem with altruism itself, its essential incoherence and destructive impracticality. The failure to solve the problem of communal altruism leaves present violence in place and it can lead, in turn, to more and greater violence in the future. In the East, the problem of altruism is indigenous to the ancient Jain ethics of *ahiṃsā*, nonviolence, subsequently found in Hinduism and in Gandhi's ashramic community; in the West, it can be traced to the slave ethics of Jesus of Nazareth, subsequently found in

King's beloved community. The problem of communal altruism is entrenched in the universal unworkability of altruistic ethics, itself, an ethic of service to others through the humbling and negating of oneself. Consider altruistic ethics at its idealistic best in the following admonition of Jesus of Nazareth:

> Whoever would be great among you must be your servant, and whoever would be first among you must be slave [*doulos*] of all. For the Son of man also came not to be served but to serve, and to give his life as a ransom for many.[209]

Here, in the oldest gospel, about 70 C.E., the very foundation of the unattainable universal ideal of Christian altruism was first laid, an ideal that was to capture the imaginations of both Gandhi and King. Jesus' challenge was probably directed only to his immediate disciples and certainly not to all of mankind: it is, after all, logically impossible, hence empirically impossible, for everyone to be just a servant or for everyone to be just a slave.

But if the ideal of altruism is impossible of attainment then any community with an altruistic ethics at its foundation is going to be a community doomed from the start. The psychological consequence of any person's supporting such an ethic that bids its followers to serve others and always to put themselves last, will inevitably be to feel guilt and shame at not measuring up to the Master's ideal of worthiness. From this failure there is a psychological tendency for resentment and hatred to arise because of that failure.

King was aware of the psychopathology of altruism and its easy leanings toward guilt and resentment. That awareness surfaced in King's last SCLC presidential address in 1967 with the concern that Christian ethics might be viewed as powerless where one simply becomes the doormat upon which everyone is invited to wipe their moral feet. His address begins with a reference to Frederich Nietzsche, who, as King was well aware, was the most frequent and harshest critic of Christian altruism. The discussion centered on power and whether a Christian could use power, that is, compulsion, that is economic, political and social power, consistently with Christian altruistic moral principles:

> [O]ne of the great problems of history is that the concepts of [altruistic] love and power have usually been contrasted as opposites—polar opposites—so that love is identified with a

resignation of power, and power with a denial of love. . . . It was this misinterpretation that caused Nietzsche, who was a philosopher of the will to power, to reject the Christian concept of [altruistic] love.

Then King cries out his warning quoted above in chapter 4:

Now, we've got to get this thing right. What is needed is a realization that power without love is reckless and abusive and love without power is sentimental and anemic.[210]

King's problem is this: How can we balance altruistic love, Christian love that is "patient and kind, that does not insist on its own way, is not irritable or resentful, that bears all things, hopes all things, endures all things,"[211] with the power to force or compel the decisions that one makes?

King, it would appear, is caught on the following dilemma of altruistic love: if altruistic love is joined with power, then it ceases to be Christian love; and if it is not so joined, then it becomes sentimental and anemic. There is no other choice: therefore, either one practices love that bears all and endures all or else one is not a Christian.

Frederich Nietzsche's (1844–1900) critique of Christian altruism is far more devastating, however, than either King or the dilemma of altruistic love suggest. In *Thus Spoke Zarathustra*, Nietzsche ironically reminds his reader,

The spirit of revenge, my friends, has so far been the subject of man's best reflection; and where there was suffering, one always wanted punishment, too.

For punishment is what revenge calls itself; with a hypocritical lie it creates a good conscience for itself.[212]

When you are wronged, you want to flee or strike back; that's natural, a celebrated instinct. But now altruistic ethics tells us to stand our ground, turn the other cheek, to love our oppressors, to do good to them that persecute us, to become the slave of all. And the altruistic ethics of Gandhi and King (or, possibly, of Leopold and the Buddha) would agree bidding us do what we cannot do, namely, go against instinct and forgive. And it is that failed attempt to forgive that causes the problems of repressed desire, guilt, shame, resentment, and hatred. Nietzsche offers an analysis of the psychology of resentment in his *Genealogy of Morals* and *Beyond Good and Evil*. He traces the repressed guilt and shame that result from not being able to live up to the impossible ideal of altruistic ethics. The feeling of anger leads to the feelings of guilt and shame toward oneself and resentment and hatred toward others in the community. The latter emotions are then repressed but find acceptable legal and metaphysical outlets in the creation of prisons and capital punishment in this life and hells and terrors in the next. What began in communal peace ends in communal violence.

Frederich Nietzsche is required reading at seminaries throughout the Judeo-Christian world. His psychology of resentment and sublimation is worth studying by all who would consider altruism a foundation on which to build community. Altruistic Christianity is the visible embodiment of the unconscious workings of massive resentment; it is probably the major punishment-dominated religion of the twenty-first century.

If altruism, because of its limited appeal, its clash with human instincts, and its dangerous psychological and social consequences, that is, because of its unworkability, its unnaturalness, and its unhealthiness, is doomed to failure, and, as a result, doomed to destroy Gandhi's ashramic community and King's beloved community, as well as to devastate Leopold's biotic community and the Buddha's karmic community, then what remains? That is to say, if community is still to be the way for solving the problems of violence and peace, then to what kind of community can we possibly turn if altruism has failed? Here's an outline of a very modest proposal.

The Solution of Communal Egoism

We began this study of insanity, violence, peace, and community by quoting from Plato's dialogue the *Apology*. Socrates' argument to his judges and jurors, denying his guilt of corrupting the youth of Athens, contained at its core a simple reminder about human nature. Socrates said, in effect, that no one in their right mind would intentionally injure oneself; and if one injures others then they will surely be injuring oneself, for those others will seek revenge; therefore, no one in their right mind would intentionally injure others. This Socratic argument led us to our Socratic community argument, trying to get people to see that they *are* those others, the community, such that when they harm those others, the community, they are really harming themselves: The Socratic community argument looked like this:

1. No one would intentionally harm oneself.
2. Oneself is those others, one's community (those corrupted youth of Athens, their relatives and friends, the entire angry city, for example, who could harm oneself).
3. Therefore, no one would intentionally harm others, one's community.

By extension from this Socratic community argument, we then obtained our two community arguments, the community violence argument and the community peace argument. Here is the community violence argument, which we have attributed to Leopold, Gandhi, King, and the Buddha:

1. No one would intentionally do violence to onself.
2. Oneself is one's community.
3. Therefore, no one would intentionally do violence to one's community.

Thus the importance of the Socratic community argument, which, with immodest license, we attributed to Socrates.

Look now to the second premise of the Socratic community argument, "Oneself *is* those others, one's community." Now, what did our Socrates mean? Technically speaking, there are three rather traditional senses of the verb "is" that must be distinguished before we can answer this question. First, there is the *is* of *identity*, which expresses the relation between objects or concepts that have all of their empirical properties in common as in the factual statements "Socrates *is* the man who married Xanthippe and had three sons" or "Socrates *is* the famous Greek philosopher who lived from 469 to 399 B.C.E." Such *extensional* identity is to be distinguished from *intensional* identity, where the relation of identity holds between the verbal meanings of the terms in the statement alone. Thus a bare inspection of the meanings of the words is sufficient to establish the intensional identity in the statements "Socrates *is* Socrates" or "Socrates the philosopher *is* a philosopher." Second, there is the *is* of *predication*, where a property is attributed to, or said to belong, to a subject but without saying that subject and property are identical as in "Socrates *is* short" or "Socrates *is* guilty of corrupting the youth of Athens." Third, there is the *is* of *existence*, where the verb asserts the being of some subject as in "Socrates *is*," that is to say, "There *is* a Socrates."

The ambiguity in, and concern over, *is* for our purposes relates either to the *is* of identity or to the *is* of predication. And when it is stated, "Oneself is one's community," it is clear that we are dealing with the *is* of predication and not the *is* of identity. Our Socrates is using the *is* of predication because he does not intend to say that there is an identity, neither *extensional* (Socrates and the community do not share all their empirical properties) nor *intensional* (the meanings of the words of "Socrates" and "community" are clearly not the same), relating himself to the community. That is to say, our Socrates did not say "The community is I," the essence of *communal identity* and also, ultimately, of communal altruism, wherein the *is* of identity is employed; but he did say, "I am the community," the essence of *communal predication* and also, ultimately, of communal egoism, wherein the *is* of predication is employed, implying that membership in the community is one of his properties but that he's not one of its properties, that is, he is included in the community but the community is not included in him (think of, "Socrates is short." Shortness is in Socrates, in some metaphorical/Aristotelian sense, but Socrates is not in shortness— thus the *is* of predication). Finally, our Socratic community argument would not hold that a right action is one that aims to benefit others (ethical altruism), but it would hold that a right action is one that aims to benefit the agent (ethical egoism).

To demonstrate the relation between the *is* of identity and ethical altruism and the *is* of predication and ethical egoism, recall the mystical metaphor of the Jewel Net of Indra in our example from Hua Yen Buddhism above. Each individual jewel in the Net was identical to the entire Net: the Net was in each jewel and each jewel was in the Net. Individualism would be lost in this metaphysical monism and were an ethic to be developed around it, that ethic would reflect the rules of conduct between or among identical jewels in the Net, a curious "ethic," indeed, where there are no "others." But altruistic ethics, itself, is rather curious. The Jewel Net of Indra is a community where only altruistic ethics could prevail because there is only the One acting toward Itself.

The difference between communal altruism and the *is* of identity, and communal egoism and the *is* of predication, might be brought out more sharply by the following example taken from the 1948 book (and the 1949 film) *Twelve O'Clock High!* The setting is an American B-17 bomber base in England in 1943. Casualties have been high, a new commander, General Frank Savage (Gregory Peck), has been assigned to find out what the problem is, whether "hard luck" is to blame, and to correct the problem and the luck. Here is General Savage upbraiding some 240 officers and enlisted personnel from his bomber group in a preraid briefing:

> I can tell you now one reason that you've been having hard luck. I saw it in your faces last night. I see it there now. You've seen a lot of air lately. You think you ought to have a rest. In short you're feeling sorry for yourselves. Now I don't have a lot of patience for this what are we fighting for stuff. We're in a war. A shooting war. We've got to fight! And some of us have got to die! I'm not trying to tell you not to be afraid. Fear is normal. But stop worrying about it and about yourselves. Stop making plans. Forget about going home. Consider yourselves already dead!

Later, in a postraid debriefing session, General Savage publicly interrogates a particular officer, Lieutenant Pettingill, for breaking formation to help out a stricken fellow B-17 pilot who had been attacked by German fighters. The pilot of the crippled plane, Ackerman, and his crew are subsequently lost:

> "Ackerman a pretty good friend of yours?"
> "My roommate, Sir."
> "So for the sake of your roommate you violated group integrity. Every gun on a B-17 is designed to give the group maximum defensive fire power. That's what I mean by "group integrity." When you pull a B-17 out of formation you reduce the defensive power of the group by ten guns. A crippled airplane has to be expendable. Let them go. Let the Jerries shoot down your own brother. The one thing which is never expendable is your obligation to this group, this group! this group! That has to be your loyalty! Your only reason for being."[213]

In addition to communal altruism, the dialogue illustrates many of the concepts that we have been dealing with in this book. We have here a communal *holism*, the bomber group is a living organism, an organized indivisible whole that when divided loses its qualitative integrity, its personality, its organic character; it is *fascist*, with a centralized authoritarian government headed by a dictatorial leader who has laid down a severe social regimentation; it is *totalitarian*, subordinating the individual to the good of the group with strict control of all its members; it reflects the relation of *identity* between crew members and the group when Savage tells them, "You are this group"; and, following from all this, it expresses a *communal altruism*, reducing the lives of its members to insignificance, to nothing—"consider yourselves already dead!"—to support the welfare of the group. Here, the group, a living being greater than the sum of its parts, shapes and forms its components to direct and satisfy its own end, which is primarily and simply to survive: every communal holism is a fascism and every fascism necessitates an altruism. Let's examine this more closely.

If General Savage is expressing a communal altruism, then Lieutenant Pettingill, the pilot who tried to save Ackerman at the expense of the group, is expressing a communal egoism. This communal egoism rejects the holism, the fascism, and the totalitarianism; it upholds a relation with the group, where the group is not "in him" but he is in the group, it is predicated of him; and with all of this it also rejects the very efficient, but all-consuming, communal altruism.

Communal altruism is also nicely expressed in one of the three principles Gandhi cites above in summarizing the essentials of community: "That the good of the individual is contained in the good of the community." General Savage would undoubtedly agree. When the group survives then the individuals in it survive. But Lieutenant Pettingill would probably have justified his act of courageous rebellion in the air by rejecting this principle of communal altruism and proclaiming in its stead this principle of communal egoism: "That the good of the community is contained in the good of the individual."

Despite the fact that General Savage might have lost the air war if communal egoism had prevailed, there are advantages to adopting communal egoism over communal altruism. One compelling advantage is that its opposite, communal holism with its accompanying communal altruism, is entirely without sense. We look at that next.

Communal Holism and Communal Altruism

Immanual Kant (1724–1804) once wrote about organic holism (with present advances in cybernetics and robotics one could now

210 ⮞ Community, Violence, and Peace

probably speak of "inorganic holism") in language (1785) that will subsequently become familiar to students of Charles Darwin (1809–1882) and organic evolution:

> In the natural constitution of an organized being, i.e., one suitably adapted to life, we assume as an axiom that no organ will be found for any purpose which is not the fittest and best adapted to that purpose.[214]

Life and living processes, according to organic holism, are the manifestation of an activity made possible only because of the quite independent organization of the system itself, and not because of that system's separate components. What survives depends entirely on what helps the system to survive. "This group! This group!" General Savage cries, "That has to be your loyalty! Your only reason for being." The group is an abstract, organized being, a living entity, to which, however, the organs, the parts, can have relations. This is not as weird as it appears. We have relations with abstractions all the time and it doesn't take a Plato or a Kant to make acceptable sense of this. But while it's true that we honor God, country, and family on a daily basis, we try to particularize each of these abstractions in such a way as to make them more epistemologically palatable. For example, *God* is anthromorphized and often given a history; *country* is called "him" or "her" and represented by a John Bull or an Uncle Sam; and *family* is given ancestors, photographs, and familiar subjective symbols to make the abstraction acceptable and understandable. Together with these abstractions for which we would be willing to die or kill or devote our time and our treasure, there are other abstractions of varying degrees of palatability, such as love, honor, salvation, truth, goodness, and, knowledge, and beauty and, finally, *community*, all of which stretch our imaginations and the acceptable limits of comprehension.

Altruistic communities can, and they have, as we have seen repeatedly, taken on dimensions that stagger the understanding and, oftentimes, even good sense. These community organic wholes are never seen, but they are there; they make demands on us and we sometimes respond; they have expectations of us of loyalty and commitment, expectations that we, like Lieutenant Pettingill, often fail to meet; we have duties to these wholes, and failure to fulfill those duties, failure to live up to those expectations, produces, as we have seen, frustration, anxiety, and guilt.

But how is it possible, first of all, to have relations toward an abstraction that no one ever experiences? Where is this invisible whole, this organized being, that is greater than the sum of all those visible parts? And how is it possible to have any sort of moral relation of concerns, obligations, and duties to such wholes? Among such duties, of course, is that of putting one's own interests last and placing the interests of the whole first. This duty of communal altruism we have found expressed in our biotic community, ashramic community, beloved community, and karmic community. We conclude this discussion by pointing to one final problem with communal wholes that generates communal altruism.

The Problem of Whole–Part

What is the nature of the relation between a greater-than-its-parts whole to its parts? The relation, so it is claimed, is one of independence and irreducibility of the whole to those parts. And the question is significant because if the relation of the organs to the organized being, of the members to the community, fails, for whatever reason, then the holistic conception of community, which defines that relation, also fails. And if communal holism fails, then communal altruism must fail, opening the way, perhaps, for a simpler, less opaque concept of community ethics—communal egoism.

"The problem of whole-part," let's call it, draws attention to the belief that the whole can exist separate from and independent of its parts. We shall try to show that the belief that there is, or can be, something greater than, independent and separate from, those parts is simply nonsense.²¹⁵ Communal whole and communal parts, like all relative concepts, as a little attention will show, simply cannot be logically separated from each other. Just as there is no concept of *up* without the concept of *down*, no *left* without *right*, no *good* without *evil*, no *bondage* without *liberation*, so also there can be no *whole* without *parts*. The point is a logical one and it is that certain concepts have meaning only in relation to their opposites, their contradictories. To separate them and pretend that each can have any meaning, or any existence—if we can move temporarily from logic to metaphysics—without its opposite is simply unintelligible. And jumping from the logically impossible, a *whole* without *parts*, to the empirically possible, a self-existent partless whole, is both nonsense and unintelligible.

If holism, because of the problem of whole–part, fails to support its splendidly isolated organic wholeness apart from its independent constituent parts, then altruism, as a duty to that whole, must also fail. And if communal holism fails, then communal altruism fails. And with these failures, perhaps community can be made safe for another ethic, one that is neither meaningless nor opaque, which, again, brings us back to communal egoism. Communal egoism is the view that when each member of a community pursues his or her own interests or advantage, then the good of the community will be secured.

Some Advantages to Communal Egoism

There are several direct advantages that come with the adoption of what we are calling "communal egoism." First, the motivation here is defensibly selfish. There is no necessity, therefore, to produce the guilt, the shame, the resentment, together with the evident hypocrisy, associated with the previous four ways of community founded on altruism. Further, and consistent with the first advantage, the way of communal egoism rests upon a naturally attractive foundation for human endeavors, psychological egoism. The moral strength of communal egoism lies in the evident instinctual and happy appeal of that easily recognized but challenging theory of human nature: all humans are going to seek their own advantage; but sometimes, communal egoism reminds us, that advantage lies in *not* seeking our own advantage first.

Further, on this view, none of the incorrigible problems dealt with in investigating our altruistic communities need occur. The problem of self-transformation need never arise since what one wishes to change is not a condition transcendent to the ordinary conscience. Peak and transformative experiences are still necessary, but now they strengthen the ego with the realization that I am the community; education expands and extends the inherent drive of self-love to now include the love and regard for others, for it is in the community, one realizes, that one's own best interests and advantage lie; and it also lies in reducing violence and bringing peace to those others.

Finally, the problem of altruistic fascism need never arise since the individual is now safe from being devoured by the community, having relinquished the belief in the identity between the self and the community with its attendant and destructive ethical altruism.

If all of this is the case, then our task would appear to be to accept the view that what benefits me will also benefit the community. In other words, since we cannot rise above the community to the dangerous and unrealistic heights of communal altruism, let's be wise enough to accept the practicality, the naturalness, and the felicity of the way of communal egoism. What leads to a decrease of violence and an increase of peace in the twenty-first century for me will lead to the same for my community; and that community is the world of living and nonliving things; therefore, it's to my advantage to reduce the violence and increase the peace in myself, first; nonviolence and peace in the community will follow because *I am the community.*[216]

We conclude this chapter and this book by anticipating several objections to this alternative to communal altruism.

Some Problems with Communal Egoism

There are several problems that have been pushed forward with the view of communal egoism. We mention three.

The problem of where's the difference? So what's the difference, a critic might say, between your communal egoism and the communal altruism that you have rejected? In the end they both come to the same thing—a moral concern for others. So what if the altruist does it by putting the interest of others first and you do it by putting your interest first. It's not a difference that makes a difference. But, then, if altruism has failed in the past, and it's not different from egoism, then egoism is bound to fail in the future. Communal egoism is guilty by being just like communal altruism, and it hasn't solved anything.

The critic is probably right in saying that the ends of altruism and egoism can be the same—promoting everyone's interest and welfare. But recall that Plato and Aldous Huxley both argued that their communities also promoted the greatest happiness for everyone; surely that alone doesn't identify them with either communal altruism or communal egoism. The differences here lie in what is acceptable and unacceptable in the means to bringing about that end, the welfare of others. Altruism, as we have been at pains to point out, leads to illogical, unwarranted, and unacceptable consequences. Communal altruism and communal egoism are similar in their ends, but where dissimilarity really counts, in their means, they are splendidly different.

The problem of communal egoism. What you are advocating here, the critic might continue, is just old-fashioned selfishness. Do you really want selfish individuals to stand at the center of the community? Wake up! That's what we've got now. The problems of violence and peace are still there. Communal egoism hasn't solved anything and it never will.

The critic is right in stating that the center of the community is, indeed, the individual. That center is not the village, the family, a particular racial, social, or economic class, nor is it the *sangha;* it is the individual. But the critic is wrong in believing that the ordinary individual with an ordinary conscience is at that center. The center of that community is the transformed individual; the center can be an Aldo Leopold, a Mohandas Gandhi, a Martin Luther King Jr., or a Gautama the Buddha. And the necessity of the transformation from an ordinary individual to an extraordinary individual is the lesson that these four community builders have left to us. It is, indeed, an extraordinary kind of selfishness, it seems to me, that they can be seen as advocating, where one's own best interest often lies in promoting the interest of others. That was the great lesson that each of them taught, which brings us to our final problem.

The problem of egoistic transformation. What you are advocating now, the critic might say, just leads to the same old problem that we've seen before that you've called either "the problem of self-transformation" or "the problem of the way to self-transformation." So what is transformed anyway? And how do you get it? If this whole buisness was opaque before, it certainly hasn't cleared up now. Communal egoism hasn't solved a thing, and it's brought us back to where we started with Plato's aristocratic philosopher-kings and Aldous Huxley's elitist Alpha plus world controllers. You've given us a new kind of elitist transformationism that produces the same old elitism. Their, and your, communal egoism hasn't solved anything.

The critic is right, once again, in stating that the center of the community is going to be the transformed individual. But the critic is wrong in believing that such transformed individuals are so rare as to constitute an elitist class. To begin with, we have examples before us of four rather ordinary individuals who, through their transformations, recognized that each one of them was the community, the center of the community. And each one of them went on to recommend that transformative experience to others. We mustn't misinterpret, it seems to me, the sheer ordinariness, the outright commonness, of what these four community builders experienced. Their transformative experiences did not point beyond themselves to abstractions and impossibilities but to the center, to themselves as that center, of the community. And what they did, anyone can do. The result was that each of them left a map, an algorithm, by following which, any individual could be similarly transformed: Get involved with education (Plato), or with the biotic community (Leopold), or with the ashramic community (Gandhi), or with the beloved community (King), or with the karmic community (the Buddha), an involvement of getting out of dark caves, of living with wild things, of prayer, of yoga, of immersing oneself in pollution, exploitation, discrimination, injustice, poverty, and suffering. Only then will the community be transformed because, once again, *you are the community*.

Notes

1. See Arthur Herman, *The Idea of Decline in Western History* (New York: The Free Press, 1997), an examination of the ubiquitous prophets of doom and their role in Western communities.

2. Erich Fromm, *The Sane Society* (New York: Fawcett Publications, 1967/1955), p. 13.

3. Ibid., p. 309.

4. Ibid.

5. Ibid., p. 312.

6. Under the descriptor "community," there are over 96,000 citations given by the U.S. Educational Resource Information Center. See the unpublished paper by Henry St. Maurice, "Constructions of Community: Aspects of a Cultural-Historical Approach to Schooling," p. 3.

7. Aristotle, *Politics* 1252a, *The Basic Works of Aristotle*, edited by Richard McKeon (New York: Random House, 1941), p. 1127.

8. Plato, *Apology* 24b, *The Collected Dialogues of Plato*, edited by Edith Hamilton and Huntington Cairns (New York: Pantheon Books, 1961), p. 10. The official charge probably was either *asebeia*, blasphemy, which officially meant desecrating an altar dedicated to the Gods of the community, saying impious things or revealing the secrets of the mystery cults, or it was *anosion*, unholiness, that is, offending the Gods of the community; either way the religious foundations were attacked and either way "treason" was entailed.

9. *Apology* 29d-30b, ibid., pp. 412–13. It is small wonder that Socrates was later called "the Jesus Christ of the ancient Greek world." See "Socrates revealed among the Greeks, What Christ Revealed among the Barbarians," 105–6 by Justin Martyr (d. 165 C.E.), in Werner Jaeger, *Early Christian and Greek Paideia* (Cambridge, Mass.: Harvard University Press, 1961), p. 118 n. 5, which cites Justin's parallels between Socrates and Jesus. Both men can be seen as exalting individualism.

10. Cf. *Laws* X.907e–910d, *The Collected Dialogues of Plato*, pp. 1463–65.

11. The argument is found at *Apology* 25a–26b, ibid., pp. 11–12.

12. Both religions and communities, on this line of reasoning, are merely problem-solving devices, *games* if you like, which, when properly played, yield the prize or the solution. Our fourfold heuristic is merely an algorithm for summarizing a strategy for successful play in both religions and communities. For a defense of this strategy, see A. L. Herman, *A Brief Introduction to Hinduism* (Boulder, Colo.: Westview Press, 1991), pp. 30–32.

13. *Republic* I.352d. Author's translation.

14. Literally, "a drinking together."

15. See Plato's *Letters* in *The Collected Dialogues of Plato*, especially letter VII. See the chapter on Plato by the greatest gossip of the ancient world, who wrote down every fact and rumor about Plato that he ever heard, Diogenes Laertius (fl. 220 C.E.), *Lives of Eminent Philosophers*, translated by R. D. Hicks, 2 vols. (Cambridge, Mass.: Harvard University Press, 1950), vol. 1, pp. 277–373. See also the bibliography and accounts of Plato's life in A. E. Taylor, *Plato: The Man and His Work* (London: Methuen, 1978/1926); W. K. C. Guthrie, *A History of Greek Philosophy*, volume 4: *Plato: The Man and His Dialogues* (Cambridge: Cambridge University Press, 1975).

16. The subject throughout the *Republic* is "What kind of life should one live?" and "What is the best life for a human being?" See especially *Republic* 344e, 352d, and compare *Gorgias* 500c. Since Plato gives no name to his community, we shall simply call it "the Republic" and thereby distinguish this unitalicized name from the book *Republic* in which the Republic is described.

17. *Republic* 414c–415c, *The Collected Dialogues of Plato*, pp. 658–59.

18. *Republic* 459c, ibid., p. 698.

19. *Republic* 462d, ibid., p. 701.

20. *Republic* 441c, d, ibid., pp. 683, 684.

21. *Republic* 473c–d, ibid., pp. 712–13.

22. *Republic* 517a, ibid., p. 749.

23. A. J. P. Taylor, *A History of the First World War* (Berkeley, Calif.: Medallion Books, 1966), pp. 82, 83, 84, 86.

24. Sybille Bedford, *Aldous Huxley: A Biography* (New York: Alfred A. Knopf/Harper & Row, 1973), p. 142.

25. J. W. N. Sullivan, *Beethoven: His Spiritual Development* (New York: Vintage Books, 1927), p. 43.

26. For more on Huxley's life, see the fine biography by his longtime friend, Sybille Bedford, *Aldous Huxley: A Biography*; see also Ronald W. Clark, *The Huxleys* (New York: McGraw-Hill, 1968), and Keith M. Kay, *Aldous Huxley* (New York: Barnes & Noble, 1972).

27. Aldous Huxley, *Brave New World & Brave New World Revisited* (New York: Harper Colophon Books, 1965), p. 169.

28. Ibid., p. 182.

29. Ibid., p. 184.

30. Ibid., p. 1.

31. Ibid., pp. 19–20.

32. K. R. Popper, *The Open Society and Its Enemies*, 2 vols. (New York: Harper Torchbooks, 1962), vol. 1, p. 102. See the source in *Laws* 739c ff. and *Republic* 424a, 462a ff.

33. Ibid., p. 103. See also *Laws* 442a, b.

34. Ibid., p. 104.

35. *Psychological egoism* is the theory that all humans are by nature self-interest–pursuing creatures, that is, each of us is naturally prone to satisfy our own interests before anyone else's. If those interests are self-realization, then we have *psychological spiritualism*, the foundation of the Republic. If those interests are pleasure, then we have *psychological hedonism*, the foundation of the World State. Each of these psychological theories are deeply imbued with individualism. And both the Republic and the World State, as communities, are rightly concerned about ego-centered individualism and the anti-community selfishness that it engenders. And both communities must, it seems, contain therein the seeds of their own demise. We will return to this matter in chapter 6.

36. For a fascinating history of ecology, see Donald Worster, *Nature's Economy: A History of Ecological Ideas*, 2nd ed. (Cambridge: Cambridge University Press, 1994).

37. Aldo Leopold, "The Land Ethic," *A Sand County Almanac with Essays on Conservation from Round River* (New York: A Sierra Club/Ballantine Book, 1970/1949), pp. 239, 240.

38. Rachel Carson, *Silent Spring* (Boston: Houghton Mifflin, 1962), p. 297. An earlier book, incidentally, *The Sea around Us* (1951), had already brought Carson fame and a small fortune.

39. These others include such now famous ecologists as Barry Commoner, Ian McHarg, and Lynn White Jr., all of whom, together with Rachel Carson, have, as J. Baird Callicott has so well put it, "with almost loving attention recited a litany of environmental ills, spoken of 'chlorinated hydrocarbons,' 'phosphate detergents,' 'nuclear tinkering,' and 'gratified bulldozers' in language once reserved for detailing the precincts of hell and abominating its seductive Prince." J. Baird Callicott, *In Defense of the Land Ethic: Essays in Environmental Philosophy* (Albany: SUNY Press, 1989), pp. 190–91.

40. Carson, *Silent Spring*, p. 189.

41. Paul Brooks, *The House of Life: Rachel Carson at Work* (Boston: Houghton Mifflin, 1972), p. 319.

42. Ian L. McHarg, *Design with Nature* (New York: Doubleday & Company, 1969), p. 26.

43. Aldo Leopold, "Thinking Like a Mountain" (1944), *A Sand County Almanac*, pp. 138–39.

44. Susan L. Flader, *Thinking Like a Mountain: Aldo Leopold and the Evolution of an Ecological Attitude towards Deer, Wolves and Forests* (Columbia: University of Missouri Press, 1974), p. 3.

45. Curt Meine, *Aldo Leopold: His Life and Work* (Madison: University of Wisconsin Press, 1988), p. 442.

46. Ibid., p. 444.

47. Quoted in Donald Worster, *Nature's Economy*, p. 272.

48. See the essay by Roderick Nash, "Aldo Leopold's Intellectual Heritage," in *Companion to A Sand County Almanac: Interpretive and Critical Essays*, edited by J. Baird Callicott (Madison: University of Wisconsin Press, 1987), pp. 77–79.

49. Aldo Leopold, "Some Fundamentals of Conservation in the Southwest" (1923), in *The River of the Mother of God and Other Essays by*

Aldo Leopold, edited by Susan L. Flader and J. Baird Callicott (Madison: University of Wisconsin Press, 1991), p. 95. Emphasis added.

50. Quoted in Donald Worster, *Nature's Economy,* p. 288.

51. "A Biotic View of the Land" (1939), *The River of the Mother of God and Other Essays,* p. 268.

52. Ibid., pp. 268–69. Emphasis added.

53. Aldo Leopold, *A Sand County Almanac,* pp. 139–40.

54. "Ecology and Politics" (1941), *The River of the Mother of God,* pp. 281, 282, emphasis added, 283.

55. "Review of Young and Goldman, *The Wolves of North America*" (1945), ibid., p. 322.

56. Michael Nelson, "A Defense of Environmental Ethics: A Reply to Janna Thompson," *Environmental Ethics* 15 (Fall 1993): 254. Charles Elton, writing in the 1920s, is responsible for the concept of the biotic community. See especially Elton's *Animal Ecology* (New York: Macmillan, 1927). J. Baird Callicott's classic works on Leopold are found in *In Defense of the Land Ethic,* and *Companion to A Sand County Almanac.* Playing Plato to Leopold's Socrates, Callicott's two beautifully written seminal works on Leopold are "The Conceptual Foundations of the Land Ethic" and "The Metaphysical Implications of Ecology" in his *In Defense of the Land Ethic.*

57. Aldo Leopold, "The Land Ethic," *A Sand County Almanac,* pp. 239, 240.

58. Ibid., p. 240.

59. Ibid., p. 262.

60. Ibid., p. 246.

61. Ibid., p. 246.

62. Ibid., p. 261.

63. Ibid., p. 258.

64. Ibid., p. 253.

65. Ibid., pp. xvii, xix.

66. Susan L. Flader, *Thinking Like a Mountain,* p. 153.

67. Ibid., p. 261.

68. Rachel Carson, *Silent Spring,* p. 218.

69. Ibid., p. 234.

70. See Kenneth Goodpaster, "On Being Morally Considerable," *Journal of Philosophy* 22 (1978): 305–25, and J. Baird Callicott's discussion in *In Defense of the Land Ethic*, pp. 82–86, for a grand defense of Leopold on this matter of "outrageous rights."

71. This possibility has alarmed at least one critic of Leopold's land ethic: "One might be genuinely concerned about the status of human (individual) rights within [this interpretation of Leopold's] ethic. Clearly, on [this interpretation], abortion, infanticide, nonvoluntary euthanasia, war, and other means for the elimination of the less fit may be unobjectionable because they are ecosystematically unobjectionable." Donald Scherer, "Anthropocentrism, Atomism, and Environmental Ethics," *Environmental Ethics* 4 (1982): 116; see also J. Baird Callicott, "Animal Liberation: A Triangular Affair," *Environmental Ethics* 2 (1980): 311–38, who offered the interpretation of Leopold that Scherer is attacking; and see Jon N. Moline, "Aldo Leopold and the Moral Community," *Environmental Ethics* 2 (1986): 99–112, for more on what "community" might have meant to Leopold.

72. Aldo Leopold, *A Sand County Almanac*, p. 240. Emphasis added.

73. J. Baird Callicott, *In Defense of the Land Ethic*, pp. 83, 84. Emphasis added.

74. Ibid., p. 84. Callicott's subsequent defense of the land ethic against vengeful holism is brilliant and insightful. Space does not permit its inclusion here.

75. Mohandas K. Gandhi, *An Autobiography, or The Story of My Experiments with Truth* (Boston: Beacon Press, 1966/1927), p. 94.

76. Ibid., p. 111.

77. The literature on Gandhi and satyagraha is immense. *Publishers Weekly* in 1985 estimates that there are over 400 biographies alone of his life. In addition, some ninety volumes of his collected works are now in print and the collection is not yet complete. Some of the more useful books by and about Gandhi will be found listed at the end of this volume. But see *A Comprehensive, Annotated Bibliography on Mahatma Gandhi*, vol. 1, compiled by Ananda M. Pandiri (Westport, Conn.: Greenwood Press, 1995).

78. Nicholas Gier, "Gandhi: Pre-Modern, Modern or Post-Modern?" *Gandhi Marg*, 18.3 (October–November 1996): 263. I have relied throughout on Gier's very fine scholarly work on Gandhi.

79. *The Collected Works of Mahatma Gandhi*, 90 vols. (New Delhi: Government of India, 1964–   ), vol. 13, pp. 524–25.

80. M. K. Gandhi, *The Way to Communal Harmony* (Ahmedabad, India: Navajivan Publishing House, 1963), p. 406.

81. Gier, *"Gandhi,"* p. 268.

82. Gandhi, *Autobiography*, p. 365.

83. Ibid., p. 372.

84. Ibid., p. 256.

85. Ibid., p. 407.

86. Gandhi, *Collected Works*, vol. 10 (1909–11), p. 308.

87. Gandhi, *Collected Works*, vol. 13, p. 91.

88. Gandhi, *Autobiography*, p. 484.

89. Gandhi, *Collected Works*, vol. 13, p. 226. The discussion comes from a key speech that Gandhi made at the YMCA in Madras on February 16, 1916. In it, after elaborating upon the satyagrahi vows in some detail, he calls upon the very enthusiastic crowd to enact the Ashram life individually and collectively by adopting the vows and rules just discussed (p. 235). The meeting is then interrupted, the reporter for the *Indian Review* states, by "loud cheers."

90. *Young India*, November 13, 1924, p. 378.

91. *Harijan*, February 1, 1942. Quoted in Joan V. Bondurant, *The Conquest of Violence*, rev. ed. (Princeton, N.J.: Princeton University Press, 1988), p. 30.

92. Ibid., p. 175.

93. Quoted in Margaret Chatterjee, *Gandhi's Religious Thought* (South Bend, Ind.: University of Notre Dame Press, 1983), p. 153.

94. Dhananjay Keer, *Mahatma Gandhi: Political Saint and Unarmed Prophet* (Bombay: Popular Prakashan, 1973), pp. 585, 588.

95. One of Conger's conversations, on November 2, 1933, has been published in *Collected Works*, vol. 56, pp. 171–73. That interview, together with two others, November 3 and 6, 1933, are in Chandrashankar Shukla, *Conversations with Mahatma Gandhi* (Bombay: Vora & Co., 1949).

96. M. K. Gandhi, *Hindu Dharma* (Ahmedabad, India: Navajivan Publishing House, 1950), p. 404. Emphasis added.

97. Margaret Chatterjee, *Gandhi and His Jewish Friends* (New York: Macmillan, 1992), p. 93.

98. *A Testament of Hope: The Essential Writings of Martin Luther King, Jr.*, edited by James Melvin Washington (San Francisco: Harper & Row, 1986), pp. 295–96.

99. Aristotle, *Nichomachean Ethics* 1099b, I.viii.17. *The Basic Works of Aristotle, Op. Cit.*, p. 945. Aristotle is not one of those "some," however; see *N.E.* 1099b, I.viii.23–24.

100. *The Papers of Martin Luther King, Jr.*, vol. 1: *Called to Serve*, January 1929–June 1951, edited by Clayborne Carson et al. (Berkeley: University of California Press, 1992), introduction, p. 10.

101. Ibid., p. 18.

102. Ibid., p. 21.

103. Ibid., p. 23.

104. *A Testament of Hope*, p. 247.

105. Martin Luther King, Jr., "Playboy Interview," *A Testament of Hope*, pp. 342–43.

106. Stephen B. Oates, *Let the Trumpet Sound: The Life of Martin Luther King, Jr.* (New York: New American Library, 1982), p. 17. The story is recounted by Lerone Bennet, a close friend of King's and a fellow student at Morehouse.

107. Ibid., pp. 31–32.

108. Martin Luther King, Jr., *Stride toward Freedom: The Montgomery Story* (New York: Harper & Row, 1958), quoted in *A Testament of Hope*, p. 485.

109. *The Papers of Martin Luther King, Jr.*, vol. 2: *Rediscovering Precious Values*, July 1951–November 1955, edited by Clayborne Carson et al. (Berkeley: University of California Press, 1994), p. 24. Throughout I express King's understanding, right or wrong, of these two theologians; they are presented as King understood them. I also wish to avoid the controversy of plagiarism of the words that expressed these understandings; the subsequent charges of plagiarism made against King are not part of this study.

110. Ibid.

111. "A Comparison of the Conceptions of God in the Thinking of Paul Tillich and Henry Nelson Wieman," Ibid., p. 519.

112. Ibid., p. 524. Emphasis added.

113. Ibid., p. 525.

114. Ibid., p. 527.

115. Ibid., p. 538.

116. "Pilgrimage to Nonviolence," *A Testament of Hope*, p. 38, a restatement really of part of chapter 6 of his *Stride toward Freedom*.

117. Ibid.

118. Ibid., p. 40.

119. *Brown v. Board of Education of Topeka*, 347 U.S. 483 (1954).

120. See Aldon D. Morris, *The Origins of the Civil Rights Movement: Black Communities Organizing for Change* (New York: The Free Press, 1984), pp. 17–22, 128–30.

121. *A Testament of Hope*, pp. 7–8.

122. Ibid., p. 20. Compare Aldo Leopold's definition of rightness: "A thing is [ethically and aesthetically] right when it tends to preserve the integrity, stability, and beauty of the biotic community."

123. Ibid., pp. 7, 8, 9. The piece is from *Christian Century* 74 (February 6, 1957) but the five points were repeated many times in the years ahead in various church and secular journals. Jesus' love and Gandhi's strategy pervade the entire method outlined here by King.

124. Ibid., p. 447.

125. Ibid., p. 16.

126. The entire letter was reprinted in *Why We Can't Wait* (New York: Harper & Row, 1963) and by the American Friends Service Committee as a pamphlet. It is probably the most well-known and often reprinted of all of King's works.

127. *A Testament of Hope*, p. 291.

128. Ibid., pp. 292, 293, 294. King obviously knew Plato's dialogue, *Crito*. All this is reminiscent, of course, of the nineteenth-century philosopher, naturalist, and pacifist, Henry David Thoreau, who, in his "Civil Disobedience" of 1849, stated: "As for adopting the ways which the State has provided for remedying the evil, I know not of such ways. They take too much time, and a man's life will be gone." Thoreau disobeyed unjust laws, went to jail, and his life and works were well known to both Gandhi and King. The Thoreauvian influence throughout this entire letter is inescapable.

129. Stephen B. Oates, *Let the Trumpet Sound*, p. 254.

130. *A Testament of Hope*, pp. 295–96.

131. This was Gandhi's name for the untouchables of India: *harijan* or "children of God."

132. Ibid., p. 302.

133. See James Q. Wilson, *American Government, Institutions and Policies* (New York: D. C. Heath and Company, 1986), pp. 411, 536, 547–49.

134. *A Testament of Hope*, pp. 219, 220.

135. From the film, *Martin Luther King, Jr.: From Montgomery to Memphis*.

136. Stephen B. Oates, *Let the Trumpet Sound*, p. 431.

137. *A Testament of Hope*, p. 20.

138. Ibid. King's interpretation of traditional *agapē* is ingenious but wrong.

139. The earliest use of the phrase "beloved community," that I can find, is in a work by the Harvard philosopher and theologian, Josiah Royce (1855–1916): "The principle of principles in all Christian morals remains this: 'Since you cannot find the universal and beloved community, create it.'" *The Problem of Christianity* (Macmillan, 1913/Archon Books, 1967), p. 359. See also Bruce Kuklick, *Josiah Royce: An Intellectual Biography* (Indianapolis, Ind.: Hackett Publishing Company, 1985), chapter 11, "The Absolute and the Community," for a discussion of Royce's Christian ideas about the beloved community which was for him the community of all Christian believers, that is, "the body of Christ." I find no reference to Royce in any of King's published papers or works.

140. Quoted in Kenneth L. Smith and Ira G. Zepp Jr., *Search for the Beloved Community* (Valley Forge, Pa.: Judson Press, 1974), p. 119. The authors make no mention of Josiah Royce (see note 139 above).

141. Ibid., p. 44.

142. Ibid.

143. *A Testament of Hope*, p. 37.

144. Ibid., p. 103.

145. Ibid.

146. Ibid., p. 118.

147. Ibid., p. 122. In his last Sunday morning sermon given on March 31, 1968, four days before his murder on April 4, 1968, the beloved community and John Donne were still on his mind. King quoted from the

seventeenth-century English poet and clergyman: "No man is an island entire of itself. Every man is a piece of the continent—a part of the main. Any man's death diminishes me because I am involved in mankind." Ibid., pp. 269–70. We are arguing, however, that King goes further than Donne and sees an identity between those pieces and parts and the continent and the main. "Involvement," for members of the beloved community, would mean identity with, and not merely participation in, community.

148. Ibid., p. 124.

149. Ibid., p. 58.

150. Quoted in Joan V. Bondurant, *The Conquest of Violence*, p. 30.

151. *A Testament of Hope*, p. 122.

152. Quoted in Alan Watts, *The Way of Zen* (New York: Vintage Books, 1957), p. 26.

153. Ibid.

154. A. L. Herman, *An Introduction to Buddhist Thought* (Washington, D.C.: University Press of America, 1983), p. 56. The sermon is from the Pāli text of the *Samyutta-Nikāya* v. 20. We have, the reader will note, used the form of the Four Noble Truths as a useful heuristic for summarizing the various views about communities throughout this book calling them "Prescriptions for Community."

155. Ibid., p. 59.

156. Ibid., p. 60.

157. Ibid., p. 61.

158. *Sangha*, "community," is from the Sanskrit meaning "to collect together."

159. *Buddhism in Translations*, translated by Henry Clarke Warren (New York: Atheneum, 1963/1896), pp. 302–3.

160. *Some Sayings of the Buddha According to the Pāli Canon*, translated by F. L. Woodward (New York: Oxford University Press, 1973), pp. 84–85.

161. Edward J. Thomas, *The Life of the Buddha as Legend and History* (London: Routledge & Kegan Paul, 1949/1927), p. 90.

162. Ibid., p. 146.

163. *Buddhism in Translations*, p. 109.

164. *Bṛhadāraṇyaka Upaniṣad* III.2.13.

165. *Bṛhadāraṇyaka Upaniṣad* IV.4.6.

166. *Chāndogya Upaniṣad* V.10.7. Kṣatriyas are the protectors, vaiśyas are the producers, and caṇḍālas are the corpse-carrying servers in the traditional Hindu community.

167. *Śvetāśvatara Upaniṣad* V.7, 11–12.

168. *Bhagavad Gītā* IV.5–8.

169. *Bhagavad Gītā* IX.31–34. Śūdras are the servers in the traditional Hindu community.

170. *Bhagavad Gītā* XVIII.64–66.

171. A "game" is merely a physical or mental contest carried out according to rules and undertaken for amusement, recreation, or winning a stake, that is, a game is any ruled activity for reaching a goal. In this sense all religions are games.

172. *Bhagavad Gītā* XVIII.71.

173. Krishna has defined the cosmic breadth of the law when he says to Arjuna that all the worlds from Brahmā the Creator downwards are subject to rebirth and therefore are governed by the law of karma. See *Bhagavad Gītā* VIII.16. Since the creation consists of all beings, including the gods, themselves, we must assume that the law of karma holds sway even over them. Only by reaching liberation and Lord Krishna, many Hindus believe, does one pass beyond the reach of the law of karma.

174. *Bhagavad Gītā* XVIII.56, 58, 62, 73.

175. On the matter of the justness of the cosmos and the place of the law of karma in it, see A. L. Herman, "Materials for an Analysis of a Just Universe," *Asian Philosophy*, 5.1 (1995): 3–22.

176. The Hindu Purāṇic tradition has provided for such things as deferred, hence stored, karma: "A man reaps that at that age, whether infancy, youth or old age, at which he had sowed it in his previous birth. . . . A man gets in life what he is fated to get, and even a god cannot make it otherwise." *The Garuḍa Purāṇa*, edited by Manmatha Dutt (Calcutta: Society for the Resuscitation of Indian Literature, 1908), in *The Pocket World Bible*, edited by Robert O. Ballou (London: Routledge and Kegan Paul, 1948), p. 68. Further, karma can be divided between *aravdha* karma, on the one hand, which is the result of actions that have begun to produce effects, and *anaravdha* karma, on the other, which is the result of actions that have not yet begun to produce effects. The latter, in turn, is divided into *prāktana* karma, the results of actions done in previous incarnations, our "stored" karma, presumably, which have not yet begun to produce effects; and *kryamāna* karma, the results of actions done in this incarna-

tion that have not yet begun to produce effects, another "stored" karma, presumably. See Troy Wilson Organ, *Hinduism: Its Historical Development* (New York: Baron's Educational Series, 1974), p. 188.

177. Karmic communalism may also be found in Theravāda Buddhism in the concept of the *saṅgha*, the community of monks. Since our interest here is in Mahāyāna and not in the history of Pāli communalism, karmic or otherwise, we'll say no more about Theravāda. But see a discussion of the Theravāda *saṅgha* as a source of merit in David J. Kalupahana, *A History of Buddhist Philosophy* (Honolulu: University of Hawaii Press, 1992): "If the disciples of the Buddha are endowed with these four characteristics [well-behaved (in Pāli, *supaṭipanno*), straightforward (*ujupaṭipanno*), methodical (*ñāyapaṭipanno*), and correct (*sāmīcipaṭipanno*)], they are worthy of veneration, hospitality, magnanimity, and respect. They represent an incomparable source of merit (*puññakkhetta*) for the world, since they are the living aspirants to the moral ideal represented by the Buddha. . . . The Saṅgha or community of disciples would then be a veritable source of merit not in its own right [which is what will happen in Bodhisattva-dominated Mahāyāna], but because it *represents* a community that cultivates a noble moral ideal (*dhamma-cārī*)," pp. 117–18, emphasis added. See also Sukumar Dutt, *Buddhist Monks and Monasteries of India* (New Delhi: Motilal Banarsidass, 1988), especially chapter 5, "Saṅgha Life and Its Organization in Early Settlements."

178. Shantideva, *Bodhicaryāvatāra* III.6–10, in Edward Conze, *Buddhism: Its Essence and Development* (New York: Harper Torchbooks, 1959), p. 149.

179. *Śikṣāsamuccaya*, 280–81 (*Vajradhvaja Sūtra*), in *Buddhist Texts through the Ages*, edited by Edward Conze et al. (New York: Harper Torchbooks, 1964), p. 131. It is important to point out at this stage of the argument that if ethical altruism fails, then communal altruism fails and then karmic communalism will fail. We shall be at some pains to point out in our final chapter that ethical altruism must, indeed, fail.

180. Edward Conze, *Buddhism: Its Essence and Development*, p. 148.

181. *Aṣṭasāhasrikā* VI, in *Buddhist Texts through the Ages*, p. 133.

182. *Śikṣāsamuccaya*, 280 (*Vajradhvaja Sūtra*), in *Buddhist Texts through the Ages*, p. 131.

183. For a fascinating look at a parallel between the ancient Yoga conception of karma and modern psychology, particularly Sigmund Freud and Karl Jung and their views of memory, motivation, and the unconscious, see Harold G. Coward, "Psychology and Karma," *Philosophy East and West*

32.1 (January 1983). For an examination of the parallels between the concept of karma and economics, banking, checking and savings accounts, interest, withdrawals, transfers and bankruptcy, see A. L. Herman, "Two Dogmas of Buddhism," in *Pāli Buddhism*, edited by Frank J. Hoffman and Deegalle Mahinda (Richmond, U.K.: Curzon Press, 1996).

184. Abraham H. Maslow, "Lessons from the Peak-Experiences," *Journal of Humanistic Psychology* 2 (1962): 9.

185. Abraham H. Maslow, *Religions, Values and Peak-Experiences* (New York: Penguin Books, 1981/1964), pp. 59–68.

186. Aldo Leopold, *A Sand County Almanac*, p. 138. Emphasis added.

187. Stephen Fox, *The American Conservation Movement, John Muir and His Legacy* (Madison: University of Wisconsin Press, 1981), p. 43.

188. D. T. Suzuki, Erich Fromm, and Richard DeMartino, *Zen Buddhism and Psychoanalysis* (New York: Harper Colophon Books, 1970), p. 3.

189. Ibid., p. 4.

190. Aldo Leopold, "The Ecological Conscience (1947)," *The River of the Mother of God*, p. 340.

191. Ibid., p. 341.

192. Ibid.

193. Ibid., p. 345.

194. Ibid. Emphasis added.

195. Ibid., pp. 345–46.

196. J. Baird Callicott, "The Metaphysical Implications of Ecology," *Nature in Asian Traditions of Thought: Essays in Environmental Philosophy*, edited by J. Baird Callicott and Roger T. Ames (Albany: SUNY Press, 1989), p. 64. Emphasis added.

197. Gandhi, *Autobiography*, p. 48. Gandhi is probably exaggerating, as he usually does in the *Autobiography*, playing to an audience of devoted readers. But it is not the first time a saint, a Mahatma, was converted by a book. Aurelius Augustine (354–430) is transformed from a whoring, drinking, vice-ridden sinner into a committed Christian when one day in his garden he hears a child saying repeatedly what sounds like the voice of God, "Take up and read; take up and read." Hearing this as a command from heaven, he takes up a book of Letters of St. Paul he chanced to have and reads, "Not in rioting and drunkenness, not in whoring and wantonness,

not in strife and envying; but put on the Lord Jesus Christ, and make no provision for the flesh to satisfy your lusts." *Confessions* VIII.xii.29. Augustine does and the rest is ecclesiastical history, as they say.

198. George Hendrick, *Henry Salt: Humanitarian, Reformer and Man of Letters* (Urbana: University of Illinois Press, 1977), p. 167.

199. Gandhi, *An Autobiography*, p. 112.

200. Louis Fischer, *The Life of Mahatma* Gandhi (New York: Collier Books, 1973), p. 49. Louis Fischer, Gandhi's biographer, adds to the remark, "[In] that frigid night at Maritzburg the germ of social protest was born in Gandhi."

201. *A Testament of Hope*, p. 509. The recounting here is from chapter 13 of *The Strength to Love* (1963), samples of King's sermons.

202. Ibid.

203. Stephen B. Oates, *Let the Trumpet Sound*, p. 90. The entire incident is recounted in *Stride toward Freedom* (1958), pp. 137–38.

204. Ibid.

205. A. L. Herman, *An Introduction to Buddhist Thought*, p. 108.

206. Ibid.

207. *Pratītyasamutpāda* is either from *samutpāda*, 'arising,' and *prati + i + ya*, 'after getting,' so literally 'an arising after getting,' that is, dependent origination or causation; or alternatively, it is from *pratītya*, 'dependent,' *sam*, 'together,' and *utpāda*, 'to come into existence,' so literally 'to come into dependent existence together,' that is, interdependent origination or causation. Either etymology is instructive as we shall see below. Ibid., pp. 67–74.

208. Francis H. Cook, "The Jewel Net of Indra," *Nature in Asian Traditions of Thought: Essays in Environmental Philosophy*, p. 214.

209. *Mark* 10.43–45, Revised Standard Version. President John F. Kennedy's "Ask not what your country can do for you; but ask what you can do for your country," is altruistic ethics in the twentieth century.

210. *A Testament of Hope*, p. 247.

211. 1 *Corinthians* 13.4–7, Revised Standard Version.

212. *Thus Spoke Zarathustra*, "On Redemption," *The Portable Nietzsche*, edited and translated by Walter Kaufmann (New York: Penguin Books, 1984), p. 252.

213. Berne Lay Jr. and Sy Bartlett, *Twelve O'Clock High!* (New York: Harper & Brothers, 1948), pp. 94, 95, 111, 112. The authors also wrote the screenplay for the film producers, Twentieth Century Fox.

214. Immanual Kant, *Foundations to the Metaphysics of Morals*, sec. I, paragraph 5. *Kant Selections*, edited by Lewis White Beck (New York: Macmillan, 1988), p. 237.

215. It is the Indian Buddhist philosopher Nāgārjuna (ca. 150–250 C.E.), whose most common expressions in his attacks on abstract concepts were *na yujyate*, "this is nonsense" and *nopadyate*, "this is unintelligible," who is setting the stage for this attempt to reduce *community* to emptiness, an emptiness to which no one can become attached. Since the argument that follows is Nāgārjunian in spirit, using his expressions here has a justification.

216. For a forceful argument defending axiological egoism, see Kenneth Goodpaster, "From Egoism to Environmentalism," *Ethics and Problems in the 21st Century*, edited by Kenneth Goodpaster and K. Sayre (South Bend, Ind.: Notre Dame University Press, 1979). There Goodpaster states that in normal ethics egoism has not needed a justification. The intrinsic value of the self has always been taken for granted; it is the value of others that is problematic and in need of defense. In other words, what we are calling "communal egoism" begins with a rather sound assumption, that self-love and egoism are in themselves intrinsically valuable; everyone recognizes the usefulness of this and the view needs no justification. Goodpaster is in good company here since David Hume, Jeremy Benthan, and Immanuel Kant appear to have shared this same view. See J. Baird Callicott, "Intrinsic Value, Quantum Theory, and Environmental Ethics," in his *In Defense of the Land Ethic*, pp. 172, 173.

Some Suggestions for Further Reading

Chapter 1. Something about Community

Sybille Bedford, *Aldous Huxley: A Biography* (New York: Alfred A. Knopf/Harper & Row, 1973). A splendid introduction to Huxley's life and works by a critical friend.

The Collected Dialogues of Plato, edited by Edith Hamilton and Huntington Cairns (New York: Pantheon Books, 1961). The *Apology* and the *Republic*, contained herein, have inspired generations of community-seekers.

Erich Fromm, *The Sane Society* (New York: Fawcett Publications, 1967/1955). A hard and damning critique of Western community, as timely and applicable today as it was over forty years ago.

Arthur Herman, *The Idea of Decline in Western History* (New York: The Free Press, 1997). An insightful analysis of the role that cultural pessimism has played in shaping solutions to the problems of violence and peace in the West.

Aldous Huxley, *Brave New World and Brave New World Revisited* (New York: Harper & Row, 1965). Huxley's invaluable look back at what all the philosophic fuss was about thirty-three years earlier together with some valuable warnings about the future.

Chapter 2. Aldo Leopold and the Biotic Community

J. Baird Callicott, *In Defense of the Land Ethic: Essays in Environmental Philosophy* (Albany: SUNY Press, 1989). Extremely well-written and moving writings about Leopold by the man who practically invented environmental ethics.

Aldo Leopold, *The River of the Mother of God and Other Essays*, edited by Susan L. Flader and J. Baird Callicott (Madison: The University of Wisconsin Press, 1991). Leopold's published and unpublished essays beautifully edited and introduced. Required reading for anyone interested in environmental ethics.

Aldo Leopold, *A Sand County Almanac* (New York: Oxford University Press, 1949). The classic work on environmental ethics and environmental aesthetics for the twenty-first century. Required reading for anyone interested in environmental ethics.

Linda Lear, *Rachel Carson: Witness for Nature* (New York: Henry Holt & Company, 1997). A full-scale examination (634 pages) of Carson's life and career and her extraordinary influence on worldwide ecological sensibilities.

Marybeth Lorbiecki, *Aldo Leopold: A Fierce Green Fire* (Helena, Mont.: Falcon Publishing, 1996). A brief, illustrated, and enjoyable read on the life of Leopold.

Curt Meine, *Aldo Leopold: His Life and Work* (Madison: University of Wisconsin Press, 1988). A highly readable, well-researched account of Leopold.

Donald Worster, *Nature's Economy: A History of Ecological Ideas*, 2nd ed. (Cambridge: Cambridge University Press, 1995). Required reading for anyone interested in environmental ethics.

Chapter 3. Mohandas Karamchand Gandhi and the Ashramic Community

P. Chenchiah, *Ashramas Past and Present* (Madras: Indian Christian Book Club, 1941). A general history of ashrams, their origin and purpose, concentrating primarily on the tradition of the stages (*ashramas*) of life.

The Collected Works of Mahatma Gandhi, 90 volumes (and counting) (New Delhi: Government of India, Publications Division: 1960–present). Contains almost everything the Mahatma ever wrote, spoke, or thought.

M. K. Gandhi, *The Village Reconstruction* (Bombay: Bharatiya Vidya Bhavan, 1966). "Just as the whole universe is contained in the self, so is

India contained in the villages." Liberation and happiness lie in the villages—here's the blueprint for that liberated, happy life.

M. K. Gandhi, *The Way to Communal Harmony* (Ahmedabad, India: Navajivan Publishing House, 1963). Compilation of Gandhi's reflections on problems of divisiveness among human beings and how the way of the ashram can solve those problems.

Mahatma Gandhi, 125 Years: Remembering Gandhi, Understanding Gandhi, Relevance of Gandhi, edited by B. R. Nanda (New Delhi: Indian Council for Cultural Relations, 1995). Sixty-four academics and laymen talk about Gandhi.

D. G. Tendulkar, *Mahatma: Life of Mohandas Karamchand Gandhi,* 3 vols. (New Delhi: Government of India Publications Division, n.d.). Drawing heavily from the *Collected Works,* this is a fine condensation of Gandhi's life in Gandhi's own words. Required reading for anyone interested in Gandhi.

Chapter 4. Martin Luther King Jr. and the Beloved Community

Lewis V. Baldwin, *There Is a Balm in Gilead: The Cultural Roots of Martin Luther King, Jr.* (Minneapolis: Augsburg Fortress Press, 1991). Downplays King's non-African-American roots and focuses on the black religious tradition in King's own church experiences.

Adam Fairclough, *Martin Luther King, Jr.* (Athens, Ga.: University of Georgia Press, 1995). A brief biography of King written with remarkable clarity and skill.

David J. Garrow, *Bearing the Cross: Martin Luther King, Jr. and the Southern Christian Leadership Conference* (New York: William Morrow, 1986). A well-researched and readable account of King and the SCLC. Required reading for anyone interested in King.

Keith D. Miller, *Voice of Deliverance: The Language of Martin Luther King, Jr. and Its Sources* (New York: The Free Press, 1992). Focuses on King's African-American heritage emphasizing its nonwhite origins.

The Papers of Martin Luther King, Jr., 3 vols. (and counting), edited by Clayborne Carson, Senior Editor, Ralph Luker, Penny Russell, and Louis R. Harlan (Berkeley: University of California Press, 1992–). King's writings collected and edited with care and brilliance. Required reading for anyone interested in King.

Chapter 5. Gautama the Buddha and the Karmic Community

Edward Conze, *Buddhist Thought in India* (London: George Allen & Unwin, 1962). A great study of early Buddhism by a fine scholar.

David J. Kalupahana, *A History of Buddhist Philosophy* (Honolulu: University Press of Hawaii, 1992). A grand introduction to the historical background and philosophical implications of the major schools of Buddhist thought.

Edward J. Thomas, *The History of Buddhist Thought* (London: Routledge & Kegan Paul, 1951/1933). The book remains the best introduction to Buddhism on the market today.

Edward J. Thomas, *The Life of Buddha as Legend and History* (London: Routledge & Kegan Paul, 1949/1927). Despite its age, it is still the best introduction to the Buddha, his life and times. Required reading for anyone interested in the Buddha.

Chapter 6. Conclusion: Community and the Twenty-First Century

J. Baird Callicott and Roger T. Ames, eds., *Nature in Asian Traditions of Thought: Essays in Environmental Philosophy* (Albany: SUNY Press, 1989). A survey of, *inter alia*, the role that personal transformations can play in the development of a responsible ecology.

Stephen Fox, *The American Conservation Movement: John Muir and His Legacy* (Madison: University of Wisconsin Press, 1981). John Muir's ecological peak experience is nicely set into context.

M. K. Gandhi, *An Autobiography, or The Story of My Experiments with Truth* (Ahmedabad, India: Navajivan Publishing House, 1948/1927). Gandhi's recounting of peak and other experiences that changed his life. Required reading for all students of Gandhi.

Kenneth Goodpaster and K. Sayre, eds., *Ethics and Problems in the 21st Century* (South Bend, Ind.: University of Notre Dame Press, 1979). A forceful defense *inter alia* of axiological egoism and its place in environmental ethics.

Martin Luther King, Jr., *The Strength to Love* (New York: Harper & Row, 1963). King's own recounting of the experience that turned him around here set into the context of many other of his finest sermons.

Abraham Maslow, *Religions, Values and Peak-Experiences* (New York: Penguin Books, 1981/1964). A brilliant survey of those all-too-common, unforgettable, indescribable experiences that some call "mystical" and others call "ennobling."

D. T. Suzuki, Erich Fromm, and Richard De Martino, *Zen Buddhism and Psychoanalysis* (New York: Harper Colophon Books, 1970). An Eastern and Western comparison of peak experiences and their implications.

Index

A

Academy, the, 17–27
Agapē, 130, 137–138
Alcibiades, 9, 10
Allegory of the cave, the, 24–25
Altruism, 74–75, 106–107, 114,
   139, 140, 143, 144, 148, 157,
   177–178, 181–182, 185, 197,
   201, 203–205, 207, 212
Altruistic community, 143–146, 210
Ānanda, 157, 158, 159, 160, 168
Anitya, 198, 200–202
Arnold, Dr. Thomas, 27
Arnold Matthew, 27
Arhat(s), 156, 168
Aristotle, 7, 14, 25, 16, 18, 33, 113
Ashram(s), 76, 82–105, 112; Phoenix
   Settlement (1904), 83–84;
   Sabarmati Ashram (1915), 86–88;
   Sevagram Ashram (1933), 88–105;
   Tolstoy Farm (1910), 84–86
Ashramic community, ix, 2,
   76–115, 116, 177, 185, 202, 215
Augustine, Saint Aurelius, 18,
   230n 197

B

Bajaj, Jamnalal, 95, 96, 97
Balance, 59–60, 68. *See also* Justice
Basho, 187–188, 189
Battle of the Somme, the, 28–29
Bellamy, Edward, 18
Beloved community, the, ix, 2, 116,
   124, 137–141, 142, 146, 173,
   175, 203, 204, 215, 226n, 139
Bentham, Jeremy, 70, 232n 216
Bhagavad Gītā, 94–95, 105–106,
   114, 162–167, 168
Biotic altruism, 74–75
Biotic community, the, ix, 2, 53,
   56–65, 71–73, 74, 109–110, 116,
   173, 175, 177, 186, 215
Biotic pyramid, the, 57–58, 71
Blackwood, Russell Thorn III, x
Bodhisattva, 169f., 172, 174, 177, 178
Bradley, Sarah Grace, 119–120
Brave New World, 2, 31–35, 39, 40
Broken community, the, 139
Buddha. *See* Gautama the Buddha
Buddhist, Buddhism, ix, x, xi, 14,
   149–180 *passim*

C

Callicott, J. Baird, 62, 71–72, 191,
    192, 220n 39, 221n 56, 222n 70,
    222n 74, 230n 196, 232n 216
Carson, Rachel, 47, 48–52, 68–69,
    220n 38
Channa, 150
Chatterjee, Margaret, xi, 108
Christian, ix, 51, 91, 94, 95, 116,
    117, 121, 122–125, 128–130,
    133, 141, 153, 185–186, 194,
    203–205, 230n 197
Christian satyagraha, 121, 128–137,
    138, 139–140, 142
Chunda, 159
Cicero, 20–21
Civil disobedience, 81
Clements, Frederic, 47
Communal altruism, x, 2–3, 45, 177,
    181, 183, 185, 186, 197, 202, 207,
    208, 209–211, 212, 213, 229n 179
Communal egoism, x, 3, 45, 202,
    205–215, 232n 216
Communal holism, 2, 182, 208,
    209–211
Community, ix, x, 1–3, 7–14, 15,
    16–27, 31–36, 37–40, 40–46
Community arguments, 11
Community peace argument, 13,
    46 (Plato, Huxley), 74 (Leopold),
    115 (Gandhi), 146 (King), 179
    (Buddha), 206
Community violence argument, 12,
    13, 44–45 (Plato, Huxley), 73–74
    (Leopold), 114–115 (Gandhi), 146
    (King), 179 (Buddha), 206
Confucius, 145–146
Conger, Agnes, 89–105 passim,
    110, 112
Conger, George Perigo, 89–105 pas-
    sim, 109, 223n 95
Congress of Racial Equality
    (CORE), 127
Connor, Eugene "Bull," 133

Conze, Edward, 171
Cook, Francis H., 201
Corinthian War, the, 26
Cote, Carolee, x, v
Coward, Harold, xi, 229n 183
Critias, 9, 10
Cynicism, 26

D

Darwin, Charles, 27, 62, 210
Dharma, 156, 157, 159, 173
Dikē. See Justice
Dilemma of community. See
    Dilemma of the individual and
    the community
Dilemma of the individual and the
    community, the, 11, 74, 85, 87,
    176
Dilemma of self-transformation,
    the, 176
Dilemma of stored karma, the, 167
Diogenes Laertius, 218n 15
Disney, Walt, 55
Donne, John, 140, 226n 147
Dostoievsky, Fyodor, 30
Dubos, Rene, 47

E

Eco-holism (organicism), 47, 48, 53,
    56, 57, 71–72, 74
Ecological conscience, 63–65, 67,
    70, 186, 189–190
Ecology, 47, 50, 51, 59–60, 62–63
Ecomystic, ecomysticism, ix, 52,
    65, 191
Ecosystem community, 47–48, 55–57
Education, 23–27 (Plato), 36
    (Huxley), 39–40 (Plato, Huxley),
    74 (Leopold), 86–113 (Gandhi),
    121–126, 142 (King), 153–155,
    180 (Buddha), 191–192, 212, 215
Ehrlich, Paul, 47

Elton, Charles, 48, 62, 69
Environmental ethics, 62
Environmental holism, 47, 57, 58
Ethical altruism, x, 1, 2, 45, 197,
    207, 229n 179

F

Fadner, Donald, xi
Federal Bureau of Investigation
    (FBI), 137
Fictional communities, ix, 45
First World War, 28, 29. *See also*
    Somme generation
Fischer, Louis, 231n 200
Forbes, S. A., 47
Four Noble Truths, the, 14, 152,
    153–155, 198, 227n 154
Freud, Sigmund, 113
Fromm, Erich, 5–6, 8

G

"Game," 228n 171
Gandhi, Mohandas K., ix, x, xi, 1, 2,
    7, 8, 11, 12, 13, 15, 76–115, 116,
    119–121, 125, 127, 129, 132, 134,
    138, 141, 142, 143, 146, 174,
    175, 181, 191, 192–195, 202, 204,
    206, 209, 214, 215, 222n 77,
    223n 89, 230n 199
Gautama the Buddha, ix, x, 1, 2, 7,
    8, 11, 12, 13, 14–15, 113–114,
    149–180, 181, 197–202, 204,
    206, 214, 215, 229n 177
Georgia Equal Rights League, 117
Ghose, Aurobindo, 104
Gier, Nicholas, 222n 78
Ginsburg, Allen, 47
Glaucon, 22–23, 24
God, 10, 34, 36, 37, 50, 51, 107,
    153, 122–126, 131, 133, 135,
    136, 183, 184, 191, 210
Gokale, G. K., 87

Good luck, 113
Goodpaster, Kenneth, 232n 216
Gore, Al, 47
Great Peloponnesian War, the, 26
Great War, the. *See* First World War.

H

Happiness, 6, 8, 15, 18, 21, 22–27,
    36, 37, 38–39, 42, 43, 44, 46, 50,
    113, 152
Hedonic egoism, 45
Hedonism, 31–35
Herman, A. L., 218n 12, 227n 154,
    228n 175, 229n 183
Herman, Arthur, xi, 217n 1
Herman, Barbara, x
Hermes, 9
Hīnayāna Buddhism. *See*
    Theravāda Buddhism.
Hindu(s), Hinduism, ix, x, 76, 79,
    81, 82, 105, 152, 153, 160, 161,
    162, 166, 167, 171, 173, 175,
    185, 228nn. 166, 173, 176
Historical communities, ix, 45
Hitler, Adolph, 93–94, 96
Hoffman, Frank J., xi, 229n 183
Holism, 47, 57, 58, 141, 209–212.
    See also Eco-holism.
Homer, 19
Hua-yen Buddhism, 201–202
Hume, David, 62, 232n 216
Huxley, Aldous, ix, 2, 15, 18, 27–46,
    72, 181, 213, 214, 219n 27
Huxley, Julia, 28
Huxley, Julian, 28
Huxley, Sir Thomas Henry, 27
Huxley, Trev, 28

I

Individualism, 9, 10–11, 40–42,
    176–177
Injustice, 26, 37, 142

J

Jaeger, Werner, 218n 9
Jemison, Theodore J., 127
Jesus of Nazareth (Christ), 89, 111,
  124, 129, 133, 202–203, 218n 9,
  230n 197
Jews, 93, 95, 96, 97, 112
Johnson, Dr. Mordecai W., 120
Johnson, President Lyndon, 137
Jopling, Jan, xi
Justice, 18–20, 21–27, 121
Justinian, Emperor, 18

K

Kalupahana, David J., xi, 229n 177
Kant, Immanual, 209–210, 232n
  216
Karma, 161, 162
Karmic altruism, 177–178, 180
Karmic Communalism, x, 168,
  169–173, 229n 179
Karmic community, the, 149,
  173–180, 215
Karmic Individualism, x, 167, 168,
  178
Karmic Saviorism, x, 167, 168–169
Kay, Keith M., 219n 26
Kierkegaard, Søren, 121, 124, 125
King, Coretta Scott, 121, 135
King, James (Jim) Albert, 118–119
King, Martin Luther, Jr., ix, x, xi, 1,
  2, 7, 8, 11, 12, 13, 15, 89, 109,
  111, 113, 115, 116–148, 173,
  175, 181, 191, 195–197, 203,
  202–205, 206, 214, 215
King, Martin (Michael) Luther, Sr.,
  116, 118–119
Kisa Gotami, 158–159
Krishna, Lord, 162–165, 166, 169,
  228n 173
Krishnamurti, Jiddu, 109
Krutch, Joseph Wood, 47

L

Leopold, Aldo, ix, x, 2, 7, 8, 11, 12,
  13, 15, 47–48, 52–74, 85, 88,
  109, 112, 114, 115, 141, 142,
  143, 144, 145, 146, 172, 173,
  174, 175, 181, 186–187,
  188–191, 204, 206, 214, 215
Land Ethic, the, 48, 62–65
Land, the, 57, 62–65. See also
  Biotic community
Lao-Tzu, 145–146
Law of karma, the, 161–164, 165,
  167, 168, 170, 171
Laws, the, 11, 18, 12, 42

M

Maharshi, Sri Ramana, 104
Mahāyāna Buddhism, x, 149,
  160–162, 168–173, 174, 177,
  179, 199, 229n 177
Marx, Karl, 18
Marxists, 154
Maslow, Abraham, 183–184, 192
McHarg, Ian, 51–52
Meine, Kurt, 54–55
Melville, Herman, 30
Miletus, 11
Moline, Jon N., 222n 71
Montgomery Improvement
  Association (MIA), 127, 128
Moore, Elizabeth, xi
Muir, John, 187, 191, 192
Muslim(s), 79, 82

N

Nader, Ralph, 47
Nāgārjuna, 232n 215
National Association for the
  Advancement of Colored People
  (NAACP), 117, 118

Naturalist, naturalism, ix
Nature mysticism, 48
Nelson, Michael P., xi, 62, 68, 221n 56
Nietzsche, Frederich, 203–205
Nirvana, 152, 156, 177, 182
Nobel Peace Prize, the, 136
Nonviolence, 96, 99, 104, 112–114, 120, 124, 129, 139, 179, 202
Nygren, Anders, 138

O

Organ, Troy Wilson, 228n 176
Organic theory of community, the, 20, 71, 138, 139, 140. *See also* Eco-holism
Orwell, George, 34, 35
Ouspensky, P. D., 56
Overholt, Thomas W., xi

P

Parks, Rosa, 127, 128
Paul, Saint, 103, 104, 124, 125, 230n 197
Peak experiences, 183–184, 192, 195, 197, 212
Peck, Gregory, 208
Peloponnesian generation, 29, 44
Peloponnesian War, the, 9, 16, 26. *See also* Peloponnesian generation, the
Persian War, the, 26
Plato of Athens, ix, 2, 8, 9, 11, 15, 15–27, 33, 36, 37–46, 72, 74, 87, 205, 210, 213, 214, 215, 217n 8, 218nn. 9, 15, 16, 225n 128
Platonism, 26, 39–40
Plutarch, 17
Polemarchus, 18
Popper, Sir Karl, 41–42
Pratītyasamutpāda, 198–200, 201, 202, 231n 207

Prescriptions for community, 14–15, 25–27, 35–36, 65–66; Plato, 25–27; Aldoux Huxley, 35–36; Aldo Leopold, 65–66; Mohandas Gandhi, 105–107; Martin Luther King Jr., 141–142; Gautama the Buddha, 173–174
Problem of altruism, the, 74–75, 106–107, 114, 115, 143–146, 202
Problem of altruistic fascism, the, 212
Problem of ashramic altruism, the, 115
Problem of communal altruism, the, x, 144, 181, 182, 202–205
Problem of communal egoism, the, 213–214
Problem of communo-fascism, the, 40–42, 143–145, 176
Problem of community limitation, the, 144–145, 173
Problem of ecofascism, the, 71–73, 176
Problem of egoistic transformation, the, 214–215
Problem of karmic altruism, the, 177–178
Problem of karmic fascism, the, 176–177
Problem of lost virtues, the, 40
Problem of the meaning of "violence," the, 108–110
Problem that nonviolence provokes violence, the, 110–111
Problem of self-transformation, the, 175–176, 181, 182–202, 214
Problem of stored karma, the, 165–166, 175
Problem of suffering, the, 14, 25, 35, 37, 65, 105–106, 154
Problem of the transfer of karma, the, 166–167, 175
Problem of the transformation of the ordinary conscience, the, 67–69, 88, 112, 145

Problem of the way-to-nonviolence, the, 112–114
Problem of the way to self-transformation, the, 145–146, 214
Problem of where's the difference?,
the, 213
Problem of whole-part, the,
211–212
Problems of karma and merit, the,
161–167, 164, 175
Problems of outrageous rights and
confused use, the, 69–71, 173
Problems of violence and peace,
the, ix, 1, 2, 3, 7, 8, 11, 13, 15,
44–46, 73–74, 114–115, 143,
147, 149, 161, 175, 179, 213
Psychological egoism, 45,
219n 35
Psychological hedonism,
219n 35
Psychological spiritualism,
219n 35

R

Rabelais, Francois, 18
Rauschenbush, Walter, 138–139
Reeb, James, 134
Republic (Plato's community), 18,
25–27, 40–46
Republic, the, 2, 15–27
Royce, Josiah, 226n 139
Ruskin, John, 83–84, 86

S

Sallinger, J. D., 31
Salt, Henry, 193, 194
Salt March, the, 99–102, 134
Saṅgha, 156, 176, 214
Satyagraha, 76, 78–81, 97–99,
101–105, 106–107, 110, 112,
120, 125, 129–130, 142
Savior, 162, 165, 166, 169, 172

Schweitzer, Albert, 70
Self-transformation, 21–25, 63–65,
67, 70, 112–114, 115, 116,
140–141, 145–147, 179, 181,
182–202, 212
Scherer, Donald, 222n 71
Shakespeare, William, 32
Shantideva, 170, 178–179
Shuddhodana, 149
Skepticism, 26
Smuts, General Jan Christian,
79–80
Socrates, 8–14, 18, 20, 22–25, 27,
39, 87, 131, 205, 206, 207
Socratic argument, the, 8, 11,
205
Socratic community argument,
the, 12–13, 205–206
Somme generation, the, 29, 44
Sousa, John Philip, 19
Southern Christian Leadership
Conference (SCLC), 119, 128,
135, 203
Spiritual egoism, 45
Stoicism, 26
Subhuti, 172–173
Suffering, 142, 150–151, 153, 154,
174
Sullivan, J. W. N., 30–31
Suzuki, D. T., 187–188
Swift, Jonathan, 18

T

Tansley, A. G., 48
Tennyson, Alfred Lord, 188
Teresias, 28
Theravāda Buddhism, 160, 168,
229n 177
Thirty Oligarchs, the, 9, 16
Thoreau, Henry David, 225n 128
Tillich, Paul, 121, 122–125
Tolstoy, Leo, 30, 85
Transformative experiences,
182–184, 185, 186–202

U

Upaniṣads, 161–162, 167
Utilitarian(ism), 50, 57, 58
Utopia, 19, 39, 42, 181

V

Violence, "violence," 5, 88, 98–99,
  108–110, 111, 129, 139, 175,
  177, 180, 213
Vollrath, John, xi

W

Wardha Ashram, x, 88, 89, 90
Warren, Chief Justice Earl, 126
Warren, Dôna, xi

Way(s) of community, the, ix, 1, 2,
  7, 14, 36, 44, 46
Wieman, Henry Nelson, 121,
  122–125
Williams, A. D., 117, 118
Williams, Alberta Christine, 116
Williams, Willis, 117
World State (Aldous Huxley's com-
  munity), 31–46
World War II, 55
Worster, Donald, 220n 36

Y

Yasa, 155

Z

Zola, Emile, 30